Books written by Jack Hartman

Trust God for Your Finances
Deep In⌐
Strong Faith ʄ
What Will Hₑ
Never, Neₗ
Soaring Above thₑ
How to Study the Bible
Quiet Confidence in the Lord
Conquering Fear
God's Will for Our Lives
One Hundred Years from Today
Nuggets of Faith
Books co-authored by Jack and Judy Hartman
Receive Healing from the Lord
Unshakable Faith in Almighty God
Exchange Your Worries for God's Perfect Peace
God's Wisdom Is Available to You
Increased Energy and Vitality

Scripture Meditation Cards co-authored by Jack and Judy Hartman

Receive Healing from the Lord
Freedom from Worry and Fear
Enjoy God's Wonderful Peace
God Is Always with You
Continually Increasing Faith in God
Receive God's Blessings in Adversity
Financial Instructions from God
Find God's Will for Your Life
A Closer Relationship with the Lord
Our Father's Wonderful Love

Comments from readers of our publications:

The following are just a few of the comments contained in more than six hundred letters we have received pertaining to our publications:

Receive Healing from the Lord

- "I am so blessed by your comprehensive book on divine healing. This book is a monumental masterpiece. The Holy Ghost has written this book. Glory be to God that you have obeyed Him. You have presented dynamic scriptural instructions for Christians who are sick that will enable them to progressively increase their faith for divine healing. You obviously have put a lot of labor into this book. Many people will be blessed by it." (Florida)

- "Your healing book is awesome. It is unbelievable. This book is so simple. It is phenomenal. I am so happy to have read it. Many people will be helped by this book." (New Hampshire).

Unshakable Faith in Almighty God

- "*Unshakable Faith in Almighty God* has amazed me. The language is so simple and very clear to understand. This book is powerful and life-changing. I will always hang on to this book. Brother Hartman, God's favour and wisdom are so great on your life. I believe this book is written on very heavy anointing from God. Your reward in heaven will be so great. All those who have sown seeds in your ministry should rejoice. When I wake up, I read this book. Before going to bed, I read it. I will continue to go through it again and again. Your ministry is a big blessing to me. You are always in our prayers." (Zambia)

- "If there is one thing that people need above all else it is *Unshakable Faith in Almighty God.* Next to my Bible, I put this book among the best. Every reader should place this book next to his or her Bible. Hundreds of Scripture references that support the challenging truths in this book will equip readers for the future. We want to help get your writings into the hands of people in the island nations. Thank you for being so obedient to the Lord. Thank you for the time and the energy that you have invested in the lives of so many." (Australia)

Trust God for Your Finances

- "I am writing to you from deep in the interior of Russia having just read your wonderful book, *Trust God for Your Finances.* I appreciate your faith, your accurate thinking and your work which helps many, many people in various countries. After reading your book I know what I must do. I will follow your instructions to the letter. I am so grateful to you. You have removed the scales from my eyes. I love you." (Russia)

- "We find your material to be so readable and upbuilding. Your writing communicates a clear and fatherly concern for the edification of the believer. *Trust God for Your Finances* is a tremendous book. Your book by far is the most thorough and systematic work I have read to date. The church here in Greece has a great need for this book." (Greece) (This book was translated into Greek.)

- "Your book *Trust God for Your Finances* is tremendous. It has helped me very, very much. I found your book so interesting and knowledgeable and it excited me so that I found myself reading too fast just to find out what was ahead. The second reading of your wonderful book has helped me tremendously. Jack Hartman, you are gifted from God. I think that every Christian should have a copy of this book. God bless you." (Illinois)

Exchange Your Worries for God's Perfect Peace

- "*Exchange Your Worries for God's Perfect Peace* is a masterpiece. I am reading this book to the people here in the Philippines. I saw tears flowing down their faces as I read them parts of this book. I must get this book translated into their language. I am reading this book for the second time. After thirty years in the ministry I have finally learned how to turn my worries over to God. I have learned more from this book in the last few months than I have ever learned in my life. I will not allow my copy of this book to leave my presence. I thank God for you." (Philippines)

- "I just want to tell you how much I appreciate you and your excellent book, *Exchange Your Worries for God's Perfect Peace*. I have read all of your books several times each. I continually go back to refer to the notes I have made in your books. I have done this for close to fifteen years and pages are falling out of your books. I read the Bible daily. Your books are a close second to the Bible. I have never found another Christian author who teaches me more about God's Word and speaks directly to my heart as your writings do. Thank you for helping me appreciate and respect the Word of God." (Wisconsin)

- "When I read your book on peace, my heart felt like something was released off of me. I have been in prison for nine years and six months. Many times I kept trying to kill myself. Life didn't even matter, but I now know that God has something He wants me to do here on earth. When I was younger, many people raped me. I grew up hating men. I pray to be delivered from this homosexual lifestyle. Please pray that God will deliver me. This book has helped me and I am passing it around to others." (Illinois)

God's Wisdom Is Available to You
- "I thank God each and every day for Jack and Judy Hartman. When I started reading your book on wisdom, everything was going wrong in my life. This book revived my spirit and my faith in God. It has changed my life. The Bible used to be like Greek to me. Now I can read it and understand it. I can't put this book down because I know I need to absorb it. I'm going through it for a second time. This book is one of the best

things that has ever happened to me. I thank you both and I thank God." (Florida)

- "You did a fantastic job on this book. It is an encyclopedia on God's wisdom. The writing style is just great. Many books don't bring the reader through the subject the way this book does. I'm very impressed with that. You have made it a real joy for me to study and re-digest Scripture. This book has been very good for me." (North Carolina)

What Will Heaven Be Like?

- "On the very first page of your book on heaven I was spell-bound. The material read so quickly and coherently that it was like having a conversation with a Christian friend. I could really feel the excitement as we talked about the throne of God and its radiance. Those who are curious about heaven will be so delighted and joyful when they read this book. I think the questions at the end of the book are a great idea. This book is a ready-made classroom treasure. I was deeply moved by the gentle loving approach and the manner this material was presented to me, the reader. I can hardly wait to read your other books. You have gained a new fan and admirer of your special way of presenting the kingdom of heaven and God's love for us." (Mississippi).

- "I've looked at several books on heaven and bought some, but none had the depth of the Holy Spirit in them as your book on heaven. I want to express my appreciation for the way the Spirit wrote through you." (Kentucky)

- "I am the Youth Director of our church and I'm leading a group of high school students in a Bible study of your book on heaven. We all respect your opinions and have found your book to be an excellent springboard for discussion. It is thought-provoking and informative. This book has much substance and is well organized." (California)

Never, Never Give Up

- "When I received your book *Never, Never Give Up*, all was well in my life. I was supposed to be married when I graduated from the higher institution of learning, but this marriage never materialized. The lady I loved so much suffered from migraine headaches and eye pain. She suffered in great pain for almost a year and then she died. In all of this journey of suffering I read your book three times. The contents are so meaningful to me and built a good strong character in me. Though my fiancé died and went to be with the Lord, God saw me through that problem. *Never, Never Give Up* was a timely book. It is written simply and is easy to understand. I pray that the Lord will continue to use your ministry to help people who are going through tough times." (Zambia)

- "Your book, *Never, Never Give Up*, is wonderful, encouraging, motivating and educational. This book is precise, accurate and clear. My faith has been so high after reading this book. God Himself has written this book, not man. Italy is a godless nation. Most of the people here have nothing but vague thoughts about salvation." (Italy)

How to Study the Bible

- "I am incarcerated at this time in a prison in Georgia. I thank you very much for your book *How to Study the Bible*. I fell in love with this book. I read it over three times before I put it down. This book has been such a positive factor in my spiritual life that I really feel super close to my God and my Lord Jesus Christ." (Georgia)

- "My wife and I are utilizing the Bible study method that you explained in *How to Study the Bible*. We are really growing spiritually as a result. Our old methods of study were not nearly as fruitful. Thank you for writing about your method." (Idaho)

- "I have read almost all of your books and they are outstanding. The one that blessed me the most was *How to Study the Bible*. The study part was excellent, but the meditation chapters were very, very beneficial. I am indebted to you for sharing these. I purchased 30 copies to give to friends. Every earnest student of God's Word needs a copy." (Tennessee)

100 Years from Today

- "*100 Years from Today* told me that going to church and doing good deeds won't get me to heaven. I believe in Jesus Christ. I believe He died for our sins and that He forgives us for what we did wrong. Heaven is where I belong. I am born again. I have a new life. This book has changed my life." (Florida)

- "*100 Years from Today* has helped me to accept Jesus as my Savior. Your book shed a whole new light on the subject. I used to think I was too bad to be a Christian. Thank you for writing this book. It has changed my life." (Florida)

Nuggets of Faith

- "As I have read through *Nuggets of Faith* I have received insights into scriptures which have escaped me in previous meditation. This is indeed a most invaluable book of vital keys and principles." (Republic of Singapore)

- "I want to tell you how favorably your excellent book, *Nuggets of Faith*, impresses me. It thrills me through and through. It gives me great comfort and inspiration. I thank God for it. You are a terrific author." (Pennsylvania)

- "We give *Nuggets of Faith* to people who are hospitalized, for birthdays, to saved and unsaved. Everyone who has received one tells us, 'It's the best little book I've ever read. It's so clear and easy to understand.'" (Indiana)

Comments on our Scripture Meditation Cards

- "My back was hurting so badly that I couldn't get comfortable. I was miserable whether I sat or stood or laid down. I didn't know what to do. Suddenly I thought of the Scripture cards on healing that my husband had purchased. I decided to meditate on the Scripture in these cards. I was only on the second card when, all of a sudden, I felt heat go from my neck down through my body. The Lord had healed me. I never knew it could happen so fast. The pain has not come back." (Idaho)

- "I had no idea when you sent me these Scripture cards on *Freedom from Worry and Fear* that I would be using them every day. We've got to get these out to the world. Thank you again for the cards. They are absolutely incredible." (Utah)

- "I am very enthusiastic about your Scripture cards and your tape titled *Receive Healing from the Lord*. I love your tape. The clarity of your voice and your sincerity and compassion will encourage sick people. They can listen to this tape throughout the day, before they go to sleep at night, while they are driving to the doctor's office, in the hospital, etc. The tape is filled with Scripture and many good comments on Scripture. This cassette tape and your Scripture cards on healing are powerful tools that will help many sick people." (Tennessee)

- "I meditate constantly on the healing cards and listen to your tape on healing over and over. Your voice is so soothing. You are a wonderful teacher. My faith is increasing constantly." (New Hampshire).

Receive Healing from the Lord

Jack and Judy Hartman

Lamplight Ministries, Inc.
Dunedin, Florida

Dedication

We dedicate this book to the six members of the Board of Directors of Lamplight Ministries. Don Eichelberger, Mike Hartman, Ed Hiers, Paul LaCroix, Terry Lemerond and John Wade have contributed greatly to this ministry. Each of these men is a pillar in our lives and a source of wisdom, counsel and friendship. We are undergirded by their prayers. Don, Mike, Ed, Paul, Terry and John, we love you and thank you for being such a blessing to us.

FOREWORD

My wife has edited my books for many years. When we stopped writing books to devote five years of our lives to writing ten sets of Scripture Meditation Cards, Judy contributed so much that she rightfully was listed as the co-author of each set of Scripture cards.

When we started to write books again, I assumed that she would edit the books as before. However, Judy made so many changes on each draft of our next book that she changed the book significantly. I concluded at that time that she legitimately should be listed as the co-author of that book. This same situation has occurred in each of our subsequent books.

I have written several portions of this book in the first person because this book is filled with principles I have taught for more than thirty years, but I want to emphasize that Judy definitely is the co-author of this book. I am indebted to Judy for hearing God and for all of the constructive writing and rewriting she has done. Thank you, my dear wife. I believe the readers of this book also will thank you as they read the following pages.

Jack Hartman

I first started using this version of the Bible when I bought a paperback version of *The Amplified New Testament* in 1975 because of the inscription on the cover. This inscription said, "…the best study Testament on the market. It is a magnificent translation. I use it constantly." (Dr. Billy Graham)

The history of this version of the Bible is very interesting. A group of qualified Hebrew and Greek scholars believed that traditional word-by-word translations often failed to reveal the shades of meaning that are part of the Hebrew and Greek words. They spent more than twenty thousand hours amplifying the Bible, clarifying and expanding the verses.

After many years of extensive Bible study I have found that *The Amplified Bible* reveals many spiritual truths I cannot find in other versions of the Bible. Because of this marvelous amplification we now use this version of the Bible exclusively in all of our books and Scripture Meditation Cards.

Please be patient with the brackets and parentheses. They are used to indicate what has been added in the amplification. The brackets contain words that clarify the meaning. The parentheses contain additional phrases included in the original language. Do not be put off by the mass of parentheses and brackets. I believe you will find, as I did, that *The Amplified Bible* is filled with specific and practical information that will help *you* to understand what the Bible says about receiving healing from God.

TABLE OF CONTENTS

Introduction

I experienced a season of ill health approximately two years before the publication of this book. I immediately sought the Lord for healing. I wrote approximately 200 healing meditations in the first person so that I could meditate continually on what the Bible says about healing.

I continued to write these meditations after my health improved. I ended up writing more than 2,800 healing meditations. These meditations served as the foundation for the *ten separate drafts* of this book that we have written over a period of 22 months.

Judy and I have labored over this book. We know that healing is a controversial subject. We know people who trusted God for healing and still died. We know people who are sick today and have not yet been healed. We are not in any way attempting to condemn any person who has not received healing.

Healing is a complex subject. There are many variables in regard to receiving healing from sickness. Our desire is to allow God to be God. We are merely reporters of what His Word says about the subject of healing.

Fox News says, "We report. You decide." We will give you hundreds of facts from the holy Scriptures pertaining to divine healing. You then can decide what *you* desire to do with these facts from the Bible regarding sickness in your body.

Every person who is reading this book either needs healing personally or knows someone very well who needs healing. This book is filled with *facts* from the Word of God that tell Christians who are sick *exactly* what your Father instructs you to do to receive the healing that Jesus Christ has provided for you.

Most Christians believe that God can heal. They know that God can do anything. Their big question is, *"Will* God heal *me?"* You soon will see in the Word of God that God *already* has provided healing for *you.*

Our Father wants His children who are sick to *know* what His Word says about healing. He expects you to *believe* that He will do exactly what He promises to do. Many Christians have suffered through agonizing sickness and died prematurely because they *did not know* what the Word of God says about divine health and divine healing. "My people are destroyed for lack of knowledge…" (Hosea 4:6).

Many Christians have gone to the same church for many years without hearing any teaching on the subject of divine healing. Some Christians belong to denominations that teach that God does not heal today. If you are sick and you need healing we pray that you will not be influenced by anything *except* the Word of God. The Word of God is the final authority.

Christians who are sick should come humbly to God with absolute reverence for His Word. "…this is the man to whom I will look and have regard; he who is humble and of a broken and wounded spirit, and who trembles at My word and reveres My commands" (Isaiah 66:2).

Will you commit to "humble" yourself before the awesome, mighty and supernatural living Word of God? Do you "tremble at God's Word?" Do you "revere" the Word of God? Please *disregard* any statement in this book pertaining to divine healing *if* we cannot prove every principle that we teach by the Word of God.

We pray that you will approach the Bible with an *open mind* regardless of any prior beliefs you may have had about divine healing. If you learn that these beliefs are contrary to what the Word of God teaches we pray that you will align yourself completely with the Bible.

You must have a solid and unshakable foundation for your prayers of faith for healing. The Word of God should be the foundation for all of your prayers. When you are asking God for healing you should base your prayer requests on specific *facts* from His Word.

You *will* pay a price one way or another if you are severely ill. If you do *not* pay the price of learning and doing what God instructs you to do to receive healing, you *will* pay the price of your body being ravaged by sickness.

Almost all sick people would *like* to be healed. Your Father wants you to do *more* than just wish to be healed. Do you have a deep, strong and compelling desire to be healed? Are you determined to do exactly what your Father has instructed you to do to receive the precious gift of healing that already has been provided for you?

The Bible does not contain specific chapters telling you how to receive healing from God. God has interspersed hundreds of promises and instructions concerning divine healing, divine health and increased faith in God throughout the Bible. We have spent hundreds of hours extracting these promises and instructions from God. We have categorized this material into subtopics and woven them together so that you can clearly see the definite promises and instructions from the Bible that have been provided for *you* to receive healing.

If you turn on a light in a dark room you can see things that were there all along even though you could not see them in the darkness. This same principle applies to facts pertaining to divine healing. This book is filled with scriptural facts about healing that have been in the Bible all along. We pray that this book will turn on a spiritual light so that you will be able to learn, understand and take action on the specific instructions and promises in the Bible pertaining to divine healing.

There is *no* question that healing has been provided for you. Your Father wants you to *know* with absolute and unwavering faith that you already *have* been healed in the spiritual realm.

God created us to live in His Spirit. You will find that this book contains many specific scriptural instructions to show you exactly what we believe you should do to bring this healing from the spiritual realm into the natural realm.

Some Christians who are sick are not so severely ill that they cannot live a relatively normal lifestyle. They are able to get by with medical assistance, prescriptions and/or over the counter medication. Many of these Christians are willing to put up with some discomfort rather than make an absolute commitment to seek divine healing wholeheartedly.

This book is not written for these Christians. This book is written for Christians who are *totally committed* to do whatever their loving Father has instructed them to do to receive the healing He has provided for them. Many of these Christians are seriously ill. Their lifestyle has been completely changed by sickness.

Words that are not born in love miss their mark. We have done our best to write this book to give you facts from the Word of God pertaining to divine healing and also to write with pens that have been dipped in the ink of our Father's love.

We believe that seeking God is *more* important than seeking healing. God created us to have fellowship with Him. We believe that an intimate relationship with God is vitally important for all Christians who are sick. We have devoted several chapters that we believe will help you to focus on your vitally important relationship with God.

We recommend that you read this book with a highlighter or a pen. We recommend that you highlight or underline all scriptural instructions in this book that you want to retain for the future. Once you have finished reading this book with highlighting or underlining, we recommend that you review this material repeatedly as you study and meditate on these facts from the Word of God until this Scripture comes up off the printed page and comes alive in your mind and your heart.

Dear Father, we pray in the name of Jesus Christ that each person reading this book will learn exactly what is needed to receive healing in his or her body. Thank You, dear Father, for the healing You have given us and for the specific scriptural instructions and promises You have given us to enable us to receive the healing that has been provided for us by our beloved Lord, Savior and Healer, Jesus Christ.

Chapter 1

You Have Been Redeemed from *Both* Sin and Sickness

In the first two chapters of this book our goal is to *definitely* establish that God *has* provided healing for you. We then have included six chapters pertaining to divine health. Once these facts have been established you then will learn from the Word of God *how* to receive manifestation of the healing your loving Father has provided for you through His beloved Son, Jesus Christ.

People who are humble, open and teachable regarding the message of eternal salvation through Jesus Christ will receive eternal salvation and live eternally in heaven. People with closed minds will not be saved. They will live in eternal damnation in the lake of fire unless they become open to the truth pertaining to eternal salvation, repent of their sins and trust completely in Jesus Christ for their salvation.

This *same* principle applies to divine healing. There was no sickness in the garden of Eden before Adam sinned. Adam and Eve enjoyed excellent health. Sickness originated with the fall of Adam. Adam's fellowship with God was broken when he sinned. The wonderful presence of God that always had been available to him no longer was available. Adam and Eve died on the inside when they disobeyed God.

Adam lost the covering that God had put around him. He became spiritually dead. The process of physical death was birthed at that time. When Adam fell, Satan was able to pull him out of the spiritual realm that God had provided for him into the natural realm of sickness, disease and death.

Because of the sin of Adam all people who lived after him have to face death (except the Christians who will be alive when the church is raptured). Jesus Christ took away the power of death. "...just as [because of their union of nature] in Adam all people die, so also [by virtue of their union of nature] shall all in Christ be made alive" (I Corinthians 15:22).

Please highlight or underline the two times the word "all" is used in this passage of Scripture. *All* of us must face death because we *all* are descendants of Adam. However, if we receive eternal salvation through Jesus Christ *all* of us will be "made alive." Spiritual and physical death no longer will have dominion over us.

All people who receive Jesus Christ as their personal Savior will live eternally in heaven because God sent His beloved Son Jesus Christ to be the second Adam. "...The first man Adam became a living being (an individual personality); the last Adam (Christ) became a life-giving Spirit [restoring the dead to life]" (I Corinthians 15:45).

Please note that Jesus is referred to in this passage of Scripture as "the last Adam." Jesus died on the cross at Calvary to atone for the sins of Adam and the sins of every person who has lived since Adam. Jesus became "a life-giving Spirit restoring the dead to life."

Every person you know is a sinner! The nicest, most decent and most wonderful person you know is a sinner. "...all have sinned and are falling short of the honor and glory which God bestows and receives" (Romans 3:23).

Please highlight or underline the word "all" in this passage of Scripture. *Every* person who has lived since the fall of Adam *is* a sinner. God does not have degrees of sin. People who have committed only a few seemingly minor sins are just as guilty before God as someone who is considered by the world as a terrible sinner. "…whosoever keeps the Law [as a] whole but stumbles and offends in one [single instance] has become guilty of [breaking] all of it" (James 2:10).

Please understand that the word "whosoever" in this passage of Scripture includes *every* person who has ever committed a sin. Every person who has ever lived is a sinner in the eyes of God. "All have turned aside; together they have gone wrong and have become unprofitable and worthless; no one does right, not even one!" (Romans 3:12).

"Not even one" person has lived a life that is good enough for that person to qualify to live eternally in heaven. Adam's sin brought punishment to *every* person. Jesus Christ has provided freedom from the sin of Adam for *every* person. Jesus came to earth to pay the *full price* for Adam's transgressions. Jesus paid the price to set *you* free from the power of death. He *also* paid the price to set *you* free from the power of sickness. (Please read the Appendix at the end of this book for additional information on eternal salvation through Jesus Christ.)

You must understand that Jesus did not provide just partial redemption. He provided *total and complete redemption* that includes freedom from death *and* freedom from sickness. If you have asked Jesus Christ to be your Savior you know Him as your Forgiver. You must understand that Jesus *also* is your Healer.

You did not earn your salvation. You do not deserve eternal salvation. You did not earn divine healing. You do not deserve to receive healing from God. God is *so loving* that He has made provision for every person to receive through the shed blood of His Son Jesus Christ the eternal salvation and divine healing we do not deserve.

You receive eternal salvation through absolute faith that Jesus paid the full price for all of your sins by the sacrifice He made on the cross at Calvary. Your Father wants you to have deep, strong and unwavering faith that Jesus *also* paid the full price for manifestation of healing in your body.

Jesus never sinned, but He took upon Himself the sins of the entire world. Jesus actually *became sin* to pay the price for *your* sins. "For our sake He made Christ [virtually] to be sin Who knew no sin…" (II Corinthians 5:21).

The same Jesus Christ Who *became sin* to pay the price for your sins also *became sick* to pay the price for the sickness in *your* body. "…it was the will of the Lord to bruise Him; He has put Him to grief and made Him sick …" (Isaiah 53:10).

How could it be "the will of the Lord" to "bruise" His beloved Son Jesus Christ? How could it be God's will to "put Jesus to grief and make Him sick?" How could it be God's will to see His beloved Son whipped and beaten to take sickness on Himself? Would it be your will to see your child going through this ordeal? Your Father in heaven willingly observed His beloved Son paying this price because He knew that Jesus had chosen to make this enormous sacrifice *so that the entire human race could be redeemed and healed.*

God's justice requires full payment for the sins of every person before we can be saved. God's justice also requires full payment for the sickness of every person before we can receive the healing He has provided for us. Jesus paid the full price for your sins. He also paid the full price for the sickness in your body. "Bless (affectionately, gratefully praise) the Lord, O my soul, and forget not [one of] all His benefits – Who forgives [every one of] all your iniquities, Who heals [each one of] all your diseases" (Psalm 103:2-3).

This magnificent passage of Scripture says that you should "gratefully praise the Lord" and "forget not one of all His benefits." You will make a big mistake if you ask Jesus to be your Savior and fail to receive Him as your Healer. This passage of Scripture clearly states that Jesus forgives *all* of your sin *and* that He also "*heals all of your diseases.*"

Please highlight or underline the words "all of your diseases." Is it not very clear that the same Jesus Christ Who provided salvation for your soul *also* has provided healing for your body? Should you believe one portion of a passage of Scripture and *not* another portion of the same passage of Scripture? If you fail to trust God to heal all of your diseases you definitely are forgetting one of the "benefits" God has provided for you.

Stop now and take time to carefully meditate on this passage of Scripture. Do *not* take this awesome promise lightly. See for yourself that the Word of God definitely *combines* freedom from sin and freedom from sickness in the *same* passage of Scripture. If *God does not* separate freedom from sin and freedom from sickness *you should not* separate freedom from sin and freedom from sickness.

We will look many times at the 53rd chapter of Isaiah in this book. This chapter often is called the Atonement Chapter. You will clearly see that healing is part of Jesus Christ's atonement just as forgiveness of sin is part of His atonement. Jesus redeemed you from sin. He redeemed you from sickness.

There is no question that healing definitely is part of the redemption Jesus paid for you. "Surely He has borne our griefs (sicknesses, weaknesses, and distresses) and carried our sorrows and pains [of punishment], yet we [ignorantly] considered Him stricken, smitten, and afflicted by God [as if with leprosy]. But He was wounded for our transgressions, He was bruised for our guilt and iniquities; the chastisement [needful to obtain] peace and well-being for us was upon Him, and with the stripes [that wounded] Him we are healed and made whole" (Isaiah 53:4-5).

Please highlight or underline the word "surely" in this passage of Scripture. This word emphasizes that Jesus *definitely* has paid the price for *your* sins and the sickness in *your* body. He has "borne your griefs, sicknesses, weaknesses and distresses." There is no question that, because of the horrible "stripes" Jesus received when He was brutally whipped by Roman soldiers, *you* "are healed and made whole."

Isaiah, writing under the anointing of the Holy Spirit, prophesied in advance that Jesus Christ the Messiah would pay the full price for your sins and for the sickness in your body. Jesus *fulfilled this prophecy* from Isaiah more than seven hundred years later. "…thus He fulfilled what was spoken by the prophet Isaiah, He Himself took [in order to carry away] our weaknesses and infirmities and bore away our diseases" (Matthew 8:17).

You have just read a statement from the New Testament that is similar to what you have read in the 53rd chapter of Isaiah. *How* can anyone doubt that Jesus Christ actually did "carry away our weaknesses and infirmities and bear our diseases?"

The apostle Peter, also writing under the anointing of the Holy Spirit, tells you that Jesus paid the full price for your sins *and* for the sickness in your body. "He personally bore our sins in His [own] body on the tree [as on an altar and offered Himself on it], that we might die (cease to exist) to sin and live to righteousness. By His wounds you have been healed" (I Peter 2:24).

All Christians agree that Jesus "personally bore our sins in His own body" by the tremendous sacrifice He made on the cross at Calvary. *You must not stop here.* This *same* passage of Scripture says that "*you* have been healed by His wounds."

You can be certain that this promise applies to the sickness in *your* body today. This passage of Scripture does not say that you *will* be healed. It says that "you *have been* healed." The full price for the sickness in your body *already has been paid.* You need to learn and obey the specific instructions in the Word of God to receive manifestation of the healing that Jesus *already* has provided for you.

Please note the past tense of the words "bore our sins" and "have been healed." Isaiah prophesied what would happen. Peter told us what *already had happened* when he wrote these words under the anointing of the Holy Spirit.

How can any Christian who trusts Jesus Christ for his or her eternal salvation not believe that Jesus *also* paid the full price for sickness? People who say that divine healing is not for today would have to take a pair of scissors and cut out parts of Isaiah 53:4-5, Psalm 103:2-3, Matthew 8:17 and I Peter 2:24. You must understand that *the full price has been paid for healing the sickness in your body.*

You must not read the Word of God selectively. You must not say or think, "I agree with the part pertaining to eternal salvation, but I disagree with the part that pertains to healing." You must believe *everything* the holy Scriptures say whether or not these facts from the Word of God line up with your previous beliefs.

Your Father clearly has shown you in several passages of Scripture that both eternal salvation and divine healing *are* part of the atonement provided by Jesus Christ. Either all of the Word of God is true or none of it is true. You are saved because the Word of God says you are saved. You are healed because the Word of God says you are healed.

The last words Jesus spoke before He died on the cross were "It is finished!" (John 19:30). When Jesus spoke these words He emphasized that He had accomplished *everything* He came to earth to do. When Jesus took every person's sin and sickness on Himself He said, "It is finished!"

When Jesus spoke these words on the cross at Calvary He proclaimed to every human being who lived then and every human being who would live in the future that the price had been paid in full for the eternal salvation of your soul *and* for the healing of your body. Jesus has provided everything you need. He has provided eternal salvation for all who faithfully call Him their Savior. He has provided divine healing for all who faithfully call Him their Healer.

God does *not* withhold forgiveness of sins from *anyone*. He does *not* withhold healing of sickness from *anyone*. The Word of God does not separate Jesus Christ the Savior from Jesus Christ the Healer. You must not arbitrarily separate what the Word of God does not separate.

God did *not* intend for you to accept the price Jesus paid for your sins and reject the price He paid for the sickness in your body. Nevertheless, this is exactly what many Christians do. Many Christians have heard so much preaching on the forgiveness of sins that they know beyond any doubt that their sins *are* forgiven. Unfortunately, many of these same Christians have heard little or no preaching or teaching on the subject of divine healing. Because they do not know these scriptural facts about healing many Christians die prematurely without receiving the healing that definitely has been provided for them.

Is Jesus Christ your personal Savior? You can be certain that He also wants to be your personal Healer. God wants everyone to live eternally with Him in heaven, but He does *not* automatically save everyone. You can only receive eternal salvation if you believe in your heart and confess with your mouth that you are absolutely certain that Jesus Christ paid the full price for your sins. This same principle applies to divine healing.

You receive eternal salvation when you believe in your *heart* that Jesus Christ paid the price for your sins and when you open your mouth and *speak* freely of your certainty of eternal salvation. "…with the heart a person believes (adheres to, trusts in, and relies on Christ) and so is justified (declared righteous, acceptable to God), and with the mouth he confesses (declares openly and speaks out freely his faith and confirms [his] salvation" (Romans 10:10).

No matter what sins you may have committed you have been given the privilege to trust completely in Jesus for forgiveness. No matter what sickness you may have in your body you have been given the privilege of believing that Jesus already has provided healing from that sickness.

You must believe that you will receive the healing Jesus has provided for you. This chapter contains many facts from the holy Scriptures to *prove* that divine healing is as much a part of your redemption as forgiveness of sin. Now that we have established these definite facts from the Word of God we are ready to move on to learn more facts from the Bible about the healing that already has been provided for you.

Chapter 2

Jesus Christ Paid an Enormous Price for Your Healing

In this chapter you will read many facts from the holy Scriptures about the tremendous price Jesus Christ paid for *you* so that *you* can receive healing from sickness. We will go back more than two thousand years to carefully observe exactly what Jesus went through so that *you* can receive the healing He *already* has provided for you.

During the night before Jesus was crucified He went to a place called the Garden of Gethsemane. Jesus agonized about the price He knew He was about to pay (see Matthew 26:36-46, Mark 14:32-42 and Luke 22:40-46). After that ordeal Jesus then was betrayed by His disciple, Judas. When Judas led Jewish soldiers to a place where they could capture Jesus His disciples fled (see Matthew 26:47-56, Mark 14:42-52, Luke 22:47-62 and John 18:1-12).

The Jewish soldiers then led Jesus to a special session of the Jewish supreme court called the Sanhedrin. The Jewish high priest, Caiphas, presided. He sought the death penalty. False witnesses lied about what Jesus had done. Jewish soldiers spat in His face, hit Him with their fists and slapped Him (see Matthew 26:57, Mark 14:55-65 and John 18:13-23).

After this farce of a trial the soldiers brought Jesus to the Praetorium which was the palace of the Roman governor, Pontius

Pilate. The Jewish court wanted Pilate to give the death penalty to Jesus. Pilate found no evidence that Jesus was guilty. In an attempt to shift responsibility Pilate sent Jesus to the Jewish King Herod. Herod also did not find Jesus guilty. He sent Jesus back to Pilate (see Luke 23:6-11).

Please focus on this excruciating ordeal that Jesus went through up to this point. Jesus agonized in the Garden of Gethsemane. He was betrayed by Judas who was one of His disciples, He was unfairly tried by the Sanhedrin where He was physically assaulted. He was sent to Pontius Pilate who did not find Him guilty. He then was sent to King Herod who did not find Him guilty and sent Him back to Pilate.

Jesus must have been exhausted. Each of these so-called trials was a mockery. Jesus had no sleep during that entire night. He was forced to go back and forth across the city of Jerusalem for these mock trials.

When Jesus came back to Pontius Pilate for the second time Pilate once again was unable to find Jesus guilty of the alleged crimes. Pilate was surrounded by a screaming mob of people who wanted Jesus put to death. Pilate was reluctant to give Jesus the death penalty.

He finally allowed the mob of people to vote by the clamor of their voices whether they wanted to set Jesus free or to free a convicted criminal named Barabbas. The crazed mob overwhelmingly told Pilate that they wanted Barabbas to be set free (see Matthew 27:16-26, Mark 15:6-15, Luke 23:17-25 and John 18:38-40).

In order to soothe his conscience Pilate actually "washed his hands" of the entire affair. "…when Pilate saw that he was getting nowhere, but rather that a riot was about to break out, he took water and washed his hands in the presence of the crowd, saying, I am not guilty of nor responsible for this righteous Man's blood; see to it yourselves" (Matthew 27:24).

After washing his hands Pilate then caused Jesus to be whipped before He was crucified. "…he set free for them Barabbas; and he [had] Jesus whipped, and delivered Him up to be crucified" (Matthew 27:26). John gives a more graphic account. "Pilate took Jesus and scourged (flogged, whipped) Him" (John 19:1).

In this chapter you will learn exactly what took place when Jesus was whipped by the Roman soldiers. As you examine the details of this horrible ordeal please be aware that this whipping took place *before* the Son of God went through the enormous price that He paid for your sins on the cross at Calvary. The Roman soldiers beat Jesus and spat in His face before He went to the whipping post. "…they spat in His face and struck Him with their fists; and some slapped Him in the face" (Matthew 26:67).

More than seven hundred years before this event Isaiah had accurately prophesied that the soldiers would spit in the face of the Messiah, pull hair out of His beard and beat Him across His back. Jesus knew exactly what He would face at the whipping post and on the cross. He had absolute faith that God would help Him through these ordeals. Jesus was determined to persevere in faith. "I gave My back to the smiters and My cheeks to those who plucked off the hair; I hid not My face from shame and spitting. For the Lord God helps Me; therefore have I not been ashamed or confounded. Therefore have I set My face like a flint, and I know that I shall not be put to shame" (Isaiah 50:6-7).

This passage of Scripture explains that Jesus knew His back would be whipped. He knew that soldiers would pull hair out of His beard. Jesus did not hide from "shame and spitting." He was "not ashamed or confounded" because He knew that He had chosen God's will.

When this passage of Scripture says that Jesus "set His face like a flint" it compares His resolve to a hard rock called a flint. This rock was extremely durable. Jesus knew His mission and He did not waver during this excruciating ordeal.

Please visualize your Savior, the beloved Son of God, going through three mock trials where He never once was proven guilty as charged. Visualize Jesus unfairly being found guilty by Pontius Pilate because of the pressure of a screaming mob of people. Visualize the Son of God putting up with people hitting Him, pulling hair out of His beard and spitting in His face as part of the price He paid so that *you* can receive the healing He provided for you.

Before we examine exactly what took place at the whipping post we will briefly review two passages of Scripture from Chapter One. Isaiah prophesied that Jesus would pay the price for the healing of all mankind by the "stripes" He suffered for you. Isaiah said, "…with the stripes [that wounded] Him we are healed and made whole" (Isaiah 53:5). This prophesy in the Old Testament was fulfilled by Jesus approximately seven hundred years later after which the apostle Peter said, "By His wounds you have been healed" (I Peter 2:24).

We will examine both of these passages of Scripture in more detail in subsequent chapters. For now we want to state that the Bible says that "*you* have been healed" by the wounds Jesus suffered from the Roman soldiers when He was tied to a whipping post.

The soldiers probably used a whip that was called a "cat of nine tails." These whips were much more severe than a whip with a single lash. Each lash had nine separate tails of leather. A jagged piece of bone or metal was attached to the end of each tail. These nine leather cords tipped with bone or metal cut deeply into the body of the person who was being whipped. These whips were lethal weapons.

Some people say that Jesus was whipped thirty-nine times because the Mosaic law limited the number of lashes that could be given to a victim. "Forty stripes may be given him but no more…" (Deuteronomy 25:3). This number was reduced to thirty-nine lashes by the time Jesus went to the whipping post. The apostle Paul received thirty-nine stripes on five occasions. Paul said, "Five times I received from [the hands of] the Jews forty [lashes all] but one…" (II Corinthians 11:24).

The Jews limited the number of lashes to thirty-nine. However, the Romans did *not* have a law that limited the number of stripes a victim could receive. Roman soldiers often whipped people until the victim bled to death.

Even though many people believe that Jesus received thirty-nine lashes, He could have received many more. Also, please realize that *each lash* Jesus received from the whip probably was equivalent to *nine lashes* because of each of the nine tails that bruised Jesus and cut into Him. Because of the nine tails of the whips the face and body of our beloved Jesus probably were cut *more than three hundred times.*

The Bible refers to the wounds where the whips tore great pieces of flesh from the face and body of Jesus as "stripes." We do not know how many times Jesus took these lashes across His back, His body and His face, but there is no question that He was beaten horribly. Jesus took these stripes on *His body* for whatever sickness *you* have in *your body.*

Jesus has paid the price for the sin and sickness of every person who lived since that time. The pain of scourging was excruciating. Isaiah referred to scourging as "…the overwhelming scourge…" (Isaiah 28:18).

Jesus' body was torn to shreds as this "overwhelming" whipping continued. Pieces of His body probably were cut loose and detached. His ribs, bones and vital organs undoubtedly showed through the numerous openings in His skin. Isaiah prophesied how badly Jesus would be whipped. "[For many the Servant of God became an object of horror; many were astonished at Him.] His face and His whole appearance were marred more than any man's, and His form beyond that of the sons of men…" (Isaiah 52:14).

The beloved Son of God "became an object of horror" for *you.* People who saw Jesus after His whipping were horrified by what they saw. Jesus was whipped *so badly* that "His face and His whole appearance were marred more than any man's." Jesus apparently was whipped *so badly* that He did not even look like a human being — "His form beyond that of the sons of men."

Jesus suffered such horrible punishment that many people who observed His whipping turned their faces away from Him. They could not bring themselves to look any longer at this hideous sight. The Bible says that Jesus was "...despised and rejected and forsaken by men, a Man of sorrows and pains, and acquainted with grief and sickness; and like One from Whom men hide their faces He was despised, and we did not appreciate His worth or have any esteem for Him" (Isaiah 53:3).

Why was Jesus "despised, rejected and forsaken?" *Why* was the Son of God "a Man of sorrows and pains?" *Why* was Jesus "acquainted with grief and sickness?" *Why* did men "hide their faces?" Jesus endured this ordeal because His Father planned for His beloved Son to receive this horrible whipping. We saw in Chapter One that "...it was the will of the Lord to bruise Him; He has put Him to grief and made Him sick..." (Isaiah 53:10).

God's will was for Jesus to go through this ordeal. God Himself "put Jesus to grief and made Him sick." Jesus Who apparently was very healthy was *made to be sick by God* because Jesus *took upon Himself* at that whipping post *all* of the sickness that *any* person has ever suffered.

Are you sick? You can be *absolutely certain* that Jesus *paid the price in full* for the healing of sickness in *your* body. In addition to being physically mutilated at the whipping post Jesus also bore the sickness of the entire world upon Himself. Other people have been horribly mutilated at a whipping post, but *no one else* ever took the sickness of the entire world upon himself or herself *in addition to* this terrible whipping.

Please visualize Jesus Christ, the Son of God, tied to a whipping post with His hands high above His head. Visualize Him being horribly whipped to *pay the price for your healing.* Jesus sealed every healing promise in the Bible when He received that brutal whipping. All of the Old Testament healing promises and all of the subsequent healing promises in the New Testament were activated when Jesus paid this price.

Jesus went through the scourging and crucifixion with the full knowledge that He could call on His Father at any time to be delivered from this ordeal. At the peak of His spiritual and physical punishment Jesus did not give in to this temptation. *He loves you so much* that He never once gave in to the temptation of being relieved from paying the enormous price He paid for *your* sins and for the sickness in *your* body.

You must *know* that an enormous price *has* been paid for your healing. You must *learn* exactly what the Bible tells you to do to receive this healing. You *must not negate* the horrible and tremendous price that Jesus paid so that you can be healed.

If someone paid your debts in full would you think that you still have to pay these debts? Would you be excited if you had a receipt showing that this person paid off the mortgage on your home and all of your other debts? You should be *much more excited* about what Jesus did for you at the whipping post and on the cross. You should be very excited to learn that Jesus has paid the complete price for your healing. You do not have to pay this price again.

Many Christians who love Jesus with all of their hearts *do not even know* what the Bible says about the horrible ordeal Jesus went through for them at the whipping post. *How* can you expect to receive healing from God if you *do not even know* about the tremendous price Jesus paid for *your* healing?

No one in the history of the world deserved to be treated better than Jesus. Nevertheless, no one in the history of the world ever was treated worse than Jesus was treated at the Garden of Gethsemane, at His mock trials, at the whipping post and on the cross at Calvary. If the sickness in your body is wearing you down go back and carefully study the facts in this chapter about the scourging of Jesus. After you have read this chapter carefully say to yourself, "Jesus paid a tremendous price for *me*. He did *not* pay this price for me to give up. I *will persevere* in faith."

In Chapter One we clearly showed that eternal salvation and healing are linked together in the Word of God. In this chapter we have examined in detail the enormous price that Jesus paid for your healing. In subsequent chapters we will look into the holy Scriptures for many additional facts to show you very clearly what God's Word says about healing.

We have shown from the holy Scriptures that Jesus *definitely* has provided healing for you. The remainder of this book contains hundreds of scriptural instructions telling you *exactly* what to do to receive the healing that already has been provided for you.

However, before we study the subject of *divine healing* in more detail we need to learn some facts about *divine health.* Divine health is God's best. Divine healing is God's second best. We believe that many Christians pray for healing *without* doing what their Father wants them to do to be as healthy as possible. There is no question that God *will* do His part. However, if you are praying for healing you also must do *your* part.

Many people who have become sick are sick because of wrong choices they have made over a period of time. If you ask God to heal you doesn't it make sense that you first of all should learn whatever you can about *why* you became sick? Doesn't it make sense that you should do *your part* to make the changes that must be made before you ask God to do His part and give you manifestation of healing?

Let me give you some obvious examples. If a man had been diagnosed with lung cancer and continued to smoke cigarettes while he obeyed every scriptural healing instruction given in this book, do you think God would heal him? If a man had severely blocked arteries and his doctor gave him a specific list of food to avoid and this man often ate fat-laden foods at fast food restaurants, should he expect God to heal him? This man may be following the scriptural healing principles that are explained in this book, but ignoring the cause of his sickness.

God has given you specific scriptural instructions pertaining to divine healing. This book is filled with these instructions and promises. How can you expect God to heal you if you continue to eat the same kind of food that caused you to get sick in the first place? God would have to perform an instant miracle every time you lift a fork to your mouth.

You can pray and pray and pray for healing, but you often must set these prayers into motion by doing your part to improve your health. You may be praying in vain if you have not done all you can do. Miraculous healings take place instantly. However, gradual healings often must be combined with *action* from the person who is praying to be healed.

We also need to consider the relationship between death and healing. We know that all people (except those Christians who go up in the Rapture) will die. Death is *the ultimate healing* for Christians. Revelation 21:4 tells us that there will not be any more pain or grief when we are in heaven because all old conditions will have passed away.

Does God determine every aspect of the time when we die? Do we have some control over the time when we die? Of course we do. Common sense tells us that people who eat healthy food, exercise regularly and follow other common sense precautions that will lead to good health will live longer on the whole than people who completely disregard these facts pertaining to good health.

Psalm 91:15-16, Proverbs 3:1-2 and Proverbs 4:10 contain specific instructions to follow if you desire to live a long life. Proverbs 10:2 and Proverbs 14:27 contain specific instructions for you to follow to be delivered from premature death.

In the following six chapters on divine health we will give you a great deal of information pertaining to good health. Some of this information is backed up by the Word of God. Other information is backed up by facts from the research of people who have carefully studied what we need to do to maintain our health. You can verify these facts on the internet and come to your own conclusion.

We will present many principles pertaining to good health that may be very different from what you believe now. We do not expect anyone to agree completely with *everything* we recommend. We also do not believe that any person reading these chapters will disagree with *everything* we say. Believe and take action on the areas that you believe will help *you* to improve your health.

Once you have done everything you can do you then will be ready to follow the precise scriptural instructions in the remainder of this book. These instructions tell you exactly what your Father instructs you to do to receive manifestation of the healing that Jesus already has provided for you.

Chapter 3

Divine Health is God's Desire for You

In this chapter I would like to share with you some things I have learned in the past seventy-four years that have helped me to walk in health. Judy has written three subsequent chapters explaining the many facts she has learned in forty-five years of intensive study on the subject of health since she was twenty-one. I will begin this chapter by sharing with you some facts about physical exercise that have been *very* beneficial to my health.

There were no school buses when I was a boy in Vermont in the 1940s. At that time I did not ride my bicycle to school. The school did not have a place to keep bicycles. I often walked to school in cold and stormy weather. I walked thirty minutes each way to and from school every day.

I also walked a lot when I caddied at a golf course. I often rode my bicycle for thirty minutes to the golf course and then carried two bags of clubs for eighteen holes. Sometimes I would caddy again in the afternoon for a total of thirty-six holes. I then would ride my bicycle back home.

I developed a love of walking when I was younger, but I stopped consistent physical exercise for approximately sixteen years from the age of twenty-five to the age of forty-one. When I was forty-one years old I came to the conclusion that I definitely would experience severe health problems if I did not exercise regularly. I knew that I had come to the time in my life where an effective exercise program was a necessity, not an option. At that time I decided to walk vigorously for forty minutes each day at least four times a week.

I decided to walk because I was overweight and I knew that jogging would put too much stress on my feet, knees and legs. Over the years I have learned a lot about aerobic walking which also has been called speedwalking, racewalking or powerwalking. For many years I averaged over four miles an hour with my walking.

I believe I have received as much aerobic benefit from this brisk walking as I would have received from jogging. I did not experience jarring impact and there was practically no risk of injury. A detailed explanation of aerobic walking is included in Chapter Four of our book *Increased Energy and Vitality*.

I stuck to a walking schedule for more than thirty years. Many times when I lived in New Hampshire I would put on a heavy parka, boots and warm gloves to walk forty minutes in cold winter weather. I did not allow weather or anything else to deter me from this exercise. I am certain I would be dead today if I had not exercised so faithfully for more than three decades.

I have never spent much time in a health club. I have gone a few times, but for me walking is all I need. Walking is simple, effective and inexpensive. I don't need to drive anywhere in my automobile to get my exercise. I don't need to change into gym clothes. I can get the exercise I need from the convenience of my own home. I simply walk approximately twenty minutes out. Then I walk approximately twenty minutes back.

I have averaged walking at least fifteen vigorous miles each week for more than thirty years. This exercise totals to an average of approximately eight hundred miles a year. I have walked vigorously more than *twenty-five thousand miles* during the past thirty-three years which is the equivalent of walking across the United States approximately *eight times*.

I am seventy-four years old. I still walk whenever I can, but surgery on both of my knees and a problem with my right foot does not enable me to walk as much as I did previously. I often use a rebounder (which is a mini-trampoline) as a regular form of exercise.

Exercise on a rebounder is three to five times as beneficial as the same exercise on the ground. The springs on the rebounder provide tremendous additional benefits. The springs absorb my weight and push my body back into the air. Rebounding gives me excellent exercise without any jarring effect. I am able to do exercises on a rebounder that I could not possibly do on the ground.

Judy and I believe that Needak rebounders are the best. We have found that they are worth the extra money. We have two Needak rebounders in our home. I often use one when I am watching television. Sometimes when I am working at my desk and I need a break I rebound for five to ten minutes. Rebounding revitalizes me.

Judy is much more of an expert on rebounding than I am. She teaches a monthly health class at our church. Sometimes she amazes people in the audience with the exercise she does on a rebounder. This physically fit sixty-six year old woman continues to teach the class while she is exercising vigorously.

I learned the hard way the importance of starting rebounding gradually. The first time I used a rebounder I jogged on it for almost thirty minutes. This was one of the biggest mistakes I ever made. I suffered from severe aches and pains for several days. If you start rebounding we recommend that you purchase a Needak rebounder instead of a cheaper one. We also recommend that you start slowly and build up gradually to whatever level you find is best for you. You can purchase a beginners video or CD from Needak. Please contact Judy if you would like more details.

I have been overweight for most of my adult life. All of my cholesterol readings and all cardiovascular tests have been excellent. I always am interested in the reaction of the nurse who takes my pulse and blood pressure when I go for a physical exam. My pulse rate has consistently been between 55 and 65. I just took my pulse as I wrote these words. My resting pulse rate at the age of seventy-four is 62. My blood pressure readings today are much better than they were when I was forty years old.

I attribute these and other favorable results on my physical exams to consistent vigorous exercise since I was forty-one years old. Exercise is vitally important to me. I intend to continue walking and rebounding regularly for the rest of my life.

Judy and I wrote *Increased Energy and Vitality* twelve years ago. This book contains more than two hundred Scripture references. It is filled with detailed facts about exercise, aerobic walking and rebounding. This book also contains several chapters on diet. The chapters on exercise are just as valid today as they were when we wrote this book. We have refined our diets since then, but we believe that this book still is a handbook for health.

We now are advocates of the Hallelujah Diet. We invite you to go to www.hacres.com if you are interested in the relationship between diet, divine healing and divine health. *Do not begin by studying what the Hallelujah Diet is.* That will come later. We recommend that you begin by studying the *testimonies* of people who have experienced great improvement in their health as a result of the Hallelujah Diet.

There are many diets in the United States today. The Weight Watchers Diet, the South Beach Diet, the Jenny Craig Diet, the Atkins Diet and the Grapefruit Diet are just a few examples. However, as far as I know, none of these diets even begin to approach the number of *healing testimonies* that you will find on www.hacres.com.

I recently was talking with a friend who asked me to pray for a woman who had been diagnosed with breast cancer. My friend did not know about the Hallelujah Diet. I gave him the website and suggested that he look up the testimonies for breast cancer while we were talking on the telephone.

My friend was surprised to find more than *thirty* testimonies from women who had experienced great improvement from breast cancer because of the Hallelujah Diet. I suggested to my friend that he pass this information on to the woman with breast cancer. He said he would.

Shortly after this telephone conversation I was talking on the telephone with a man who recently had been diagnosed with diabetes. He said that this condition caused him to wake up constantly throughout the night to go the bathroom. The effects on his health since being diagnosed with diabetes were so severe that he told me he thought his life could be shortened by as much as twenty-five years by this disease.

I suggested that this man should go to www.hacres.com and look for testimonies regarding diabetes. He went to the website while we were talking on the telephone. Suddenly he said, "I cannot believe what I am seeing. There must be at least fifty testimonies from people who have been helped with diabetes from this diet." I told this man that some people might consider the Hallelujah Diet to be extreme. He said, "I don't care what I have to do. I am desperate."

At the time I am writing these words hacres.com contains the following testimonies:

Ailment	Number of testimonies
Arthritis	105
Heart disease	102
High cholesterol	73
Headaches	65
Diabetes	56
Depression	49
High blood pressure	44
Allergies	39
Breast cancer	34
Prostate cancer	33

I have only listed the top ten testimonies. Many other testimonies are available at this website. Do you know of any other diet that provides testimonies like these?

See for yourself. First, we suggest that you click on the link on the sidebar titled "Testimonials." This link will take you to the section where you can select from almost one hundred different categories of illness. You can choose from the drop-down list or search for a specific disease. You will be able to read many testimonies from people whose health has dramatically improved as a result of the Hallelujah Diet.

We believe you will be *amazed* by the tremendous number of testimonies from people all over the world whose health has dramatically improved as a result of the Hallelujah Diet. If you suffer from a specific illness be sure to go to the category of that illness. You probably will be very encouraged by the testimonies you read.

Once again I want to emphasize that, before you see exactly what the Hallelujah Diet is, you first must see what the Hallelujah Diet *has done* for many people. Please do not underestimate the Hallelujah Diet. The results from this biblically based and scientifically validated diet are remarkable.

This diet originates from a Christian organization named Hallelujah Acres in North Carolina that was founded by Rev. George Malkmus. One of the basic concepts of Hallelujah Acres is that each church should have a Health Minister. At this time more than six thousand Health Ministers have been certified by Hallelujah Acres in all fifty states in the United States and in fifty-seven foreign countries. More than two million people are following the Hallelujah Diet.

Hallelujah Acres has expanded tremendously in recent years. Hallelujah Acres Canada, Hallelujah Acres United Kingdom and Europe, Hallelujah Acres Australia and Hallelujah Acres New Zealand are separate arms of this non-denominational Christian ministry. Hallelujah Acres can provide you with a tremendous variety of information pertaining to divine health. You also can learn a great deal of additional information from the many books that Hallelujah Acres recommends.

Judy and I do not tell anyone what they should eat. Each person must make his or her own decisions regarding health. The fact that I have been overweight for many years clearly indicates that I do not stick to the Hallelujah Diet completely. I stick to it partially. Judy sticks to this diet very closely. We present the Hallelujah Diet. You may be blessed by it. Once again, begin with *facts* from testimonies and only examine what the diet consists of *after* reading these testimonies.

As I have said I am seventy-four years old and Judy is sixty-six years old. Unlike most senior citizens neither of us takes any medication whatsoever. I have occasionally used a prescription for an antibiotic. Judy has never taken even an aspirin.

Judy is the healthiest senior citizen I know. She recently passed the examination to be a Certified Personal Trainer. In the following chapters Judy will share just a few of the many things she has learned about divine health in the last forty-five years. You can contact Judy for a list of health teachings and for information on how to receive Hallelujah Acres free bimonthly *Back to the Garden* newsletter and/or their weekly internet health tip.

In this chapter I have given several facts about physical exercise. The Bible goes one step further. "...physical training is of some value (useful for a little), but godliness (spiritual training) is useful and of value in everything and in every way, for it holds promise for the present life and also for the life which is to come" (I Timothy 4:8).

This passage of Scripture clearly indicates the importance of being spiritually fit in addition to physical fitness. It says that "physical training is of some value, useful for a little." It goes on to say that "spiritual training is useful and of value in everything and in every way."

The words "everything" and "in every way" include *your health*. This passage of Scripture, I Corinthians 4:16, Proverbs 4:20-23 and III John 2 explain the relationship that definitely exists between divine health and faithfully immersing yourself in God's Word every day. This passage of Scripture says that daily Bible study and Scripture meditation "hold promise for the present life." Consistent Bible study and Scripture meditation *also* will provide you with eternal benefits throughout "the life which is to come."

This book is primarily devoted to divine healing. We have devoted forty-five chapters to divine healing and six chapters to divine health. We are *not* trying to minimize divine health. Divine health is even more important that divine healing. Divine health is God's best.

Divine health will help you to not get sick in the first place. Divine health will help you to receive divine healing. Divine health will help you to maintain divine healing after you have received it. Please read *Increased Energy and Vitality*. Also take full advantage of the many books on health that are offered by Hallelujah Acres and the extensive health information that Judy recommends.

Judy has written the next three chapters. She will explain facts about the Hallelujah Diet in more detail. Judy is a very healthy person who is filled with energy at the age of sixty-six. I hope you will read these chapters with an open mind.

Chapter 4

You Are Responsible
for Your Own Health

I have been studying and applying information pertaining to health, fitness and nutrition since I was twenty-one. I am now sixty-six years old and I enjoy excellent health. I do not take any medications. I feel so blessed to be so healthy. I want to bless you with what I have learned. My heart's cry is to provide information that may prevent cancer, heart disease, osteoporosis, diabetes and other degenerative diseases of affluence before a crisis occurs.

I plead with you to consider the statistics for people on the Standard American Diet. One of two will die of heart disease. One of three will die of cancer. The rest will die of complications with one of the other degenerative diseases according to statistics.

A treasured friend died suddenly with a heart blockage this year. Another friend who is like a sister to me is now unable to speak coherently or use her body fluidly because of a stroke. A lady who is like a mother to me lies in a bed in a full-care facility drugged daily and weighing less than one hundred pounds.

I teach a monthly class on health, fitness and nutrition in our church. In this first chapter I will briefly share several facts pertaining to health and fitness. The next chapter will be devoted to just a few of the facts I have learned pertaining to nutrition.

At the age of sixty-six I feel just like an eagle, soaring and strong! Every day I move closer to reaching the fitness level that I perceive will be best for me to complete my life in health and victory for the glory of God.

God gave us instructions for health. The body is so miraculous that it can reverse the most severe of diseases if given the proper tools. The body is self-healing. In these chapters I will try to bring together the natural with the supernatural to help you to keep your body fit for the King, Christ Jesus, to complete the assignment He has given you.

I do not provide any counsel in the medical area. I only provide health education to anyone who wants to bring his or her body into homeostasis, the place of balance where the body can heal itself. I teach what I have lived and what I have spent my life learning, perpetual learner that I am. I must include a disclaimer that you are responsible for any action you take as a result of reading the health education information I am presenting. You have every right to take responsibility for your own health.

The Bible refers to your body as God's temple. God gave specific instructions in the Old Testament for the temple. He is very specific as well regarding the temple where He dwells from the moment we acknowledge Jesus Christ as our Messiah. Most disease is directly related to an unclean temple or tabernacle, the body, caused by toxicity or malnutrition.

I will begin this chapter by giving you some general facts pertaining to exercise. People who are reading this book face different degrees of sickness. Please apply these comments on exercise as well as you can based upon your current physical condition.

Your muscles do not age. Joints age, but if you keep your body moving and do not eat toxin-forming foods, your joints will serve you well. Your number one goal should be to move your body as much as you possibly can based upon your current health status.

I have recently become a Certified Personal Trainer, primarily for my own education and fitness, but also to help others begin a simple plan of exercise that will help to insure a quality of life until the last breath is taken. Your body was created to move. Your heart requires your body to move aerobically for a minimum of thirty minutes three times a week. That is absolutely a minimum. How much kinder we are to our bodies if we move them at least an hour every day in a consistent way.

Our muscles atrophy through lack of use. Your muscles will continue to strengthen and become more flexible as you use them. As important as nutrition is, the person who keeps his or her body in shape is likely to be healthier than the person who eats properly but does not exercise. Of course, both are keys to health.

One of the most important benefits of exercise is sweating. Your cells are able to remove toxins from your body through perspiration. Do your best to exercise to work up a sweat and still keep your heart rate in the proper range for your age and health condition.

I believe that walking is the best exercise. A health goal is to walk a mile in fifteen minutes, then three miles in forty-five minutes. Start by walking to the door or to the mailbox. Do what you can. Any distance at any time is of great value to your body, especially your heart. Starting slowly and not overdoing is best. The key is to *move*! Our two legs are the best exercise tools, the handiest and the least expensive.

Jack and I use a rebounder (mini-trampoline) almost every day. This activity exercises every cell in the body through acceleration, deceleration, and gravity. The lymph system does not have its own pump. The lymph system can be pumped through rebound exercise. Toxins will move through your body as you rebound.

I believe that the rebounder is the best form of exercise after walking. It was created by NASA for the astronauts. I believe that a rebounder is an essential piece of equipment for optimum health.

Aerobics, weight training and stretching all can be done with the rebounder.

Do not purchase a cheap rebounder. It can damage your back. Jack has mentioned that we believe in the quality of the double-spring Needak rebounder. I have a free fact sheet with ways to use the rebounder that I will send you if you request it.

We need to strengthen our muscles every day as well as stretch them. I am currently in the process of becoming a T-Tapp instructor, the exercise of the new millennium. I am doing this for the benefit of my own body, but also to teach others the most comprehensive, non-impact exercise I have found. I am becoming more limber and flexible every day.

T-Tapp incorporates at least five muscle groups in each exercise. The exercise essentials (aerobics, weight training and stretching) are all included in T-Tapp exercise. Teresa Tapp has developed the "Wellness Workout That Works." Please go to www.ttapp.com and see all that is there. You can download free exercises.

Teresa's book, *Fit and Fabulous in Fifteen*, will be available in bookstores about the same time this book is published. Doing T-Tapp fifteen minutes a day three times a week can keep you fit. T-Tapp becomes progressively more difficult the more you do it. You do not need any equipment.

The primary nutrient of the body is oxygen. Without oxygen we cannot live longer than about three minutes. If we do not breathe from the diaphragm, we starve the body of oxygen. Breathing deeply as we exercise is a major way to oxygenate the body. Vigorous physical exercise oxygenates the body and removes waste through perspiration.

If your health permits and the weather where you live cooperates, try to be out in the sunshine for at least fifteen minutes every day. The sun provides nutrients, especially Vitamin D, for your physical health as well as the beauty of light for your mental health. We know that plants do not create chlorophyll without light. Light is very important to your health.

We know that all plants require sunshine to grow. We are living beings and require sunshine as well. We must be concerned about skin cancer. Many sunscreens contain toxic chemicals that penetrate the skin and can *increase* the risk of disease. Sunscreen can block the skin's ability to make Vitamin D by more than 95%. When I use sunscreen, I use a natural sunscreen from the health food store with a pH no higher than fifteen that contains no chemicals, such as mineral oil, that block my pores from breathing.

Any topic I mention can be researched on the internet at www.google.com. If you want to know more about a subject such as "sunscreen, danger" just request it.

Vitamin D is essential for a healthy heart, for growing cells properly, for calcium absorption, and for growing strong bones. Increased blood levels of Vitamin D are associated strongly with a decreased risk of many forms of cancer. The body requires Vitamin D intake.

When you are out in the sun for long periods of time, you should protect your skin from burning by wearing a cap or hat and covering your skin. You also can increase your antioxidant level by eating fresh vegetables and berries. Eating tomatoes and cruciferous vegetables and legumes also helps to optimize your immune system.

Drinking plenty of pure water is very important. The more you exercise, the more you will desire to drink water. We recommend distilled water, especially when you are cleansing or detoxifying your body. The water in fruits and vegetables is naturally distilled water and is excellent lubrication for the body. The brain needs pure water to function.

Fluoride is a waste product from industrial companies. Years ago a terrible misrepresentation was made. The assumption that this fluoride waste product would do the same as naturally occurring fluoride found in water was made. A deal was made to dump this waste product into drinking water.

This waste product is not natural. It is a heavy metal that researchers report to be more toxic than lead and red dye #3 and just slightly less toxic than arsenic. Much information can be found on the internet (go to google.com and put in fluoride, dangers and press Enter).

Fluoride is poisonous to humans. Read the label on the tube of toothpaste. Too much fluoride has been linked to thickening of bones even resulting in spinal fusion, bone, mouth and throat cancer, respiratory problems similar to emphysema, skin lesions, damage to the liver and kidney, neurological disorders, hyperactivity and many other ailments.

The brain is eighty-five percent water. Dehydration is a major issue that compromises health. The eyes need water as does the entire body. I recommend that you sip pure water all day long. The brain especially needs pure water to function properly.

A good way to determine how much water to drink is to take your weight in pounds, divide it by two, and drink that many ounces of water a day. Most people need eight to ten glasses of water a day as a minimum.

In this chapter I have given you very brief information on exercise, oxygen, sunshine and water. In the next chapter I will share several facts with you about nutrition and the relationship between nutrition and health.

Chapter 5

The Hallelujah Diet

Consuming certain substances can almost be considered slow suicide. These substances are white sugar, white flour, table salt, packaged foods with toxic chemicals added, cheese with hormones, fertilizer and chemicals added, milk and animal flesh. You can find information about each of these in the internet through www.google.com. List the subject with a comma followed by "dangers."

Have you been to a nursing home or rehabilitation center to visit with elderly people? Most of these people do not have any quality of life. We all must look closely at the end result of lives spent consuming the Standard American Diet. Dear friends, we are not destined to end our lives with diapers and drugs in a nursing home. We can feed our bodies living nutrients so that we can live in a perpetual state of the self-healing of the body.

Jack and I have not consumed animal products for thirteen years. The reason we stopped eating meat was that Jack could no longer digest meat. I was already a total health food person, but did not get the whole picture of the harm of animal products until we teamed up with George and Rhonda Malkmus and Hallelujah Acres.

Both Jack and I have completed Health Minister training at Hallelujah Acres in North Carolina. I have been back for subsequent intensive training at lease once each year for the past eight years and I plan to continue this yearly training. Please contact me if you would like to attend Health Minister training at Hallelujah Acres. You simply need to have a desire to learn more about God's plan for optimum health.

Every one of the trillions of cells in our bodies was created to utilize living food that was just picked from the garden. The greater the time lapse from the garden to our mouths, the greater is the loss of nutrients in the living food.

God originally created our bodies to eat living plants. "And God said, See, I have given you every plant yielding seed that is on the face of all the land and every tree with seed in its fruit; you shall have them for food. And to all the animals on the earth and to every bird of the air and to everything that creeps on the ground-to everything in which there is the breath of life-I have given every green plant for food. And it was so" (Genesis 1:28-29).

We can see the original plan of God. We know that God has allowed us to eat meat since the time of the Flood. We know that Jesus ate fish and served it to the disciples. We know that most, if not all, of the earth's fish today is contaminated with mercury which is poison to us.

I choose to consume a plant-based diet. My body functions best with the nutrients provided by whole foods created by God. I recommend the book, *The China Study, Startling Implications for Diet, Weight Loss and Long-Term Health*, by T. Colin Campbell, PhD. with his son, Thomas M. Campbell. Dr. Campbell has spent forty years in nutritional research. This book reveals the relationship between diet and disease world-wide. The conclusion is that animal-based nutrition leads to disease and plant-based nutrition leads to health.

The United States is an overfed, undernourished nation. We are spreading our diseases around the globe as our fast food companies populate the world. Where these diseases were practically non-existent, they began to rise with the arrival of the meat-based diet imported from the United States.

Jack and I consume freshly extracted carrot juice plus powdered barley leaf alive with enzymes daily. We consume fresh fruit and large vegetable salads. We have about 15% of our nutrients in cooked foods such as steamed vegetables with sesame seeds and walnuts. We have a huge array of locally grown organic produce available. I currently am working on an organic garden where I will be able to harvest our daily salads. I use the Hallelujah Diet in meal planning with 85% raw food that God made and 15% cooked food, made from whole food.

Studies show that organic produce contains more vitamins and minerals than produce laden with toxic chemicals to preserve them. Organic produce is more expensive, but the nutrient value per ounce greatly exceeds that of non-organic produce. We do our best to avoid genetically engineered produce. We do not know what will result from consuming produce with tampered genes.

Because we live in Florida, our goal is to be able to harvest our own organic produce all year long. For more information on organic produce, we refer you to the book *Square Foot Gardening*. This book can be obtained from Hallelujah Acres.

You may be very surprised by how delicious raw food tastes when it is prepared creatively. For simplicity you can carry fruit with you and a small packet of nuts and seeds. Eat raw food all day long and a huge salad for dinner followed by a cooked dish. Because your body is receiving the nutrients it needs, you will not be hungry.

Any food you like can be translated into a living food. I love to create recipes for people from the foods they like. Hallelujah Acres provides many books with health-building recipes that I believe are far superior to recipes that destroy the body. Please contact me if you would like a booklet of my recipes.

Some people wonder where protein and calcium come from in a raw food diet. What produces protein or calcium for a gorilla or a cow? These huge animals and many other animals exist solely on a plant-based diet.

Just as the world is filled with open and accepted-by-society sin, the world is filled with food contamination that is accepted by society. We must be the guards of what we choose to use for fuel for our bodies. Would you put diesel fuel in a vehicle that takes regular gasoline? We must learn what fuel was designed for our bodies and choose that food for our fuel.

My extensive study during the past forty-five years has led me to the conclusion that the best nutritional plan for optimum health is to eat a plant-based diet. Jack has mentioned Hallelujah Acres in a preceding chapter. I have briefly mentioned Hallelujah Acres here. If you have not already done so, I invite you to go to www.hacres.com for vital instructions pertaining to the relationship that exists between a plant-based diet and optimal health. I will be excited to hear that you have contacted Hallelujah Acres, so please let me know!

The person who prepares meals in the home has an opportunity to present healthy food in a very appealing manner. The person preparing the food should plan the nutrients for the day, being careful to include protein, carbohydrates, and fat as well as the major vitamins and minerals. An easy way to prepare meals is to choose only items that God has created.

As I observe grocery carts, I conclude that most people do not know the fuel that was designed for the human body: living food. All sickness comes from toxicity or malnutrition, including dehydration. We must evaluate our lives to determine the toxicity and to provide living nutrients for our bodies which are made up of trillions of hungry cells. Each cell eats, digests and eliminates just as the body does. These cells must have living nutrients in order to function optimally. When the cells are replaced, they can only be replaced with the nutrients the body has provided.

Each succeeding generation since the inception of the meat-based, long-shelf-life way of eating has produced children with weaker cells. Today infants are born with degenerative diseases that previously appeared in old age. These diseases were nonexistent or infrequent before the meat-based, long-shelf-life way of eating was chosen.

We are familiar with having to have the correct pH balance in a swimming pool. Our bodies are 76% water with blood being 94% water. Just as the body must maintain a temperature of about 98.6, the body must maintain a blood pH of 7.36. Problems such as aches, pains, digestive ailments, weight issues, fatigue, and lack of energy occur when the pH is out of balance. Consuming acid-forming foods as well as toxins and not eliminating regularly create an imbalance in pH.

To create the proper pH balance, add more fresh fruits and vegetables to your diet. Consume approximately 85% raw food and 15% cooked food as we do on the Hallelujah Diet. A balanced pH body is full of vim, vigor, and vitality, thinks clearly, and is fit with little or no excess fat. Basically, fresh fruits and vegetables are alkaline-forming in the body and all cooked food is acid-forming. Legumes, grains (except millet) and most nuts, except almonds, are acid-forming. To test your pH, purchase test strips from a pharmacy or on the internet for saliva and urine.

Drinking freshly extracted vegetable juice gives the body the nutrients it needs to go beyond the daily functions. The extra nutrients enable the body to tackle unfinished business – all wounds and leftovers from every sickness you ever had. The body cleans house and sends workers to the areas where there was a weakness and corrects the imbalance.

Jack and I also take supplements to supercharge our health. Jack takes a multi-vitamin with a high percentage of bilberry extract and lutein for his eyesight. We each take a probiotic to populate our intestines with good bacteria. We take digestive enzymes to break down the food we eat. We take an anti-oxidant to fight any invader in our bodies. We take Vitamin B-12, B-6 and folic acid supplements. We also consume powdered living barley leaves each day.

I know that the Bible warns us not to judge people for what they choose to eat. "One [man's faith permits him to] believe he may eat anything, while a weaker one [limits his] eating to vegetables. Let not him who eats look down on or despise him who abstains, and let not him who abstains criticize and pass judgment on him who eats; for God has accepted and welcomed him" (Romans 14:2-3).

God frees us to eat whatever we choose. God particularly warns us not to allow food to create a division between people. We must never criticize another person's eating choices. This issue creates a problem when the husband or wife knows that the other is eating food or drinking liquids that are harmful to the body.

Most often the person should only pray and not say anything. We are not responsible for anyone else's body. We have a huge job being responsible for our own. Only when people are close and have a covenant to help each other to be all that they can be for God should one offer suggestions to another. I cannot emphasize enough the importance of not letting food create a division in a family or in relationships. Food should not be the focus of life. The more we plan our meals and our food intake, the less we need to focus upon food.

Some of my family members believe that my views on nutrition are extreme. I choose to impart what I have learned through study and experience to anyone who would like to hear, but I never attempt to force what I have learned on anyone. I only present to those who want to hear the research that is now available with thousands of studies revealing the health of a plant-based diet and the disease results of an animal-based diet. Each person must decide for himself or herself what to eat.

There are Christian groups today insisting that the body must have meat. Each person must decide for himself or herself what to do. Study for yourself and test your own body. Hallelujah Acres has two documented cases of people who were doing well in a health crisis on a plant-based diet. They were convinced to return to eating meat and died.

Dr. T. Colin Campbell reports in *The China Report* that even a small amount of meat can lead to serious health issues. I am the reporter of what I believe. You must decide for yourself what is best for your body.

Chapter 6

Additional Facts Pertaining to Your Health

In this chapter I will point out several additional facts that can affect your health. Please read each of these facts and decide for yourself whether they are helpful to maintaining your health. I would like to begin by making the general statement to beware of chemicals. In our rush for convenience without any knowledge whatsoever of the consequences that could be forthcoming, many of us can cause severe problems with our health.

Hairstylists and other beauty operators are at a greater risk of developing cancer of the salivary glands because of the toxic chemicals they breathe every day. You will inhale toxic chemicals if you walk down the cleaning product aisle of the grocery store or the pesticide section of a home supply store. Breathing toxic chemicals on a regular basis, such as in giving permanents and dying and spraying hair, can cause serious problems.

Please forgive me, ladies, but I want to save your life. As I observe older women, I believe that about 80% of the ladies color their hair. Does creating an illusion of youth while ingesting chemicals that may result in premature death or a lingering life without quality make any sense? The head is made up of pores through which whatever is placed on it enters. Why not use avocado for hair conditioner and a slice of cucumber for a facial mask? We can replace chemicals with natural, living plants that promote health and have no dangerous results. Contact me for a booklet on natural health and beauty aids.

Antiperspirants and deodorants can cause health problems. Most antiperspirants contain a form of aluminum. Many lumps in the breast are in the area where antiperspirants have been applied. Aluminum also is associated with Alzheimer's Disease. I do not believe we should cook with aluminum pots, use aluminum foil in cooking or storing food or drinking from an aluminum can. Check all labels to see if aluminum is contained in the product.

Why would we want to stop the pores under our arms from releasing toxins? Sweating is good for us. When we perspire, we release waste. If we close pores with antiperspirants and deodorants, aren't we creating a buildup of toxins just under the skin? You must decide whether you want to put toxic chemicals into your body through your skin or through your mouth by inhaling them.

Mineral oil slows down cell replacement and is a likely cause of premature aging. It may promote skin, colon and breast cancer. It actually suffocates the skin, preventing the skin from receiving necessary oxygen or releasing carbon dioxide. Mineral oil is found in sunscreen, shampoo, soap, bubble bath, laundry detergents and facial cleansers. Why not change to coconut soap from the health food store? Why not moisturize your body with coconut butter?

I am continually finding new ways to improve the environment of our home which is free of toxic cleaning substances. Our swimming pool and our spa are sanitized and pH-balanced by an ionizer rather than with chemicals. Studies have shown that household chemicals are the cause of many illnesses and even death in the United States each year. Please contact me if you would like information regarding a pool or a spa ionizer.

I have written a report on the dangers of chlorine entering the body through the skin from a shower, a bath or a pool and the value of ionization as a water purifier. I also have a report on how to replace poison-laden cleaners with natural substances. Please write to me if you would like to receive these reports.

I have done much of my research on the internet. You can do the same thing. Find a replacement for every chemical product you use. You often can use much less as well.

Many ladies will not want to read this part. Cosmetic products contain preservatives to extend shelf life. These poisons can penetrate the skin. How much time passes before extreme damage is done? The tragedy is that people do not connect the poisons of cosmetics and beauty supplies with life-threatening diseases. Years may pass before symptoms appear.

Look at the warning messages on all cosmetics. Look for sodium laurel sulphate or sodium laureth sulphate, an ingredient in many cosmetics and almost all toothpaste. This chemical is linked to cataracts in adults and the prevention of children's eyes developing properly. It is used in medical laboratories to actually damage skin before testing with products to heal the skin. It is shown to react with other chemicals to create cancer-forming substances. I can share information with you on a natural bubble bath, toothpaste, shampoo, shaving cream, and other beauty and health products.

Many household products as well as beauty products contain phthalates which can cause many health issues including liver and kidney damage, changes in blood pressure, and heart problems. Phthalates are believed to have a serious effect upon fetuses by causing testicular atrophy and reduced sperm count in male fetuses. Phthalates are found in nail polish, lipstick, and perfumes. They also are found in children's toys.

The cosmetic industry has taken industrial chemicals that have been banned and provided them in beauty products. Many moisturizers contain propylene glycol which is an industrial anti-freeze. Studies have shown that when this product has penetrated the skin, it has caused damage to the liver and kidneys.

Carbonated soft drinks ultimately can lead to significant health problems. The average twelve ounce carbonated soft drink contains approximately eleven teaspoons of sugar. Sugar greatly compromises the immune system.

A recent study reveals a strong link between drinking these soft drinks and obesity in children. Another study shows a direct link between soft drinks and tooth decay. Acid begins to dissolve tooth enamel in twenty minutes. Phosphorus, a common ingredient in carbonated soft drinks, is known to deplete bones of calcium which can result in weak bones. A serious issue ensues.

The caffeine in soft drinks can cause severe health problems. If a child is dependent on the caffeine in these drinks, there is a potential for impairment of brain development. Many Americans consume tremendous amounts of caffeine. They do not understand the long term effects that caffeine can have on their health. Excessive caffeine intake can result in cerebral allergy with symptoms including lack of focus, mood swings, hallucinations and paranoia. Significant caffeine intake can lead to toxic dementia.

Drinking carbonated soft drinks is linked with obesity, heart disease, diabetes, food addictions, dysfunction of neurotransmitters, nutritional deficiencies and neurological and adrenal disorders from excessive caffeine. There are many more issues with phosphoric acid, citric acid, and artificial flavors. (see www.ghchealth.com/soft-drinks-america.html.)

Many Americans, in a desire to lose weight, consume large amounts of diet soft drinks containing aspartame. They do not realize that large amounts of aspartame can be more dangerous than the huge amounts of white sugar the aspartame replaces.

Aspartame side effects can occur gradually or immediately. They include blindness in one or both eyes. Please go to http://www.sweetpoison.com/aspartame-side-effects.html for a list of the side effects of aspartame relating to the eyes, ears, nerves, the mind, the chest, the digestive system, the skin, metabolism and glands.

Because the buildup of aspartame in the body is gradual, when the symptoms occur, the person often does not associate aspartame consumption with the symptom. The above website says that the most critical symptoms are "death, irreversible brain damage, birth defects including mental retardation, peptic ulcers, aspartame addiction, increased cravings for sweets, hyperactivity in children, severe depression, aggressive behavior, and suicidal tendencies."

Many people are unaware of the hazards of microwave ovens. I removed the microwave from our home many years ago. Dr. Mercola (www.mercola.com) reports about a lawsuit in Oklahoma in 1991. A nurse chose to warm the transfusion blood in a microwave oven. The patient died. A study showed that microwave cooking so changes the nutrients that the result is changes in the blood which lead to the breakdown of systems in the body.

The electromagnetic radiation of microwave heat causes atoms, molecules and cells to reverse the polarity from one to one hundred billion times a second. Molecules are deformed; thus quality is impaired. The result can be a marked increase in white blood cells. Cholesterol may increase rapidly because of the stress factor of ingesting microwaved food (even foods containing no cholesterol).

I now would like to switch emphasis to a more positive area. Proverbs 4:20-23 and other Scripture references that will be explained in detail in the remainder of this book show the relationship between Bible study, Scripture meditation and good health. I believe that Bible study and Scripture meditation are essential for good health.

God has provided us with spiritual food for our redeemed spirits. God's holy Word was written by men but inspired by God Himself. Do not allow a day to go by without having a special time with God, talking to Him, reading His Word and meditating upon it which means chewing it until it is part of you.

God has a plan that is taking place. He has given us the written record of His past history, His present activity, and His future activity. He has a part for each of us to complete. God's Word, the Bible, is essential fuel for living in optimum health.

The Bible is daily manna for my spirit and provides instruction for the care of my body, the temple of the Holy Spirit. He came to reside within me when I made the decision to surrender my life to Jesus Christ, the Messiah, King of kings and Lord of lords.

I must feed my spirit the Word of God daily. If I do not, I am like a feather blowing in the wind, being tossed to and fro by the whims of my mind and my body and the circumstances I face. I must know what the Bible says about mental and physical health.

The power of God resides in the Word of God. The Bible is not just words; it is life. When we read it, study it or meditate on it, we are filling ourselves with God. I cannot read the Bible without meditating on it. It penetrates every fiber of my being. I love the Word of God so much. I feed my spirit by my time with God in prayer and Bible study and meditation.

I am sixty-six years old, so the King James version of the Bible is my friend. I am very comfortable in it. I use the *Amplified Bible* to glean more information for many verses of Scripture. I wouldn't be without a *Thompson Chain Reference Bible*. I use *Strong's Exhaustive Concordance* often to gain understanding of the original Hebrew and Greek meaning of a word. My treasured prayer resource is *The Hour That Changes the World* by Dick Eastman.

In these chapters I have given you a glimpse of the areas of health that I believe must be in balance in order to live in vibrant health. If any of these areas are out of balance, disease may develop. Often disease develops slowly so that, when you finally are faced with a disease, you do not know how you acquired it.

I am aware that many of the statements I have made in these three chapters will sound very extreme to some people. However, if you are sick and you are struggling to regain your health, you might look carefully at some, most or all of these statements in a much different way than you would have before you became sick. If you are sick, you owe it to yourself and to Jesus to leave no stone unturned.

Read these three chapters again very carefully. Look up the documentation on the indicated websites. Be determined to make any and all changes that you believe will enable you to do everything you can do to regain your health. Carefully study and obey all of the scriptural instructions on divine healing that are in this book.

My heart breaks over the sickness that plagues the body of Christ. We should be serving as examples of health for others. The facts in these chapters are only a few of the facts that I teach in my classes on health and fitness. If you would like to receive the written material that I distribute on health and fitness, please contact me.

I have an accountability health class in my home on Mondays. I am in the process of writing and testing a booklet that will be titled *Fat Loss in a Nutshell*. Through diet and exercise each person can achieve a healthy amount of body fat.

Sometimes a person is too set in his or her ways to make the changes that are required to save this person's life. Are you too set in your ways to make changes in your life? My heart is to help each person find his or her place and assignment in God's kingdom. You need to be vibrantly healthy in body, mind and spirit to be and do what God asks. My great joy is to provide you with health information for the glory of God.

We have so many testimonies of lives changed through making simple changes. We do not give any medical advice or recommendations, only simple health education for you to consider as you take responsibility for your own health.

I would be glad to tell you the juicers I recommend, the rebounder mini-trampoline, the dehydrator, the water distiller, the high speed blender and the food processor. If you request it, I will email you my Twelve Day Challenge for instructions on how to begin your own long-term care today. I pray that everyone who reads this book will live a fulfilling life that is filled with energy and the joy of the Lord.

Chapter 7

Your Emotions and Your Health

You have just read one chapter that I wrote and three chapters that were written by Judy. In this chapter we will look into the Word of God for specific information pertaining to your *emotions* and your health.

Some people suffer from medical problems that cannot be diagnosed by an x-ray, stethoscope or any other diagnostic device. Many doctors run exhaustive tests without being able to find any physical reason for the sickness of their patients. Most physicians agree that a significant percentage of their patients suffer from illness that has a mental or emotional origin.

The truth is that many of their patients come to them with sickness that is primarily caused by failure to know, understand and do what the Word of God instructs them to do regarding their emotions. They would have been healthy if they had learned to direct the cumulative effect of their emotions over a period of time.

The fast paced lifestyle that many people lead today leads to a great deal of stress that was not present in our grandparents' day. The origin of the word "stress" comes from engineers who are able to measure the amount of resistance a steel beam could bear. Many things have limits. Bridges have limits for the number of tons they can hold. Elevators have limits for the number of pounds they can safely carry. Airplanes have limits for the number of people and the weight of cargo they can carry.

Your body is similar. When God created you He built within you the ability to withstand a certain amount of stress with your human capabilities. The emotional stress that is so prevalent in the world today is far too much for many people to process. We must learn to live in the Spirit and to see every situation as an opportunity to observe God at work.

Unbelievers do not have any scriptural instructions that will help them to deal effectively with stress. They must attempt to use the world's methods for dealing with stress. *Christians do have an alternative.* If you have faithfully obeyed your Father's instructions to fill your mind and your heart daily with His Word, you will steadily build up a spiritual reservoir in your mind and your heart that will sustain you when you face stressful situations.

If you are a Christian you have the Holy Spirit living in your heart. He can and will help you to deal with stressful situations if you trust Him so much that you actually will yield control of your life to Him (see Galatians 5:16-26).

You will learn to welcome trials as friends, knowing that God will work His will through your life because you love Him and serve Him. Reaction to stress in a way that does not obey God's instructions ultimately can weaken your immune system. As your immune system becomes weaker sickness will be able to obtain a foothold in your body. You must learn how to yield to the Holy Spirit to walk in the divine health your Father planned for you.

Stress can affect your digestion. Stress can cause your muscles to tighten up. Stressful situations cause some people to become short of breath. Some people perspire profusely when they are stressed. Many people find that their heart rate and their blood pressure increase. Sometimes stress causes nausea. Some people experience dryness in their mouths when they face stressful circumstances. The cumulative effect of these different reactions to stress can cause you to lose your health.

Extreme fatigue can be caused by the cumulative effect of negative emotional reaction over a period of time. This emotional fatigue is much different than the physical fatigue caused by hard work. Your body produces hormones when you react negatively to stressful situations. These hormones can cause you to become extremely fatigued.

God gave you adrenal glands when He created you. Some people react so negatively to stressful situations that they continually secrete adrenalin because they are agitated and upset. People whose bodies have secreted a substantial amount of adrenalin over a period of years often experience significant repercussions pertaining to their health.

Cumulative unscriptural reaction to stress definitely can cause sickness. People who are constantly agitated because of worry, fear, anxiety, anger, arguments and all other negative emotions live in a continual state of alert. People who do not know or do not obey God's instructions on reaction to stressful situations ultimately will pay a severe price with their health. A chain is only as strong as its weakest link. Something has to give – usually the weakest area in your body. Poor health often can be compared to a rubber band that snaps when it is stretched too far.

God created you with emotions. He could have created you without emotions. What kind of life would an emotionless person live? *Your Father wants your emotions to work for you, not against you.* The Word of God teaches you how to control your emotions instead of allowing your emotions to control you.

Some people live on an emotional rollercoaster. They expend a tremendous amount of emotional energy because of their continual emotional ups and downs. There is *no* place in the Bible where you are instructed to go through emotional ups and downs. *Many* places in the Bible instruct you to be calm, quiet and steady because of your close relationship with the Lord and your absolute and unshakable trust in Him.

Some people are more emotional than others because that is how God created them. No matter how high strung you may be, you *can* learn from the Word of God how to direct your emotions. Immature Christians often experience more emotional ups and downs than mature Christians. Mature Christians learn to respond spontaneously to the Word of God and the Spirit of God living in their hearts.

You must understand that many of the health challenges that seem to come on you suddenly actually are caused by the cumulative effects of negative emotions over a period of years. Negative emotions are as poisonous as a venomous snake. You cannot do anything that is worse for your health than to allow negative emotions to dominate your life over a sustained period of time.

Worry, anxiety and fear are negative emotions that definitely can cause you to lose your good health and become sick. Heart disease, high blood pressure, ulcers, migraine headaches, digestive problems, constipation, fatigue and insomnia often are caused by worry, anxiety and fear. Many people who are being treated for illness would be much better served if they would learn how to go to the Great Physician and carefully study His prescription for entering into His rest instead of allowing worry, anxiety and fear to dominate their lives (see Hebrews 4:8-11).

Sometimes we hear people say, "I'm worried sick about..." or "I'm worried to death about..." Constant worry and fear ultimately will rob you of the good health your Father wants you to have. Continued worry and fear can cause serious illness that ultimately will lead to death.

There is no question that worry can cause premature aging. Dr. Charles Mayo, the founder of the famous Mayo Clinic in Minnesota once said, "Worry affects the circulation, the heart, the glands, the whole nervous system and profoundly affects the heart." We all have known people who are constant worriers. Compare the health of these people with mature Christians of approximately the same age who refuse to worry and, instead, constantly rejoice and praise the Lord.

Other negative emotions that can cause severe problems with your health are jealousy, envy and arguing. "...wherever there is jealousy (envy) and contention (rivalry and selfish ambition), there will also be confusion (unrest, disharmony, rebellion) and all sorts of evil and vile practices" (James 3:16).

Please highlight or underline the word "wherever." This all-inclusive word includes the cumulative effect of "jealousy, envy, contention, rivalry and selfish ambition." Anyone who gives in to these negative emotions ultimately will experience "confusion, unrest, disharmony and rebellion." You *will* give Satan a foothold in your life if you react this way. You will open yourself to "all sorts of evil and vile practices."

The Bible teaches that you are spiritually immature if you allow negative emotions to control your life. "...you are still [unspiritual, having the nature] of the flesh [under the control of ordinary impulses]. For as long as [there are] envying and jealousy and wrangling and factions among you, are you not unspiritual and of the flesh, behaving yourself after a human standard and like mere (unchanged) men?" (I Corinthians 3:3).

You are "unspiritual" if you are jealous and argumentative. You exhibit "the nature of the flesh." Your words and actions will indicate that your carnal nature is in control of your life. Your Father does *not* want you to be "unspiritual, having the nature of the flesh and under the control of ordinary impulses." He does *not* want you to "behave after a human standard like mere unchanged men." He wants you to grow and mature so that you will be able to walk in divine health instead of giving in to these negative emotions and allowing them to control your life.

Your Father strongly emphasizes the importance of learning how to be set free from all negative emotions. "Let all bitterness and indignation and wrath (passion, rage, bad temper) and resentment (anger, animosity) and quarreling (brawling, clamor, contention) and slander (evil-speaking, abusive or blasphemous language) be banished from you, with all malice (spite, ill will, or baseness of any kind)" (Ephesians 4:31).

Look carefully at the negative emotions that are listed in this passage of Scripture. Do you often experience "bitterness and indignation?" Do you often allow "wrath, passion, rage and bad temper" to dominate your emotions? This passage of Scripture lists several other negative emotions such as resentment and slander. Your Father tells you that all of these negative emotions should be "banished from you." They only can be banished through the Word of God and the presence of God permeating your life, not through your human will.

The Bible emphasizes through repetition. Your Father gives you similar instructions in the Book of Colossians. "...put away and rid yourselves [completely] of all these things: anger, rage, bad feeling toward others, curses and slander, and foulmouthed abuse and shameful utterances from your lips! Do not lie to one another..." (Colossians 3:8-9).

This passage of Scripture lists many of the same negative emotions that you read about in Ephesians 4:31. Colossians 3:9 also tells you that you should not lie to other people. Jesus, speaking of Satan, said, "...there is no truth in him. When he speaks a falsehood, he speaks what is natural to him, for he is a liar [himself] and the father of lies and of all that is false" (John 8:44).

Satan "is a liar." He is "the father of all lies and all that is false." All untruth in the world comes as a result of the influence of Satan. If you lie you are influenced by Satan. You are disobeying your Father's specific instructions because He said, "Do not lie to one another."

Your Father wants you to be healthy. Satan wants you to be sick. Satan and his demons will do their best to influence you in any way they possibly can. Satan and his demons are able to exert a high degree of control over some people through their emotions. Some people are very prone to emotional ups and downs. Satan's demons consistently hammer away at these people, trying to get them to react negatively.

Your Father wants you to learn how to control your thoughts and emotions. He does not want you to allow negative emotions to damage your health. You cannot control your emotions through human willpower. You only can control your emotions by the surrender of your whole self to God.

This chapter contains basic information about your emotional reaction to stressful situations and the resulting effect on your health. If you want more scriptural information on controlling your emotions, you will find hundreds of scriptural instructions in our books titled *Unshakable Faith in Almighty God, Exchange Your Worries for God's Perfect Peace, Quiet Confidence in the Lord* and *Never, Never Give Up.* A great deal of additional scriptural instruction can be found in our Scripture Meditation Cards and cassette tapes titled *God's Wonderful Peace, Freedom from Worry and Fear, A Closer Relationship with the Lord, Your Father's Wonderful Love, Receive God's Blessing in Adversity* and *God is Always with You.*

Chapter 8

Your Health and the Decisions You Make

God gave you the power to choose. Throughout your life you have made continual choices that determined much of what took place in your life. The cumulative effect of many of the choices you have made determine whether you will walk in health or experience sickness.

God gave Adam and Eve freedom of choice just as He has given you freedom of choice. Adam and Eve made a choice that caused them great anguish and brought anguish to the entire human race after that time. This choice allowed sickness that never had been experienced in the garden of Eden to come into the world.

You would be a robot if God did not give you the power to choose. You must understand the importance of continually making choices that will enable you to walk in divine health. The apostle Paul said, "Everything is permissible (allowable and lawful) for me; but not all things are helpful (good for me to do, expedient and profitable when considered with other things). Everything is lawful for me, but I will not become the slave of anything or be brought under its power" (I Corinthians 6:12).

God did *not* place limits on you because "*everything* is permissible, allowable and lawful for you." However, "all things are not good for you." Some people use the freedom of choice God has given them to make decisions that stop them from walking in the divine health He intended for them. Your Father does not want you to allow yourself to "become the slave of anything or be brought under its power."

We each are responsible for the effect of the choices we make. Most people know many of God's laws pertaining to health. They know what they should and should not eat. They know that they should exercise regularly. They may have some knowledge of what the Bible says about negative emotions. There is no lack of general knowledge in the world today regarding what we should do to be healthy.

However, knowing what to do and *actually doing* these things are very different. The apostle Paul said, "...I am a creature of the flesh [carnal, unspiritual], having been sold into slavery under [the control of] sin. For I do not understand my own actions [I am baffled, bewildered]. I do not practice or accomplish what I wish, but I do the very thing that I loathe [which my moral instinct condemns]" (Romans 7:14-15).

You have a part of yourself that is "a carnal and unspiritual creature of the flesh." You often may do things you know you should not do. You may "not understand your own actions." Sometimes you may be "baffled and bewildered" by what you do. You may "do the very thing which your moral instinct condemns."

Paul went on to say, "...I can will what is right, but I cannot perform it. [I have the intention and urge to do what is right, but no power to carry it out.] For I fail to practice the good deeds I desire to do, but the evil deeds that I do not desire to do are what I am [ever] doing" (Romans 7:18-19).

Willpower often is insufficient. Tens of millions of New Years resolutions are made at the beginning of each year, only to be discarded within a few weeks. You may have learned that you "can will what is right," but you do not always do what you know you should do. You may have good intentions, but the "power to carry out" these good intentions often is lacking. You may "fail to practice the good deeds you have to do" and find that you do things "you do not desire to do."

One of the best ways to walk in divine health is to continually study and meditate on the Word of God to program yourself with God's Word so that you will be able to do what you often would not do if you made choices with your carnal nature. You also must learn how to continually yield control of your life to the Holy Spirit so that He will guide you and help you continually.

There is no question that your loving Father wants you to be healthy. Your Father wants each of His children to be healthy just as parents here on earth want their children to be healthy. "Beloved, I pray that you may prosper in every way and [that your body] may keep well, even as [I know] your soul keeps well and prospers" (III John 2).

These words that John spoke to a man named Gaius apply to you today. Your Father wants you to "prosper in every way." He wants "your body to be kept well." Please highlight or underline the words "even as your soul keeps well and prospers." This portion of Scripture explains the relationship between divine health in your body and divine health in your *soul*. Infusing your soul with the Word of God is an important key to divine health.

There is no question that a relationship exists between your soul and your body. Your soul consists of your mind, your emotions and your will. Your mind controls what you think, your emotions control your reaction to the circumstances you face and your will controls the decisions you make. The cumulative result of what you think, how you feel and what you decide often determines the ultimate condition of your health.

If you want to walk in divine health, you must learn how to keep your *mind* free from the cumulative effect of thoughts that will cause you to be sick. If you want to walk in divine health, you must learn how to keep your *emotions* free from reactions that ultimately could cause you to be sick. If you want to walk in divine health, you must learn to make the *decisions* your Father wants you to make so that you will be healthy and live your life the way He wants you to live.

Your mind and your heart should be filled with the Word of God. Your emotional reaction to circumstances should be in agreement with the instructions your Father has given to you. The decisions you make should be consistent with the instructions you have been given in the Word of God.

In subsequent chapters we will study in detail about the relationship between divine healing, Bible study and Scripture meditation. Some Christians are sick because they have *ignored* God's instructions to renew their minds *each day* in His Word (see Romans 12:2, II Corinthians 4:16 and Ephesians 4:23) and to meditate on the Word of God *continually* throughout *each day and night* (see Joshua 1:8 and Psalm 1:2-3).

The same renewal of your mind and daily Scripture meditation that will cause you to receive manifestation of healing in your body also is required for you to consistently walk in divine health. Divine health is the result of a prosperous soul. A prosperous soul is a soul that is continually infused with the Word of God.

The Word of God is eternal. It is supernatural in its power. You must understand the definite relationship that exists between your mind and your heart being filled with God's Word and walking in divine health.

Continual encouragement over a period of months and years has a positive effect on your health. Continual discouragement over a period of time ultimately will damage your health. You will constantly encourage yourself when you immerse yourself in the Word of God each day. You will allow yourself to be discouraged if you continually react negatively to the challenges you face instead of responding to God's supernatural Word that is alive in your mind and your heart.

Your Father wants the Word of God and the Holy Spirit living in your heart to control your life, but *you* must make this continual choice. You decide each day whether you will allow the circumstances you face and the carnal part of your human nature to control you. You decide each day whether you will program yourself with the Word of God so that your life constantly will be yielded to God.

We now are ready to look at a passage of Scripture that we will study carefully in a subsequent chapter pertaining to divine healing. In this chapter we will study what this passage of Scripture teaches about divine *health*. "…attend to my words; consent and submit to my sayings. Let them not depart from your sight; keep them in the center of your heart. For they are life to those who find them, healing and health to all their flesh. Keep and guard your heart with all vigilance and above all that you guard, for out of it flow the springs of life" (Proverbs 4:20-23).

This passage of Scripture tells you to pay careful attention to the Word of God. You should consistently "consent and submit" to the instructions your Father has given you. You should not allow the Word of God to "depart from your sight." If you truly desire to walk in divine health, you should meditate on God's Word throughout the day and night. You must keep the Word of God "in the center of your heart."

Your life ultimately could depend upon how much of God's Word you have in your heart. This passage of Scripture promises "healing and health to your flesh." Please highlight or underline the word "health" in this passage of Scripture. You must understand the relationship between the spiritual contents of your heart and walking in divine health.

The supernatural power of God's living Word will constantly rise up inside of you *if* you obey your Father's instructions to renew your mind each day and to meditate continually on His Word. You must understand the direct correlation that exists between walking in divine health, renewing your mind in the Word of God daily and meditating continually throughout the day and night on the holy Scriptures.

You must "guard your heart" vigilantly, "above all that you guard." The "springs of life" flow out of your heart. There is no question of the relationship that exists between your health and the spiritual condition of your heart.

You *will* be able to increasingly submit control of your life to the Holy Spirit if you continually fill your eyes, your ears, your mind, your heart and your mouth with the supernatural living Word of God. An important factor in divine health is keeping your mind and your heart so full of the Word of God that you *gladly yield control* of your life to the Holy Spirit.

The Holy Spirit lives in the heart of every person who has asked Jesus Christ to be his or her Savior (see Galatians 4:6). If you trust the Holy Spirit enough to continually yield control of your life to Him, He will control your life and guide you to constantly make the decisions you need to make to walk in divine health. You should "…walk and live [habitually] in the [Holy] Spirit [responsive to and controlled and guided by the Spirit]…" (Galatians 5:16).

You should "walk and live habitually in the Holy Spirit." If you truly want to make the decisions you must make to walk in divine health, you should be "responsive to and controlled and guided by the Spirit." Your walk in divine health requires that you yield control of your life to the Holy Spirit.

We now have completed six chapters on divine health. If you would like more information about God's laws pertaining to health, please ask Judy for her recommendations for additional reading. The remainder of this book will be devoted to a thorough study of hundreds of additional Scripture references pertaining to *divine healing*.

Chapter 9

Jesus Christ Heals Today

In this chapter we will briefly examine what we believe is incorrect teaching on divine healing. Some religious denominations teach that God does not heal today. Some pastors teach that God only heals selectively. We touched on this subject in the Introduction, but we must examine in more detail exactly what the Bible says in this area.

Many Christians have not learned *facts* from the Word of God pertaining to divine healing. Errant religious beliefs about divine healing have been handed down from one generation to another. Some Christians have a difficult time believing that God will heal them because their parents, their grandparents and their church have taught them that divine healing is not available today.

Religious tradition says that healing was only for the early church. Jesus made a strong statement about religious tradition when He said, "…for the sake of your tradition (the rules handed down by your forefathers), you have set aside the Word of God [depriving it of force and authority and making it of no effect]" (Matthew 15:6).

Jesus made this statement to a group of Scribes and Pharisees, but these words also apply to you today. Some Christians are so indoctrinated in erroneous traditional teaching that has been handed down from generation to generation that they have "set aside the Word of God, depriving it of force and authority and making it of no effect."

Religious tradition can cause the mighty supernatural power of the living Word of God to be ineffective. Please do *not* make this mistake. If you are sick you must be certain that your belief about divine healing lines up exactly with what the Word of God says about this vitally important subject.

You have been *set free* from religious tradition if you have asked Jesus Christ to be your Savior. You have been given the ability to understand the *facts* that are presented in the Word of God. "...you were redeemed (ransomed) from the useless (fruitless) way of living inherited by tradition from [your] forefathers..." (I Peter 1:18).

You must learn for yourself exactly what the Bible says about divine healing. You must *not* allow traditional religious beliefs to stop you from learning the Truth from the Word of God. Jesus said, "...you will know the Truth, and the Truth will set you free" (John 8:32).

These words that Jesus spoke to His disciples more than two thousand years ago apply to you today. What was Jesus referring to when He spoke of the Truth? Jesus was speaking of the Word of God. At a later time He said, "...Your Word is Truth" (John 17:17).

You *can be set free* from error by learning exactly what the Word of God says about health and about healing. If you have any doubts about healing allow the Word of God to be the final authority. Your Father does not want you to block Him with erroneous doctrine. He wants you to have a humble and teachable heart that will receive the wonderful truth of His healing promises.

Some people believe that the healing miracles that were recorded in the New Testament only lasted until the end of the apostolic age. The Word of God teaches that just the opposite is true. "...the Lord is good; His mercy and loving-kindness are everlasting, His faithfulness and truth endure to all generations" (Psalm 100:5).

God did *not* place promises in the Bible that would only last for a short period of time. Divine healing did *not* end with the apostolic age. Divine healing dwindled and disappeared because of ignorance and unbelief caused by spiritual darkness during the Middle Ages and the Dark Ages. Your loving and merciful Father's magnificent healing promises "endure to all generations." God does *not* change His promises. He said, "My covenant will I not break or profane, nor alter the thing that has gone out of My lips" (Psalm 89:34).

When God promises that He will do something He will do it forever. Your Father does not stop doing what His Word says He will do. "…whatever God does, it endures forever, nothing can be added to it or anything taken from it…" (Ecclesiastes 3:14).

There is no question that Jesus healed multitudes of people during His earthly ministry. *Jesus has not changed.* He still heals multitudes of people today. "Jesus Christ (the Messiah) is [always] the same, yesterday, today [yes] and forever (to the ages)" (Hebrews 13:8).

Jesus is "the same" today as He was during His earthly ministry. The gospels of Matthew, Mark, Luke and John recount more than sixty instances where Jesus healed people from sickness. Jesus has not grown weaker. His healing power is just as great today.

If Jesus did not want you to be healed today *why* would He have paid the tremendous price that He paid at the whipping post? *Why* would He have undergone that horrible mutilation? *Why* would He have taken upon Himself all of the sickness of all of the people who were alive then and all of the sickness of people who would live after them? Jesus did *not* pay this horrible price so that *only* the people who lived in the next generation after He ascended into heaven could be healed.

I was blessed to be able to see a powerful and unforgettable manifestation of divine healing when I was a new Christian. A friend of mine asked if I would be interested in driving from New Hampshire where I lived at that time to Rhode Island to attend a Kathryn Kuhlman miracle healing service. He told me some very interesting facts he had read about her ministry. I agreed to go with him.

My friend picked me up about 6:00 on a Saturday morning. We drove from New Hampshire to Lowell, Massachusetts where we met a group of people outside of a church to ride in a bus to the Kathryn Kuhlman meeting. As the bus traveled from Massachusetts to Rhode Island many people shared healing testimonies over a portable microphone that was passed around. The detailed and specific facts in these healing testimonies amazed me. I was a new Christian. I had never heard anything like these statements.

I remember one woman from Franklin, New Hampshire who told of a miraculous healing she had received at a Kathryn Kuhlman meeting. This woman worked in a shoe factory. She was so simple in her faith and so honest and sincere that I *knew* she was telling the truth. I went over to her afterward and asked her many questions about her healing. She replied to each question forthrightly.

When we arrived in Providence, Rhode Island, buses surrounded the Providence Civic Center for as far as I could see. I am not certain what the seating capacity of that auditorium was, but I believe it was approximately twelve thousand people. Soon after we entered I saw that every seat was filled. We sang Christian worship songs for more than thirty minutes.

Kathryn Kuhlman then made her appearance. She was a very small woman. She appeared to be approximately five feet tall. Miss Kuhlman began by telling everyone in the audience that they should not give any credit whatsoever to her. She explained that the Lord had given her an anointed healing ministry and that the Holy Spirit deserved all of the credit. She said that she could not cure even the most minor illness herself.

Miss Kuhlman then had several people come to the platform to give testimonies of the miraculous healings they received the last time she held a healing crusade in that area. I remember a mother who brought her little boy in front of the audience. She said that her son had cancer before the last time Kathryn Kuhlman came to the area. The doctors gave her no hope for this boy.

At the time of the previous crusade her son was completely bald from chemotherapy treatments. He received a miraculous healing at the previous Kathryn Kuhlman crusade. His hair grew back. Doctors documented his miraculous healing. This young boy came up front with his mother. He obviously was happy, healthy and very energetic. The crowd erupted into applause at the end of his mother's testimony.

Many other people came up to give their testimonies. Each testimony had been documented by physicians. Letters from these physicians were read to show this documentation. There was no question whatsoever in the minds of the people in the audience about the authenticity of the healing testimonies we heard.

Kathryn Kuhlman then began to call out specific individuals from the audience. She would point to a section of the auditorium and, with a word of knowledge from the Holy Spirit, mention a person in that section who had a specific illness. She told each person to get up from his or her seat to come to the stage at the front of the auditorium. She said that each of these people had been healed by God.

She continued to call out specific individuals in many different sections of the auditorium. I saw people who were sitting near me get up and walk down to the stage. Many times friends and family members gasped because of the amazing authenticity of her statement regarding this sick person.

I will never forget that day. I saw people get out of wheelchairs and walk. I saw people throw aside crutches. I remember one lady jumping up and down and running across the stage with tears streaming down her cheeks. I remember one mother standing next to her son as he took the braces off his legs and ran out on the stage.

Several physicians were stationed next to the stage. They were there to eliminate people who had not actually been healed. They carefully questioned all of the people who said they had received a healing before they allowed them to go on the stage. One thing that convinced me of the absolute authenticity of these healings was that three Catholic nuns went up to the stage to give testimonies of healing they had received.

Anyone who does not believe that Jesus Christ heals today could not have explained everything I saw and heard that day. I am *so thankful* that I was able to see with my own eyes and hear with my own ears this tremendous documentation of the healing power of Jesus Christ.

Kathryn Kuhlman has been dead for many years, but you can obtain information on her ministry at www.kathrynkuhlman.com. Even though Kathryn Kuhlman is with the Lord now you can still order her book *God Can Do It Again* which is a collection of testimonies of ordinary people who experienced God's incredible healing power. Each chapter contains one person's testimony. Each of these ordinary people, having nowhere else to turn, experienced the willingness of God to touch them with His mighty healing power.

Read these tremendous testimonies. Believe that God can and will heal you. If you search the web you can find her books, videotapes and audio tapes featured on many websites. You might want to go to www. faithcenteredresources.com. Her book, *God Can Do It Again,* can be ordered on this site.

I developed a deep belief that divine healing *is* for today during my impressionable early days as a Christian. This belief has never changed. I have believed in divine healing for more than thirty years. As a result of writing this book my faith for divine healing is at an all-time high.

After that meeting in Rhode Island I saw many sick people receive healing from God. I particularly remember a woman who had cancer. She came to one of the early Bible studies I taught in the cafeteria of a junior high school in Manchester, New

Hamphsire. Several of us prayed for her when she came to the front of the room after the Bible study. She received a miraculous healing. She went to her doctor for verification. The doctor gave her this verification.

The Bible is *filled* with numerous promises that contain words such as "all," "every" and "always." We will list just a few of these promises so that you can see for yourself that God's promises are all-inclusive. On one occasion Jesus said, "…whatever you ask for in prayer, having faith and [really] believing, you will receive" (Matthew 21:22).

If healing was not included in this promise, shouldn't there be an asterisk or a statement that the word "whatever" includes everything except healing? *All* of the promises in the Bible that tell us what God *always* will do for us would have to be eliminated if healing was not included in these all-inclusive promises from heaven. "…my God will liberally supply (fill to the full) your every need according to His riches in glory in Christ Jesus" (Philippians 4:19)

Please focus on the words "your every need" in this passage of Scripture. Personalize this promise. Put your name in this promise. *Know* that your loving Father Who promises to provide *everything* you need includes healing in this all-inclusive promise.

Your Father repeatedly promises to meet all of your needs. There is *no* qualifying statement in the Bible that says these promises do not include healing. "…they who seek (inquire of and require) the Lord [by right of their need and on the authority of His Word], none of them shall lack any beneficial thing" (Psalm 34:10).

You are instructed to "seek" the Lord. Please note the emphasis that is placed on seeking the Lord when the word "require" is used in the amplification. When something is required, it is absolutely necessary. Your Father wants you to seek Him aggressively, fervently and unceasingly with your whole heart.

Why should you seek the Lord in this manner? You should seek Him aggressively because of your "need." Healing is not a nice to have when you are very sick. Healing is a have to have. How should you "seek the Lord?" You should seek Him "on the authority of His Word."

Please highlight or underline the words "any beneficial thing." Isn't healing of the sickness in your body a "beneficial thing?" These all-inclusive words *must* include divine healing.

There is no question that God has provided divine healing for you just as He has provided everything else you will need throughout your life. "...His divine power has bestowed upon us all things that [are requisite and suited] to life and godliness, through the [full, personal] knowledge of Him Who called us by and to His own glory and excellence (virtue)" (II Peter 1:3).

Do you believe that the words "all things" include healing of the sickness in your body? Are you willing to do everything you can to walk in divine health? Are you willing to obey the scriptural instructions contained in this book to receive the healing that is included in the words "all things?"

If you believe that God gave up His only Son to take the sins of the entire world on Himself on a cross at Calvary, you also can be assured that your loving Father will provide everything else you need. "He who did not withhold or spare [even] His own Son but gave Him up for us all, will He not also with Him freely and graciously give us all [other] things?" (Romans 8:32).

God gave His very best when He sent His only beloved Son to earth to die on the cross to pay the price for the sins of mankind. Because God gave us this greatest of all gifts He also has "freely and graciously" promised to give us "all other things." These all-inclusive words definitely *include* healing. God did *not* say, "I will send My Son to earth to pay the price for your sins and I will meet all of your needs except for healing the sickness in your body."

When you add the scriptural *facts* in this chapter to the scriptural *facts* in the first two chapters you have the beginning of a solid foundation to believe God for manifestation of healing in *your* body. In the next chapter we will look into the Word of God for additional *facts* to encourage you that your loving Father has provided healing for *you.*

Chapter 10

You *Already* Have Been Healed

In the initial chapters of this book we have mentioned several times that healing *already* has been provided for you. In this chapter we will look into the Word of God so that you can see for yourself that the Bible says that you *already* have been healed because of the price Jesus Christ paid for you.

In the last chapter you saw that the Word of God is the Truth (see John 17:17). You saw that this Truth will set you free (see John 8:32). Christians who are sick can be set free from sickness *if* they thoroughly know and absolutely believe what the Bible says about the freedom Jesus has given us from sickness and disease. "…if the Son liberates you [makes you free men], then you are really and unquestionably free" (John 8:36).

This statement that Jesus made to a group of Jews more than two thousand years ago applies to the sickness in your body today. Jesus paid a tremendous price to enable you to walk in freedom from both sin and sickness. However, this freedom is *not* automatic. Jesus wants every person to live eternally in heaven, but every person will not live in heaven. You must *believe in your heart* and *confess with your mouth* that Jesus has paid the complete price for your sins (see Romans 10:9-10).

The same principle applies to freedom from sickness. Every person is not automatically set free from sickness. You must *release your faith* for the healing Jesus has provided for you by *believing in your heart* that you have been healed because of the enormous price Jesus paid at the whipping post and on the cross at Mount Calvary. You must confess with your mouth this great truth that you believe in your heart to receive and walk in the manifestation of the healing Jesus has provided for you. You must faithfully obey the scriptural instructions on divine health that are contained in Chapters Three and Eight.

God wants you to be healthy. Satan wants you to be sick. During His earthly ministry a leper came to Jesus to ask if He was willing to heal him. "...a leper came up to Him and, prostrating himself, worshiped Him, saying, Lord, if You are willing, You are able to cleanse me by curing me. And He reached out His hand and touched him, saying, I am willing; be cleansed by being cured. And instantly his leprosy was cured and cleansed" (Matthew 8:2-3).

When Jesus said, "I am willing" these words apply to *you* just as much today as they applied to that leper more than two thousand years ago. Jesus has not changed. There should be no doubt whatsoever in your heart. Your prayers for healing always should be anchored on your absolute certainty that God's will is to heal you.

If you knew that you were in a wealthy relative's will, wouldn't you be very interested to see what you inherited after this person died? The Bible is God's will. It is His testament. The Old Testament and the New Testament tell you exactly what your Father in heaven has provided for you.

Your Father has given you healing in addition to many other blessings. Divine healing and the other precious gifts your Father gives you are *much greater* than any financial gift you could ever inherit.

Carefully study God's will and testament. Find out for yourself exactly what the Old Testament and the New Testament say about healing. See for yourself that your loving Father in heaven has given *you* the gift of healing. Receive this precious gift through *unwavering faith* that God *has* provided healing from the sickness in your body.

God has given each of us the ability to choose. We all would be robots if we could not choose. If you sincerely desire to receive manifestation of divine healing, you must make the choice to carefully study what the Word of God says about divine healing. *You should obey God's specific instructions and believe in God's promises wholeheartedly* to receive the healing that has been provided for you.

Many religious denominations believe that God can heal sick people. They pray asking God to heal "if it is Your will." You have just seen that the Word of God definitely states that healing *is* God's will for you. Jesus and His disciples did not use the words "if it is Your will" when they prayed for the sick. This phrase has been created by well-meaning people, but it does *not* line up with the teaching of the Word of God.

You should remove the word "if" from your prayer request whenever you pray for healing. Your Father wants you to be *certain* that it *is* His will to heal you. Christians who use the words "if it is Your will" are praying in a way that is not pleasing to God. There is no question that God has provided healing for you. You must not express any words of doubt and unbelief when you pray for manifestation of healing from the sickness in your body.

Your faith for divine healing should *not* be limited to the belief that God *can* heal you. Your faith should be solidly anchored on your absolute certainty that God *already* has healed you. We have previously looked at the theme passage of Scripture on the cover of this book that says, "...by His wounds you have been healed" (I Peter 2:24).

We now will examine this verse in more detail. The word "have" in this passage of Scripture is in *the past tense*. You should *not* wonder *if* God will heal you. You can be certain that you "*have* been healed." Jesus gave you total victory over sickness by the price He paid at the whipping post. Jesus gave you total victory over sin by the price He paid by shedding His precious blood on the cross. You are *not* trying to win a victory. You should receive by faith manifestation of the victory that Jesus *already* has won for you.

Healing was provided for you many years before you were born. You came into this world with healing *already* provided for you. You do not need to beg and plead to receive what Jesus already has provided for you.

Would you beg and plead to receive what already has been provided for you in another person's will? You can be just as certain that you already have been healed as people here on earth can be certain after they learn what was left to them in another person's will.

When some Christians hear that they already have been healed, this statement does not make sense to them. They wonder how anyone can say they already are healed when they *still have* symptoms, pain and discomfort from sickness.

Manifestation of healing from sickness may be in the future, but you must believe in the present that you already have been healed just as the Bible says. You should not say, "The Lord is going to heal me." You should say, "The Lord already has healed me." You should believe that you will receive manifestation of this healing that *already* has been provided if you persevere with unwavering faith until you receive manifestation of this healing.

You saw in Chapter One that Isaiah prophesied more than seven hundred years before the birth of Jesus Christ that Jesus "surely has borne our griefs, sicknesses, weaknesses and distresses" (see Isaiah 53:4). Even though Isaiah was prophesying about the future he used the words "has borne" which are in the past tense. You can be certain that Jesus already has paid the price for healing. The word "surely" is a strong word. This word adds emphasis to the fact that Jesus already has borne the sickness in your body.

God gave Isaiah the ability to look into the future to see what Jesus would provide for us. You saw in Chapter One that Jesus *did* exactly what Isaiah prophesied He would do. "…He fulfilled what was spoken by the prophet Isaiah, He Himself took [in order to carry away] our weaknesses and infirmities and bore away our diseases" (Matthew 8:17).

This passage of Scripture tells you what Jesus did with the disease in *your* body. Jesus "carried away" this sickness. He "bore away your diseases." If Jesus already has carried your infirmities you do *not* need to carry sickness yourself. If Jesus bore away your diseases *why* would you think you have to carry this sickness yourself?

Do you believe that Jesus has taken the heavy load of *your* sickness and carried it away as the Bible says He has? The past tense in these declarative statements from Scripture in Isaiah 53:4 and Matthew 8:17 leave no doubt whatsoever that Jesus *already* has paid the complete price for your healing and that He already has *carried away* the sickness in your body.

If Jesus takes disease away from you, you do not have this disease. You may have evidence of disease in the natural realm, but you do not have this disease in the spiritual realm. You must believe this great spiritual truth and persevere in faith until God's promises of divine healing come into manifestation in the natural realm.

You will make a big mistake if you hold on to any sickness. You should not attempt to do anything that Jesus already has done for you. If you were weak and someone offered to carry a heavy load for you, would you insist on attempting to carry the load yourself? If Jesus bore *all* of your sickness there is *no* additional sickness for you to bear. Jesus loves you *so much* that He bore your sickness for you. You actually will insult Jesus if you attempt to carry the burden of sickness by yourself.

Our goal in these initial chapters is to firmly establish that healing *has been provided* for you. Once this fact has been established the remainder of this book will be filled with hundreds of scriptural instructions telling you exactly what God instructs *you* to do to receive the healing that already has been provided for you.

Your loving Father wants you to have total, absolute and unwavering faith in *each* of His promises. "…Know in all your hearts and in all your souls that not one thing has failed of all the good things which the Lord your God promised concerning you. All have come to pass for you; not one thing of them has failed" (Joshua 23:14).

You can depend completely on every promise your Father has given you concerning healing because "*not one thing*" that God has promised to you has failed. Your loving Father *always* does exactly what He says He will do. "…it is impossible for God ever to prove false or deceive us…" (Hebrews 6:18).

Your Father wants your heart to be filled to overflowing with the many healing promises He has given you in His Word. He wants you to have *absolute faith* that He stands behind every one of these promises if you do what the promise requires. He wants you to be certain that it is absolutely "impossible for Him to prove false or deceive you."

Please think of a person who loves you very much. If this person promises to do something do you believe he or she will carry out this promise? If you can trust human beings to do what they promise to do, you certainly can trust your loving Father to provide the healing He has promised to you. "God is not a man, that He should tell or act a lie, neither the son of man, that He should feel repentance or compunction [for what He has promised]. Has He said and shall He not do it? Or has He spoken and shall He not make it good?" (Numbers 23:19).

God is very different from human beings – "He is not a man." God cannot lie. Every healing promise and every other promise in the Bible is completely dependable – "has He spoken and shall He not make it good?"

If you can trust other people who love you to do what they promise to do, you certainly can trust your loving Father to give you manifestation of the healing He has promised to you. "God is faithful (reliable, trustworthy, and therefore ever true to His promise, and He can be depended on)…" (I Corinthians 1:9).

God's healing promises are *conditional*. God has *done* His part. *You must do your part*. You must learn *exactly* what His Word says about divine healing. You must *develop your faith* to the level where you *will* be able to receive manifestation of the promises of healing that God already has given to you.

Contrary to the belief of some denominations, God does *not* pick and choose who He wants to heal. God has provided healing for *everyone*. *We* are the ones who do the picking and choosing. *You decide* whether you will carefully study the scriptural facts in this book to learn exactly what the Word of God says about divine healing. *You decide* whether you will continually strengthen your faith for divine healing to the level where you will receive manifestation of the healing Jesus already has provided for you. You decide whether you will do everything you can to walk in divine health. Believe and receive and rest in God.

What more could you ask your Father in heaven to do? What more could you ask His beloved Son Jesus to do? Complete provision has been made for every person on earth to receive eternal salvation through Jesus Christ. Complete provision has been made for every person on earth to receive healing through Jesus Christ. *We each decide* whether we will receive salvation. *We each decide* whether we will receive healing.

The Word of God is filled with specific instructions telling you exactly what to do to be healed. Will you fail to learn and believe wholeheartedly in God's wonderful promises pertaining to healing? Will you fail to do your very best to walk in divine health?

We believe that the facts about healing in these initial chapters have given you a solid foundation to develop your faith for healing. Please go back and carefully review the scriptural facts in this chapter until you are *absolutely certain* that God has provided healing for *you*.

Chapter 11

You Must Obey Your Father's Specific Instructions

You have read many facts in these initial chapters telling you that Jesus Christ has provided healing for *you*. Do you have absolute certainty of this great scriptural truth in your heart? If you can answer this question affirmatively you are ready to proceed. If you do not have this deep inner certainty please go back and carefully study and meditate on the scriptural contents of these chapters.

Take as long as you need to firmly establish this certainty in your mind and your heart. You are not ready to learn what the Scriptures instruct you to do to receive manifestation of healing from God without first being absolutely certain that your loving Father has provided healing for you.

I want to make clear at this point that some people receive healing from God *without* following the specific scriptural instructions you will read in the remainder of this book. The Bible tells us that God has many ways of healing people such as healing miracles and the laying on of hands. When hands are placed on a person for healing, the hands of a Christian with strong faith for divine healing are placed on the person (usually on the shoulders or on the head) while praying for this person to be healed. I gave you several examples of healing miracles in the chapter concerning Kathryn Kuhlman's ministry.

Do not hesitate to ask your pastor and other Christians in your church with strong faith in God to lay hands on you. If you are sick and someone with a gift of healing comes to your area, you should attend this meeting. Do everything you can to receive manifestation of healing in any way you can. However, you must *not* give up if these attempts do not result in immediate improvement. Rest in faith and your absolute certainty that Jesus Christ is your Healer.

Your Father has shown you in His Word exactly what to do to steadily increase your faith in Him to receive manifestation of healing even if you are not healed in any other way. This book is filled with specific scriptural instructions pertaining to divine healing. Many Christians who are sick *do not know* what the Word of God instructs them to do to receive healing.

Some people ignore the instructions they receive from a manufacturer. They buy a product and pay little or no attention to the written instructions that come with the product. They attempt to assemble their purchase by doing what seems right to them.

Some of us have learned the hard way that we would have been a lot better off if we had read the manufacturer's instructions and followed them exactly. This same principle applies to receiving manifestation of the healing God has provided for you. "There is a way which seems right to a man and appears straight before him, but at the end of it is the way of death" (Proverbs 14:12).

You will make a severe mistake if you do "what seems right" to you instead of learning and doing what God instructs you to do. These efforts can lead you to "the way of death." This passage of Scripture refers to spiritual death, but you also can cause premature physical death if you do what seems right to you instead of learning and doing exactly what your Father instructs you to do in the areas of divine health and divine healing.

Many sincere and well-intentioned Christians who love God wholeheartedly have died prematurely because they did not know and obey God's instructions for health and healing. Ignorance of and/or disobedience to God's laws of health often cause illness. Ignorance of and/or disobedience to God's instructions for health and healing often block God from healing us. Many of God's faithful leaders go home early.

If you are sick and need healing, you should be absolutely determined to carefully study your Father's instructions pertaining to healing and follow these instructions exactly. We have done a great deal of work for you. We have spent hundreds of hours finding all of the Scripture references in this book. We have prayerfully woven them together so that you will be able to learn exactly what your Father instructs you to do to receive manifestation of the healing that Jesus already has provided for you.

You should have *great determination* to follow God's instructions exactly. The Great Physician has given you a prescription for healing. You must not ignore the instructions He has given to you.

You can compare following God's specific instructions to using a road map when you are preparing to go on a long trip. If you were going to a distant place where you had not been before and you were given a detailed road map with exact instructions telling you how to get to this location, would you ignore that map? Would you just drive in the general direction of the place or would you carefully plot your trip and follow these directions exactly?

The Bible is God's road map for you. Your loving Father has given you specific, exact and detailed instructions telling you exactly what He wants you to do to receive the healing that has been provided for you by His beloved Son. Your Father wants you to follow these instructions even more carefully than you would follow instructions on a road map when you go on a long trip.

Many of the scriptural instructions in this book may sound quite unusual to you if you have not previously spent many years studying the Word of God. You must understand how much higher and different God's ways are from what may seem right to you.

"...My thoughts are not your thoughts, neither are your ways My ways, says the Lord. For as the heavens are higher than the earth, so are My ways higher than your ways and My thoughts than your thoughts" (Isaiah 55:8-9).

God's thoughts "are *not* your thoughts." God's thoughts are "higher than your thoughts." God's ways are "higher than your ways." Make up your mind that you will do *exactly* what your Father instructs you to do whether or not His instructions make sense to the limitations of your human understanding.

You must understand that Satan and his demons are in the atmosphere around you. They will do everything they can to try to stop you from receiving the healing Jesus has provided for you. They often will attempt to influence you to do what seems right to you. They do not want you to follow God's instructions exactly until you receive manifestation of the healing Jesus has provided for you.

Your loving Father has promised that He will bless you if you are obedient. "If you are willing and obedient, you shall eat the good of the land; but if you refuse and rebel, you will be devoured by the sword. For the mouth of the Lord has spoken it" (Isaiah 1:19-20).

Please note the two times the word "if" is mentioned in this passage of Scripture. The results depend upon what *you* do. Are you "willing and obedient?" Are you willing to carefully study to learn and obey your Father's specific instructions pertaining to divine healing? You will "eat the good of the land" (receive manifestation of healing) if you do not "refuse and rebel." "You will be devoured" by the sickness in your body if you insist on doing what you want to do.

Some Christians are spiritually lazy. They attend church most Sundays. They spend a few minutes each day in prayer. They may study the Bible occasionally. They may attend occasional Christian meetings or concerts. This casual Christian lifestyle is *not* sufficient for Christians who are sick or for anyone else in these last days before Jesus returns.

You should be absolutely determined to learn and obey God's instructions. You often will be required to obey these specific instructions for more than just a few days or a few weeks. These instructions from God should be a way of life for you.

If you are very serious about receiving the healing that Jesus already has provided for you, make the decision now to spend tremendous amounts of time poring over the scriptural instructions contained in this book. Be determined to learn everything you can about the specific instructions your Father has given you. Make the decision to follow every one of these instructions exactly.

Jesus is your example in every area of your life. You should be just as obedient to your Father's instructions for healing as Jesus was obedient to every one of His Father's instructions throughout His earthly ministry. Jesus said, "…I do not seek or consult My own will [I have no desire to do what is pleasing to Myself, My own aim, My own purpose] but only the will and pleasure of the Father Who sent Me" (John 5:30).

You should "have no desire to do what is pleasing" to you. You must be determined to do exactly what your Father has instructed you to do. "Blessed (happy, fortunate, to be envied) is everyone who fears, reveres, and worships the Lord, who walks in His ways and lives according to His commandments. For you shall eat [the fruit] of the labor of your hands; happy (blessed, fortunate, enviable) shall you be, and it shall be well with you" (Psalm 128:1-2).

Please highlight or underline the word "everyone" in this passage of Scripture. God is speaking to *you*. Do you "fear, revere and worship the Lord?" Are you absolutely determined to "walk in His ways" and live according to His specific instructions?

We pray that you will be humble and teachable and that you will be determined to follow exactly the specific scriptural instructions for divine healing that are contained in this book. If you are humble and teachable your Father will show you exactly what He wants you to do. He will teach you continually. "He leads the humble in what is right, and the humble He teaches His way" (Psalm 25:9).

We pray that you will humbly approach the scriptural instructions for divine healing in this book by saying something like, "Dear Father, show me Your healing power through Your Word. Help me to be obedient to Your specific instructions. My heart's desire is to be obedient to You because I love You, dear Father. I know that You already have provided for my healing through Your Son Jesus. Thank You, dear Father."

You must not make the mistake that the Pharisees made during the earthly ministry of Jesus Christ. Jesus said, "You disregard and give up and ask to depart from you the commandment of God and cling to the tradition of men [keeping it carefully and faithfully]. And He said to them, You have a fine way of rejecting [thus thwarting and nullifying and doing away with] the commandment of God in order to keep your tradition (your own human regulations)!" (Mark 7:8-9).

You must not "disregard" God's instructions in any area of your life, including divine healing. You must not "cling to" human "tradition." You can fail to receive manifestation of the healing that already has been provided for you if you insist on clinging to traditional beliefs and customs instead of learning and obeying the specific instructions your Father has given to you.

This chapter has given you a scriptural foundation for absolute commitment to obeying God's instructions pertaining to healing. In the next chapter you will learn about the mighty power of God's medicine and exactly what you should do to partake of the wonderful spiritual medicine your loving Father has provided for you.

Chapter 12

God's Mighty and Powerful Medicine

This book is filled with specific scriptural instructions pertaining to divine healing. These instructions will only benefit you if you obey them. "...be doers of the Word [obey the message], and not merely listeners to it, betraying yourselves [into deception by reasoning contrary to the Truth]" (James 1:22).

This passage of Scripture says that you must *do* what the Word of God tells you to do. You must "obey" God's instructions. You will "betray yourself" if you only "listen" to these instructions. You can be deceived by Satan and his demons because of "reasoning contrary to the Truth."

God's Word is the Truth (see John 17:17). You must not attempt to receive divine healing from sickness through human reasoning that does not obey God's specific instructions. You cannot expect to receive manifestation of healing if you merely read these instructions from God and fail to do what your Father tells you to do.

The instructions in the Word of God are *God's medicine*. God's medicine is much more effective than any medicine in the world. No doctor in the world can prescribe a medicine that even remotely approaches the effectiveness of the Great Physician's supernatural medicine. If you have a holy Bible you have in your possession the most powerful medicine that exists, but you must partake of this medicine from God throughout every day and night until you receive healing in your body. "He sends forth His Word and heals them…" (Psalm 107:20).

This passage of Scripture explains the medicinal healing power of the Word of God. When this passage of Scripture says that God sends His Word and heals you it could accurately say that He sends His medicine and heals you. "Keep my commandments and live, and keep my law and teaching as the apple (the pupil) of your eye" (Proverbs 7:2).

God is telling you that the way to live is found in the Bible. You should be determined to "keep God's commandments" – to follow His instructions exactly. When you speak of someone as "the apple of your eye" you are speaking about someone who is very special to you. Your Father wants His Word to be "the apple of *your* eye."

Every aspect of your life should revolve around the supernatural Word of God that should fill your heart to overflowing. You should be *absolutely determined* to partake *continually* of the magnificent spiritual medicine your Father has provided for you. This book will give you specific scriptural instructions to tell you what to do to continually fill your mind and your heart with the supernatural medicine of the Word of God. "A happy heart is good medicine and a cheerful mind works healing, but a broken spirit dries up the bones" (Proverbs 17:22).

You will have a "happy heart" regardless of the sickness in your body if you continually fill your heart with the mighty supernatural power of the living Word of God. A heart that is filled with God's Word is filled with "good medicine" from God. You will have "a cheerful mind" if you obey your Father's instructions to consistently renew your mind in His Word. Your happy heart and your cheerful mind ultimately will "work healing."

You may have "a broken spirit" if you fail to obey your Father's specific instructions. God says that a broken spirit will "dry up the bones." You are much less likely to receive healing *if* you are worried and discouraged. Your Father is looking for you to exhibit deep, strong and unwavering faith in Him.

Some of the medicine that you purchase as a result of a doctor's prescription carries a disclaimer. These prescriptions often warn you of potential side effects that could take place in your body if you take this medicine. You can be absolutely certain that there are *no* side effects to God's medicine.

When a doctor gives you a prescription you usually are limited as to how much of this medicine you can take. The Great Physician does *not* limit His medicine. You *cannot overdose* on God's medicine. God's medicine will never hurt you in any way. You can take as much of God's medicine as you desire throughout every day and night of your life. You must not limit the amount of God's medicine that you take.

The Great Physician tells you how often He wants you to take His medicine. Your Father does not want you to just take His medicine three or four times a day. Joshua 1:8 tells you to take God's medicine throughout the "day and night." Psalm 1:2 tells you to take God's medicine "by day and by night." II Corinthians 4:16 tells you to take God's medicine "day after day." Ephesians 4:23 tells you to take God's medicine "constantly." If you are very sick you should take *massive doses* of God's supernatural medicine throughout every day and night of your life.

The world's medicine gives temporary relief, often with side effects. It does not cover the symptom unless it is taken internally. God's medicine also will not work unless it gets inside of you. The Word of God is *internal medicine*. Your Father's prescription is to constantly fill your mind and your heart with the medicine of His supernatural living Word.

You usually take the world's medicine orally. Sometimes you receive this medication by a needle being injected into your skin. You take God's medicine by constantly filling your *eyes* and your *ears* with the supernatural medicine of His living Word.

Some religious people cannot even begin to comprehend what the Word of God teaches about healing. "…[although] they hold a form of piety (true religion), they deny and reject and are strangers to the power of it [their conduct belies the genuineness of their profession]. Avoid [all] such people [turn away from them]" (II Timothy 3:5).

The word "piety" refers to pious people who are zealous in the area of religious ritual. These religious people may attend church regularly, but they "deny and reject and are strangers to the power of" the Word of God. You must "turn away" from ritualistic religious people who do not understand what the Bible says about healing.

If you are boldly speaking God's Word, what you are saying will sound like a foreign language to your family members and friends who have not consistently renewed their minds in the Word of God. Do not be surprised if some of your family members and friends tell you that what you are doing is extreme. The scriptural principles we are talking about in this book *are extreme* from a worldly perspective. You have seen that God's ways are *very different* from the ways of the world (see Isaiah 55:8-9).

You must not allow your family members, your unsaved relatives and your friends to talk you out of receiving healing from God. Do you allow your unsaved relatives and friends to talk you out of your eternal salvation through Jesus Christ? Do not allow unbelievers and religious people to sway your faith for divine healing. You should be *just as certain* of what God's Word says about healing as you are about what God's Word says about eternal salvation.

Your family and friends undoubtedly mean well, but they are wrong if they do not know what the Word of God says about healing. Unfortunately, many Christians who are sick allow their thinking to be distorted by the things that well-intentioned people say to them. "Blessed (happy, fortunate, prosperous, and enviable) is the man who walks and lives not in the counsel of the ungodly [following their advice, their plans and purposes]..." (Psalm 1:1).

You will be "blessed" by the Great Physician if you do *not* follow the advice of people who have no knowledge of what the Word of God says about divine healing. These well-meaning people are totally indoctrinated into the world's system of healing. You must not "follow their advice, their plans and their purposes" and ignore the specific instructions your Father has given you. Instead, you should do what the next two verses (Psalm 1:2-3) instruct you to do. You should meditate continually on the supernatural living Word of God.

Many times over the years I have seen unbelievers or Christians who do not understand God's principles of healing look incredulously at Christians who say they are healed while they obviously still had symptoms of sickness. These people were focusing on evidence from their senses instead of focusing on God. They were walking by sight, not by faith (see II Corinthians 5:7). These well-intentioned people were in the natural realm, not the spiritual realm. They will attempt to advise you according to the limitations of their human understanding.

Sometimes Christians are concerned that they may offend their friends and loved ones by emphatically obeying scriptural healing instructions that make no sense whatsoever to these people. *You must* establish your priorities if you are sick. *Why* would you ever choose to turn away from God's scriptural healing principles because you do not want to offend someone who is opposed to doing what God has instructed you to do?

Jesus understood the necessity of turning away from people who did not believe. You can see that He did this on one occasion when He went to a home where a little girl had been pronounced dead. "When they arrived at the house of the ruler of the synagogue, He looked [carefully and with understanding] at [the] tumult and the people weeping and wailing loudly. And when He had gone in, He said to them, Why do you make an uproar and weep? The little girl is not dead but is sleeping. And they laughed and jeered at Him. But He put them all out, and, taking the child's father and mother and those who were with Him, He went in where the little girl was lying" (Mark 5:38-40).

Jesus did not want to be surrounded by people who did not believe He could raise this child from the dead. Jesus "put them all out." He did not want their unbelief to be present. He then went into the little girl's bedroom and raised her from the dead. "Gripping her [firmly] by the hand, He said to her, Talitha cumi—which translated is, Little girl, I say to you, arise [from the sleep of death]! And instantly the girl got up and started walking around—for she was twelve years old. And they were utterly astonished and overcome with amazement" (Mark 5:41-42).

You must not allow other people's doubt and unbelief *to pull you down* when you are sick. You cannot afford to be influenced by people who do not understand what the Bible says about healing. We are talking about *your* life. Refuse to allow these people to influence you with their unscriptural beliefs. These people are the same people who will come to your funeral if you die prematurely because you listened to their traditional beliefs instead of turning away from doubt and unbelief to place *all* of your faith in Jesus Christ and doing all that you can to enable your body to heal itself.

Jesus is your personal Savior. Jesus is your personal Healer. You must not allow what other people think to affect your deep, strong and unwavering faith in Jesus as your Healer. These people are talking about *your* body. They are talking about *your* health. Be determined to do what *God tells you to do* to receive manifestation of the healing that Jesus already has provided for you.

Chapter 13

Keep the Lord in First Place

We have established a solid scriptural foundation for divine healing. We will continue to carefully examine the Word of God to help you build on this foundation so that you will understand how God already has provided for your healing through Jesus Christ. In this chapter we will look carefully at doctors, the world's medicine and the world's system of healing.

I do not believe the Bible teaches that you should abstain from going to physicians. However, the Bible does explain the mistake you will make if you put physicians ahead of the Lord when you are sick. "In the thirty-ninth year of his reign Asa was diseased in his feet – until his disease became very severe; yet in his disease he did not seek he Lord, but relied on physicians. And Asa slept with his fathers, dying in the forty-first year of his reign" (II Chronicles 16:12-13).

Asa who succeeded his father, Abijah, as the King of Judah did what many sick people do today. He "did not seek the Lord" when he had a severe disease in his feet; instead, Asa "relied on physicians." Asa died approximately two years later.

The New Testament tells us about a woman who turned to physicians before she turned to Jesus. "…there was a woman who had a flow of blood for twelve years, and who had endured much suffering under [the hands of] many physicians and had spent all that she had, and was no better but instead grew worse" (Mark 5:25-26).

This woman "endured much suffering under the hands of many physicians." After spending all the money she had she was "no better but instead grew worse." After twelve years of suffering this woman was miraculously healed by Jesus.

This woman did not give up even though she had not been healed by physicians. "She had heard the reports concerning Jesus, and she came up behind Him in the throng and touched His garment, For she kept saying, If I only touch His garments, I shall be restored to health. And immediately her flow of blood was dried up at the source, and [suddenly] she felt in her body that she was healed of her [distressing] ailment" (Mark 5:27-29).

This woman had complete faith that Jesus would heal her if she could just "touch His garments." When she touched the clothes of Jesus, "immediately her flow of blood was dried up at the source" and she was healed.

Jesus knew that someone with strong faith had touched His clothes. "...Jesus, recognizing in Himself that the power proceeding from Him had gone forth, turned around immediately in the crowd and said, Who touched My clothes? And the disciples kept saying to Him, You see the crowd pressing hard around You from all sides, and You ask, Who touched Me?" (Mark 5:30-31).

The reason Jesus knew that someone with strong faith had touched His clothing was because He knew that the healing "power proceeding from Him had gone forth." When Jesus asked who touched Him His disciples were surprised. He was surrounded by a crowd of people. Many people had touched His clothing.

Jesus persevered in His quest to find the person with strong faith who had touched His clothing. "Still He kept looking around to see her who had done it. But the woman, knowing what had been done for her, though alarmed and frightened and trembling, fell down before Him and told Him the whole truth" (Mark 5:32-33).

When the frightened woman "fell down before Him and told Him the whole truth," Jesus then explained *why* she had been healed. "...He said to her, Daughter, your faith (your trust and confidence in Me, springing from faith in God) has restored you to health. Go in (into) peace and be continually healed and freed from your [distressing bodily] disease" (Mark 5:34).

This woman was *not* healed because she touched the clothing of Jesus Christ. She was healed because "her trust and confidence" in Jesus "springing from faith in God restored her to health." The hem of His garment was merely the point of contact between her faith in Jesus and His mighty healing power.

This same principle applies to *you* today. You must not place all of your faith in physicians and the world's system of healing. You should have complete faith in Jesus as your Healer. When your faith is ignited you partake of the atonement of Jesus. You partake of both His suffering and His victorious power over sin and sickness.

Jesus did *not* say that you should not go to a doctor when you are sick. I believe that Jesus actually said that some people who are sick should go to a doctor. He said "...Those who are strong and well (healthy) have no need of a physician, but those who are weak and sick" (Matthew 9:12).

In order to comprehend exactly what Jesus said here I would like to add a few words to this passage of Scripture in an attempt to explain the full context of these words. I have added the words "have need of a physician" to the end of this passage of Scripture. Here is how it looks now. "...Those who are strong and well (healthy) have no need of a physician, but those who are weak and sick have need of a physician."

I believe this is exactly what Jesus meant. He said that people who are strong and healthy do not need a physician, but those who are weak and sick do need a physician. If you are weak and sick do not believe that you should not go to a doctor. Do not feel guilty if you go to a physician. The disciple Luke was a physician. He was very close to Jesus. The Bible refers to him as "…Luke, the beloved physician…" (Colossians 4:14).

If you decide to go to a physician, prayerfully seek a physician with the wisdom and experience of Dr. Luke. If possible, go to a physician who prays, trusts in God and is an instrument of the wisdom and excellence of God.

Some people make their doctors into little gods. They place far too much dependence on physicians and medical science and far too little dependence on the Great Physician. I do not agree with people who say we should forsake doctors and medicine completely. On the other hand, there is no question that we make a *big* mistake if we place any doctor ahead of Dr. Jesus. "It is better to trust and take refuge in the Lord than to put confidence in man" (Psalm 118:8).

Sometimes God uses physicians to help us. On other occasions the Great Physician heals us Himself. All healing actually comes from God because God has provided each of us with a miraculous self-healing body that can heal itself. You should explore every avenue of healing that is available to you.

Whenever you are sick all of your words and actions should clearly indicate that God is *first* in your life. I do not believe you should call a doctor immediately when you initially are threatened by sickness. You already should have been renewing your mind in the Word of God each day and meditating on God's Word throughout each day and night if you have been doing what your Father has instructed you to do throughout each day and night of your life.

You should *pray immediately* when you first notice symptoms of sickness. You should significantly increase your Bible study and Scripture meditation. You should take massive doses of God's medicine. You should focus *all* of your Bible study and meditation on Scripture about divine healing and increasing your faith in God.

If you know what caused the sickness in your body and what to do to reverse it, make that change immediately. Many times the symptoms of sickness in your body will dictate significant changes in your diet, exercise or your general lifestyle. Check your life for stress and for unforgiveness.

You should ask the elders in your church to lay hands on you and pray for you (see James 5:14-15). You should pray to God with faith for healing. If you do go to a doctor you should continue to pray asking the Lord to heal you. You connect with your Healer. He does not suddenly decide to heal you. He already has done it.

You must understand that all Christians have the greatest Doctor the universe has ever known living inside of them. If you are a Christian your own personal physician, Dr. Jesus, makes His home in your heart (see Galatians 2:20). He is with you every minute of every hour of every day. He is on call twenty-four hours a day.

Dr. Jesus does *not* charge a fee for His services. In these days when so many people are concerned about the increasing cost of healthcare, you must understand that Jesus *paid the price* for your healthcare more than two thousand years ago. All that He requires is that you turn to Him as your Healer with complete faith in Him and that you learn and obey the specific instructions He has given to you to receive healing.

Some Christians who are sick make the mistake of spending far too much of their time, effort and energy seeking healing from the world's medical system when they absolutely should put God in first place ahead of anything else. Jesus said, "…seek (aim at and strive after) first of all His kingdom and His righteousness (His way of doing and being right), and then all these things taken together will be given you besides" (Matthew 6:33).

When Jesus spoke these words during His Sermon on the Mount He was referring to the basic needs of life. He was referring to such things as food and clothing when He said that "all these things" will be given to you. This same principle applies to every need you have. Jesus instructs you to put God first and keep Him first and to trust Him completely with every challenge you face.

If you truly seek God first your relationship with Him will be more important than anything or anyone else. You will seek Him continually throughout every day and night of your life. Every aspect of your life will revolve around Him. You will constantly be aware of His indwelling presence. You will not allow anyone or anything to come ahead of Him. You will not allow the symptoms of sickness in your body to come ahead of Him.

You will not try to find time for the Lord. You will do just the opposite. You will *make time* for Him. Everything else in your life will come after the Lord. You will put the Lord in first place where He belongs and keep Him in first place. You must understand the absolute necessity of staying close to the Lord. "...set your mind and heart to seek (inquire of and require as your vital necessity) the Lord your God..." (I Chronicles 22:19).

The amplification of this passage of Scripture tells you that the Lord is your "vital necessity." You must not put Jesus Who paid such a tremendous price for your healing in any place except in first place where He belongs. You should live "...so that He alone in everything and in every respect might occupy the chief place [stand first and be preeminent]" (Colossians 1:18).

This passage of Scripture says that Jesus should "occupy the chief place." The amplification says that He should "stand first and be preeminent." Jesus should be in first place throughout every day and night of your life whether you are sick or healthy. You should be like the psalmist who said, "...I have no delight or desire on earth besides You" (Psalm 73:25).

You should seek the Lord actively and consistently with every fiber of your being. The Lord should be an absolute "delight" in your life. No personal "desire" should come ahead of your commitment to stay close to Him at all times. Jesus should be at the center of everything you think, everything you say and everything you do. "...Christ, Who is our life..." (Colossians 3:4).

If you are extremely sick you must understand how inadequate you are. Jesus has provided for all of your needs. You should focus on Him continually. "…from Him and through Him and to Him are all things. [For all things originate with Him and come from Him; all things live through Him, and all things center in and tend to consummate and to end in Him.]…" (Romans 11:36).

Healing and the fulfillment of every other need come from Jesus. You should hold Jesus in absolute awe and reverence at all times. "…unto you who revere and worshipfully fear My name shall the Sun of righteousness arise with healing in His wings…" (Malachi 4:2).

This passage of Old Testament Scripture prophesies about Jesus. When you fear the Lord, you revere Him. You worship Him. Every aspect of your life revolves around Him. If you truly fear Jesus and hold Him in constant reverence and awe He will "arise with healing in His wings."

The Lord truly is in first place in your life when you fear Him. When you fear the Lord you have such great awe and reverence toward Him that you trust Him completely to give you manifestation of healing and to meet every other need you have. A definite relationship exists between fearing the Lord and having deep trust and confidence in Him to heal you and to provide everything you need. "In the reverent and worshipful fear of the Lord there is strong confidence…" (Proverbs 14:26).

You cannot have deep, strong and unwavering faith in the Lord if you do not fear Him. You will only fear the Lord (revere Him and hold Him in absolute awe) when you realize how mighty, magnificent and powerful He is. You *will* have "strong confidence" in the Lord if you constantly fear Him and reverently worship Him.

The next verse shows you the relationship between reverence and fear of the Lord and avoiding premature death. "Reverent and worshipful fear of the Lord is a fountain of life, that one may avoid the snares of death" (Proverbs 14:27).

When you fear the Lord and keep Him in first place at all times, a spiritual "fountain of life" is established in your life that will enable you to "avoid the snares of death." Please focus on the scriptural relationship between fearing the Lord, receiving healing from Him and not dying prematurely. "...the Lord's eye is upon those who fear Him [who revere and worship Him with awe], who wait for Him and hope in His mercy and loving-kindness, to deliver them from death and keep them alive in famine" (Psalm 33:18-19).

The psalmist says that "the Lord's eye is upon those who fear Him." When you fear the Lord you "wait for Him." You place all of your "hope in His mercy and loving-kindness." You trust Him completely to "deliver you from death" and to "keep you alive" in spite of the challenges you face.

In this chapter you can clearly see the emphasis that the Word of God places on putting the Lord first, fearing Him with reverent awe, receiving healing and avoiding premature death. Your precious Lord *will* provide manifestation of healing and every other need *if* you fear Him and worship Him continually. "O fear the Lord, you His saints [revere and worship Him]! For there is no want to those who truly revere and worship Him with godly fear" (Psalm 34:9).

Please highlight or underline the words "there is no want." *These words include healing from the sickness in your body.* You will not lack *anything* if you keep your precious Lord in first place, fear Him with reverent awe and worship Him continually.

Does the sickness in your body seem overwhelming to you? You have seen that you should place all of your hope in the Lord whenever you face severe sickness or any other problem. You will not be afraid of anything if you truly fear the Lord. You will not be overwhelmed by sickness if you revere the Lord and hold Him in absolute awe at all times.

The prophet Isaiah explained this wonderful spiritual truth. He said that the Lord "...warned and instructed me not to walk in the way of this people, saying, Do not call conspiracy [or hard, or holy] all that this people will call conspiracy [or hard, or holy]; neither be in fear of what they fear, nor [make others afraid and] in dread. The Lord of hosts – regard Him as holy and honor His holy name [by regarding Him as your only hope of safety], and let Him be your fear and let Him be your dread [lest you offend Him by your fear of man and distrust of Him]" (Isaiah 8:11-13).

You must *not* be afraid of sickness. You must *not* give in to fear when you face sickness or any other adversity. When you fear the Lord you "regard Him as holy and honor His holy name." The amplification of this passage of Scripture says that you "will regard Him as your only hope of safety" when you fear Him. You must not fear sickness or anything else. Our precious Lord will honor the faith of every person who truly fears Him. "He will fulfill the desires of those who reverently and worshipfully fear Him..." (Psalm 145:19).

When this passage of Scripture speaks of "fulfilling the desires" of people these desires include healing for people who are very sick and fervently desire to be healed. If you want to receive manifestation of healing you cannot do anything that is more beneficial than to constantly spend large amounts of time drawing closer to your precious Lord because you reverently and worshipfully fear Him.

Are you sick? Where are you putting your trust? Are you putting your trust in human knowledge ahead of God? Or are you putting your trust in God ahead of human knowledge? Medical science and trust in God are not mutually exclusive. There is a place for both medical science and divine healing. However, you must be absolutely certain that you place your emphasis *first* of all on the Lord and *then* receive any help that is available to you through human knowledge.

Chapter 14

Trust Completely in Your Father's Great Love for You

You are moving steadily forward toward learning all of the scriptural instructions your Father has given you to receive divine healing. We have established that God *already* has provided healing for you. You have learned many facts about good health. You have learned that you should be humble, teachable and open-minded. You have learned that your loving Father has provided you with the supernatural spiritual medicine you need. We have discussed the importance of putting God in first place ahead of doctors, medicine and any other method of healing.

We now are ready to look at *the one thing* that should be the foundation for divine healing more than anything else – a deep and constant awareness of your Father's great and incomprehensible love for you. In this chapter we will look into the Word of God to learn that God has awesome love for every person on earth. You will be greatly encouraged as you meditate on what the Bible says about your Father's magnificent love for *you*.

Awareness of and continually abiding in God's love is *vitally important* to receiving healing from God. The cornerstone of your faith in God should be your Father's tremendous love for you. Faith in God that is not solidly anchored on the certainty of God's love for you will not be able to persevere if your body aches with pain and it seems as if you cannot possibly be healed.

You might hesitate to ask God to heal you because you think you are not good enough to receive healing. You are *absolutely correct*. *No one* is good enough to receive healing from God. Healing is a gift that your Father has made available to you because He loves you. You cannot earn healing from God. You do not earn gifts. You receive gifts.

Come to God for healing with a complete sense of unworthiness. Healing is available to you *only* because of your Father's love and grace and the enormous sacrifice that Jesus made for you because He loves you.

Every person who has asked Jesus to be his or her Savior is a beloved son or daughter of their Father in heaven. On the other hand, every person who has not asked Jesus to be his or her Savior is a child of the devil. "…It is made clear who take their nature from God and are His children and who take their nature from the devil and are his children…" (I John 3:10).

There are two spiritual families on earth – the family of God and the family of Satan. Satan wants you to believe that there is no God or that God is a cold, foreboding and distant God. Some people were brought up with misguided statements about all of the terrible things God would do to them because of the things they did wrong. These thoughts have become imbedded in the minds and hearts of these people.

Your Father in heaven *loves you*. He is not cold, distant and foreboding. God showed how much He loves you by making provision for everyone on earth to become beloved members of His family. "See what [an incredible] quality of love the Father has given (shown, bestowed on) us, that we should [be permitted to] be named and called and counted the children of God! And so we are!…" (I John 3:1).

Please highlight or underline the words "incredible quality of love." If you have asked Jesus Christ to be your Savior you can be absolutely certain that *you* are "named and called and counted as a child of God." If you are sick you cannot focus on anything that is more important than a constant focus on scriptural facts that explain your Father's incredible love for you.

You were an outsider looking in before you were saved. You were a member of Satan's family. Once you ask Jesus Christ to be your Savior you "…are no longer outsiders (exiles, migrants, and aliens, excluded from the rights of citizens), but you now share citizenship with the saints (God's own people, consecrated and set apart for Himself); and you belong to God's [own] household" (Ephesians 2:19).

You are a member of "God's own household" if you have received Jesus Christ as your Savior. Because of the sacrifice of Jesus, God in heaven actually is your loving Father. God is referred to as our Father more than two hundred times in the New Testament. The Bible refers to Him as "…the Father of our Lord Jesus Christ, for Whom every family in heaven and on earth is named [that Father from Whom all fatherhood takes its title and derives its name]" (Ephesians 3:14-15).

All human fathers receive the title of father from our loving Father in heaven. The same God Who sits on His throne in heaven and rules the entire universe *knows you personally*. God is omniscient. He knows everything about you and everything about every one of the billions of people on earth. The Bible says that omniscient God knows every hair on the head of every person on earth (see Matthew 10:30). Your loving Father knows every thought in your mind. He knows everything you say. He knows everything you do. "…I will be a Father to you, and you shall be My sons and daughters, says the Lord Almighty" (II Corinthians 6:18).

Open your mouth and say, "God in heaven actually is *my* loving Father. I am His beloved child. I am absolutely secure in my Father's tremendous love for me." God actually is both your spiritual father and mother. Your Father offers comfort to each of His beloved children just as a loving mother here on earth comforts her children. "As one whom his mother comforts, so will I comfort you…" (Isaiah 66:13).

When your body aches with pain and discomfort you can be certain that God *will comfort and encourage you* because He said "I will comfort you." Your Father is the source of all comfort that ever has been given to any person on earth. He wants you to receive this comfort and encouragement from Him by faith because His Word speaks of "...God [Who is the Source] of every comfort (consolation and encouragement), Who comforts (consoles and encourages) us in every trouble (calamity and affliction)..." (II Corinthians 1:3-4).

You can be certain that every person who comforts and encourages you in any way receives this ability to comfort and encourage you from God. Your Father *will* "comfort, console and encourage *you* in every trouble." The word "every" in this passage of Scripture *includes* whatever discomfort you are experiencing as a result of sickness. Receive your Father's comfort by faith.

You must be absolutely certain that you really are a son or daughter of Almighty God. Jewish people who receive Jesus Christ as their Messiah become natural children of God. Gentiles who receive Jesus as their Savior are adopted into the family of God. "...you have received the Spirit of adoption [the Spirit producing sonship] in [the bliss of] which we cry, Abba (Father)! Father! The Spirit Himself [thus] testifies together with our own spirit, [assuring us] that we are children of God" (Romans 8:15-16).

You can insert *your name* when this passage of Scripture says that "*you* have received the Spirit of adoption." The word "Abba" in this passage of Scripture is a Hebrew word that is similar to our English word "Daddy." God wants each of us to be absolutely certain that He is our loving Father. He wants each of His beloved children to come to Him with the need for healing and every other need just as children on earth reach out to their loving parents with complete faith and trust to meet their needs.

Your knowledge that you actually are a member of God's family should increase steadily as you grow and mature as a Christian. You will become better able to hear the voice of the Holy

Spirit Who will "assure you that you are a child of God." You can be absolutely certain that Jesus has paid the price for you to be a son or daughter of God. "…in Christ Jesus you are sons of God through faith" (Galatians 3:26).

Would you expect to receive special privileges if you were a member of the royal family in England? The special privileges of royalty in a country *cannot begin to compare* to the special privileges that are available to *you* as a member of God's royal family. By faith you can believe that your loving Father will supply every one of your needs just as children on earth trust their loving parents to supply everything they need.

Your Father in heaven wants you to depend on Him completely just as beloved children on earth depend completely on their loving parents. Believe that your loving Father will reward your faith in Him. Jesus said, "…According to your faith and trust and reliance [on the power invested in Me] be it done to you" (Matthew 9:29).

Your faith in God is a key to receiving His love for you. Your faith in God is a key to receiving healing from sickness. You must not block your loving Father through doubt and unbelief (see Mark 6:1-6).

God showed His love for you when He sent His only Son to earth to pay an enormous price for your eternal salvation and for your healing. *Jesus showed His love for you* by the tremendous ordeal He went through for you at the whipping post and on the cross at Calvary. Jesus was not held on the cross by the nails in His feet and the nails in His wrists. Jesus was held on the cross by His magnificent love for every person on earth.

Your Father loves you with great and incomprehensible love in spite of all of your faults and shortcomings. He knows each person intimately. God knows exactly what your faults and shortcomings are. He still loves you with *unconditional love*.

Most of us know some of the faults we have. God knows *all* of your faults and shortcomings. Not only does your Father love you in spite of your faults, but He loves you with a love that is so great, so wonderful and so magnificent that His love for you is totally, completely and absolutely beyond the limits of human comprehension. Your Father loves you as if there was no one else in the world to love. His love for each of us is great and constant.

Love is not only something that God has for you. *God is love.* Your Father wants you to be so conscious of His love for you that you will not allow sickness to overwhelm you. You should "...know (understand, recognize, are conscious of, by observation and by experience) and believe (adhere to and put faith in and rely on) the love God cherishes for us. God is love, and he who dwells and continues in love dwells and continues in God, and God dwells and continues in him" (I John 4:16).

This passage of Scripture explains the relationship between God's love for you and your faith in Him. You are told that "God is love." Your Father wants you to "dwell and continue" in constant awareness of His love for you. If your body aches with pain and discomfort caused by sickness, your Father wants you to focus continually on His great love for you. You should "believe, adhere to and put faith in and rely on the love God cherishes for you." If you "dwell and continue in love and dwell and continue in God, God will dwell and continue in you." You will persevere with unwavering faith in your loving Father until you receive manifestation of healing from Him.

As you continually draw closer to God His love for you will be perfected. "In this [union and communion with Him [love is brought to completion and attains perfection with us, that we may have confidence for the day of judgment [with assurance and boldness to face Him], because as He is, so are we in this world" (I John 4:17).

Fear can *block* love from doing its work in you. You must *get rid of fear* so that your faith for healing will be deep, strong and unwavering. You saw in I John 4:16 that your Father wants you to "dwell and continue in love." The amplification of I John 4:17 tells you that "this union and communion with Him will cause love to be brought to completion and attain perfection in us."

You will "have confidence" in God if you focus continually on His love. You will trust your Father completely. This confidence and trust in God will keep fear at bay. "There is no fear in love [dread does not exist], but full-grown (complete, perfect) love turns fear out of doors and expels every trace of terror! For fear brings with it the thought of punishment, and [so] he who is afraid has not reached the full maturity of love [is not yet grown into love's complete perfection]" (I John 4:18).

This passage of Scripture explains that you will *not* be afraid if you continually experience the perfect love of God. Some Christians who are very sick could easily be afraid because of the dire prognosis doctors have given them and the aches, pains and discomfort in their bodies. I John 4:18 says that "there is *no fear* in love." The amplification of this passage of Scripture says that "dread *does not exist.*" If you are continually conscious of your Father's great love for you, you will *not* dread what could happen in the future because "full-grown, complete, perfect love turns fear out of doors and expels every trace of terror."

You must understand the relationship between perfect love and the *complete absence of fear, dread and apprehension of what the future might hold.* If you are afraid you "have not reached the full maturity of love." You have "not yet grown into love's complete perfection."

Perfect love is God's love. The more you learn about the love of God and the more you meditate on what the Bible says about the love of God, the less opportunity fear will have to get at you. The love of God will sustain you in spite of pain and discomfort caused by sickness. You will persevere in faith if every aspect of your life is centered on your Father's great love for you. Your Father wants you to have absolute faith in Him. He is love. The antidote to fear is love. Fear cannot exist in the presence of God's love.

You will *not* be afraid if you will meditate continually on these facts from the Bible about your Father's great love for you. You will know that you are deeply loved. You will be filled with God's peace regardless of your physical condition. You will be able to rest in your Father's supernatural peace because of your absolute certainty that He loves you. "...O man greatly beloved, fear not! Peace be to you! Be strong, yes, be strong..." (Daniel 10:19).

You are "greatly beloved." Your loving Father says, "Fear not." He wants you to receive His supernatural peace. He wants you to "be strong." He wants so much for you to "be strong" that He repeats these words a second time for emphasis.

Unfortunately, many Christians do not feel loved by God because they have not invested the time to develop a close relationship with Him. Your Father wants you to be *so close to Him* that you *know* that healing is a completed work of the redemption that Jesus has provided for you.

Your Father wants you to *release your faith* in Him to receive manifestation of the healing He has provided because He loves you so much. Your Father has great compassion for you. "...His [tender] compassions fail not. They are new every morning..." (Lamentations 3:22-23).

God's "tender compassions fail not." You can trust completely in God, knowing that He is full of compassion for you. Each and every morning your Father makes a fresh supply of His compassion available to you. "The Lord is gracious and full of compassion, slow to anger and abounding in mercy and loving-kindness" (Psalm 145:8).

Please highlight or underline the words "the Lord is gracious and full of compassion." You *can* depend on your Father's grace, mercy, compassion and love. Your Father "abounds in mercy and loving-kindness." "The Lord is good to all, and His tender mercies are over all His works [the entirety of things created]" (Psalm 145:9).

This passage of Scripture tells you that "the Lord is good to all." The word "all" includes *you*. Your Father is good to you. He has provided healing for you. Trust *completely* in God Who has great love, compassion and mercy. Absolutely *refuse* to give up.

The Bible often speaks of the compassion of Jesus. Jesus healed sick people throughout His earthly ministry because of His great love and compassion for them. "When He went ashore and saw a great throng of people, He had compassion (pity and deep sympathy) for them and cured their sick" (Matthew 14:14).

There is no question that Jesus had "compassion, pity and deep sympathy" for sick people during His earthly ministry. Jesus healed these people because of His compassion. You have seen that Jesus is the same today as He was then (see Hebrews 13:8). Jesus has the *same* love and compassion for *you* today.

Focus continually on Jesus and you will receive His love and compassion. Look to Him for healing in your body just as He healed so many people during His earthly ministry because of His great love and compassion for them (see Matthew 9:35-36, Matthew 20:34 and Mark 1:41).

Jesus knows *exactly* what *you* are going through with the sickness in your body. "...we do not have a High Priest Who is unable to understand and sympathize and have a shared feeling with our weaknesses and infirmities and liability to the assaults of temptation, but One Who has been tempted in every respect as we are, yet without sinning. Let us then fearlessly and confidently and boldly draw near to the throne of grace (the throne of God's unmerited favor to us sinners), that we may receive mercy [for our failures] and find grace to help in good time for every need [appropriate help and well-timed help, coming just when we need it]" (Hebrews 4:15-16).

This passage of Scripture tells you that Jesus *does* "understand and sympathize" with you and what you are going through. Jesus wants you to "fearlessly and confidently and boldly draw near to the throne of grace" to "receive mercy" and to find the help you need "just when you need it."

This portion of Scripture should be extremely encouraging to you. When this passage of Scripture tells you that Jesus will help you with "every need," the word "every" *includes* the sickness in your body. Persevere in faith knowing that you will receive manifestation of healing from your loving Father in His good timing.

Your Father wants you to continually study and meditate on His Word to learn everything you can about His love for you. He wants you to trust Him completely. "...God is faithful [to His Word and to His compassionate nature]..." (I Corinthians 10:13).

Your Father is "faithful to His Word and to His compassionate nature." You must have absolute faith in His love, compassion and grace. Your Father loves you *so much* that His love and mercy are available to you throughout every hour of every day of your life. "...goodness, mercy and unfailing love shall follow me all the days of my life..." (Psalm 23:6).

Focus on these magnificent words. Personalize them by referring to yourself when you say, "Goodness, mercy and unfailing love shall follow *me* all the days of *my* life." Experience these wonderful blessings in your life right now. Speak these magnificent words again and again and again. Every time that you are tired and weary because of the sickness in your body, open your mouth and speak these glorious words repeatedly. Meditate continually on this great spiritual truth.

If you will take the time to open your Bible and read Psalm 136, you will see that this one psalm tells you *twenty-six* times that God's mercy and loving-kindness "endure forever." Any Christian who is sick should meditate continually on these facts. You have seen that God emphasizes through repetition. *How much more* could your Father emphasize to you how loving and merciful He is than to repeat this great truth twenty-six times in one psalm?

This chapter is filled with facts from the Word of God about your Father's great love, compassion, grace and mercy for you. Christians who are sick cannot spend their time more profitably than to meditate again and again on these truths from the holy Scriptures. Go back over the Scripture in this chapter repeatedly. Open your mouth and speak these passages of Scripture about God's great love for *you*. Personalize them. Let *your ears* hear *your mouth* continually speaking of your Father's great love for *you*

Enjoy God. Enjoy His goodness, His grace, His mercy, His compassion and His love for you. He loves you so much that He already has provided healing for you. Your faith in God *will* increase steadily as this process *continues* over a period of time. Your Father wants you to continually learn more and more about His great love and compassion for you.

The awareness of your Father's great love should be the rock-solid foundation for believing that the healing has been provided for you by Jesus Christ. This chapter on the love of God is the foundation for the remainder of this book. Be sure to spend an ample amount of time studying and meditating on the Scripture references in this chapter. These facts on your Father's great love and compassion will help *you* to steadily increase *your faith* in God.

Chapter 15

Love, Forgiveness and Divine Healing

Now that you have learned about the relationship between your Father's love for you and His healing nature, you are ready to take the next step. In this chapter you will learn what the Bible says about the relationship between your love for others, forgiving others, living in divine health and receiving healing from God.

In the last chapter you saw that faith works by love (see Galatians 5:6). I believe that this statement pertaining to love applies both to your deep and continual awareness of your Father's love for you and your unconditional love toward others. Some people who are sick are cranky, cantankerous and unloving. You are not in a position to have your prayers answered if you are continually unloving toward others. If you deeply desire to receive manifestation of healing from God you must not allow yourself to react in this way.

Faith in God for divine healing is very powerful, but the Bible teaches us that love is *greater* than faith. "…faith, hope, love abide [faith – conviction and belief respecting man's relation to God and divine things; hope – joyful and confident expectation of eternal salvation; love – true affection for God and man, growing out of God's love for and in us], these three; but the greatest of these is love" (I Corinthians 13:13).

When God says that faith works by love and that love is greater than faith you must understand that your faith for divine healing will *not* work if you are unloving toward others. Jesus said, "This is My commandment: that you love one another [just] as I have loved you. No one has greater love [no one has shown stronger affection] than to lay down (give up) his life for his friends" (John 15:12-13).

Love is not an option. Jesus has *commanded* you to love others just as He loves you. Jesus showed His great love for *you* by the price He paid at the whipping post and by giving His life for *you* on the cross at Calvary.

The Old Testament contains the Ten Commandments. However, the New Testament shows us that loving others is the *only* commandment you will need because loving others includes all of the Ten Commandments. "...he who loves his neighbor [who practices loving others] has fulfilled the Law [relating to one's fellowmen, meeting all its requirements]. The commandments, You shall not commit adultery, You shall not kill, You shall not steal, You shall not covet (have an evil desire), and any other commandment, are summed up in the single command, You shall love your neighbor as [you do] yourself" (Romans 13:8-9).

Loving others as God loves them is a result of becoming more like God. As you continually draw closer to God you will become more and more like Him. The more you take upon yourself the nature of God, the more you are able to partake of God's provision of healing.

The apostle Paul told us how important loving others is to God when he said, "...if I have [sufficient] faith so that I can remove mountains, but have not love (God's love in me) I am nothing (a useless nobody). Even if I dole out all that I have [to the poor in providing] food, and if I surrender my body to be burned or in order that I may glory, but have not love (God's love in me), I gain nothing" (I Corinthians 13:2-3).

Once again you can clearly see that faith works by love. If your faith in God is *so strong* that it actually can move mountains, but God's love is not being expressed through you "you gain *nothing*." The amplification says that each person who does not love others is a "useless nobody."

If you gave everything you had to the poor or "surrendered your body to be burned," these sacrifices would have *no* effect without God's love flowing through you to others. You can block yourself from receiving healing from God by being unforgiving, bitter and unloving. Your body chemistry changes because of these emotions and disease is able to maintain its foothold.

Sometimes you have to deal with people who are extremely difficult to love. *How* can you love these unreasonable people so that you remain in God's presence and receive His healing? The answer is that, when your human love is insufficient, you *can* love them *with the perfect love of God* that has been placed in *your heart* by the Holy Spirit. "...God's love has been poured out in our hearts through the Holy Spirit Who has been given to us" (Romans 5:5).

You always should be conscious of God's love for you. You should yield constantly to God to allow your Father's love to flow through you to others. "Love bears up under anything and everything that comes, is ever ready to believe the best of every person, its hopes are fadeless under all circumstances, and it endures everything [without weakening]. Love never fails [never fades out or becomes obsolete or comes to an end]..." (I Corinthians 13:7-8).

Please highlight or underline the words "anything and everything." These words include the sickness in your body. You can persevere in faith and love even though you are sick and you may not feel well. You can "believe the best of every person." Your love for others should "never fail." You may feel irritable when you do not feel well. God can transcend this crankiness and create a loving you.

Love and forgiveness are similar. The Word of God also tells you that forgiveness is part of unshakable faith in God. In a subsequent chapter we will carefully study Mark 11:22-24 where Jesus tells you that your faith can be so strong that it can move mountains. Jesus went on in the next two verses to say, "...whenever you stand praying, if you have anything against anyone, forgive him and let it drop (leave it, let it go), in order that your Father Who is in heaven may also forgive you your [own] failings and shortcomings and let them drop. But if you do not forgive, neither will your Father in heaven forgive your failings and shortcomings" (Mark 11:25-26).

Jesus spoke these words about forgiveness right after He spoke about mountain-moving faith. There is no question that you can fail to receive the healing Jesus has provided for you if you are unloving and unforgiving.

Sometimes Christians who do not forgive others feel justified in their unforgiveness. Perhaps this person has done something to you that is very unfair. The other person clearly is wrong. You must *not* feel justified in your failure to forgive because of the magnitude of what this person did. You must not allow yourself to indulge in what the world calls righteous indignation.

Your Father forgave you for *all* of your sins when you asked Jesus to be your Savior. Throughout your life you can *constantly* repent of what you have done and continue to receive forgiveness from God (see I John 1:9). You must forgive others regardless of what they have done just as your Father has forgiven you and will continue to forgive you for everything you do.

Jesus explained the importance of always forgiving others. "...Peter came up to Him and said, Lord, how many times may my brother sin against me and I forgive him and let it go? [As many as] up to seven times? Jesus answered him, I tell you, not up to seven times, but seventy times seven!" (Matthew 18:21-22).

Peter asked if seven times was the number of times to forgive another person. Jesus told Peter that he should forgive seventy times seven. When Jesus said he should forgive someone seventy times seven He did not mean that you should forgive a person exactly 490 times. He meant that your forgiveness should be infinite – there is no limit to the number of times you should forgive others.

You should be gentle and forgiving toward other people just as God has forgiven you for all of your sins. "Be gentle and forbearing with one another and, if one has a difference (a grievance or complaint) against another, readily pardoning each other; even as the Lord has [freely] forgiven you, so must you also [forgive]" (Colossians 3:13).

This chapter is not intended to be a thorough and detailed study of loving others and forgiving others. The purpose of this chapter is merely to explain the definite relationship that exists between forgiveness of others, loving others and receiving healing. All of these scriptural principles also apply to divine health. Christians who faithfully obey these instructions are much likelier to be healthy and not become sick.

You do *not* have to get even with people if they treat you unfairly. If you make this mistake you are attempting to do what *only God can do*. "If possible, as far as it depends on you, live at peace with everyone. Beloved, never avenge yourselves, but leave the way open for [God's] wrath; for it is written, Vengeance is Mine, I will repay (requite), says the Lord" (Romans 12:18-19).

You should never attempt to "avenge yourself" when you have been treated unfairly. You should trust God to make things right. Your Father wants you to love others and forgive others regardless of what they do to you. When you love others and forgive others with God's love that is in your heart, you will not block your loving Father's flow of healing power that has been provided for you. I believe that just the opposite will happen. I believe that manifestation of healing will be accelerated if you are constantly loving and forgiving toward people who are very difficult to love and forgive.

You should examine yourself continually to see if you are blocking God from giving you manifestation of healing from sickness. If you think you have hidden faults and you do not know what they are you should pray as the psalmist prayed when he said, "Who can discern his lapses and errors? Clear me from hidden [and unconscious] faults" (Psalm 19:12).

You should focus continually on God's love for you. You should constantly reach out to others with love and forgiveness regardless of how they treat you. The last two chapters are filled with *facts* from the Word of God about your Father's love and forgiveness for you and your love and forgiveness toward others.

Rest in God and His Word. Trust Him with your life. You will find that knowing more about God's love for you will increase your faith in Him greatly. You may find that an awareness of being unloving and unforgiving will cause you to change your ways and that you then will know that unforgiveness is not blocking you from receiving the healing that Jesus already has provided for you.

Chapter 16

Without Faith It is Impossible
to Please God

You have learned that the basic foundation for your faith for divine healing is a deep and constant awareness of your Father's love, mercy and grace. You have learned that you can block your Father from giving you healing if you fail to love others and forgive others. Now we are ready to study the holy Scriptures to learn the importance of faith in God. You will learn exactly what your Father instructs you to do to increase your faith in Him.

You have seen that Jesus *already* has provided healing for you. Your loving Father definitely wants you to receive manifestation of the healing that already has been provided for you. He wants you to have deep, strong and unwavering faith in Him. "…without faith it is impossible to please and be satisfactory to Him…" (Hebrews 11:6).

Please highlight or underline the word "impossible" in this passage of Scripture. The word "impossible" emphasizes the high priority your Father places on your faith in Him. You *cannot* please your Father if you do not have faith in Him.

Why is it impossible for you to please God without faith in Him? If you are a parent would you be pleased if one of your children *ignored* your instructions? Would you be pleased if your child did *not* believe you would do what you promised you would do?

Faith is not believing that God can heal you. Faith is *knowing* that Jesus already *has* healed you. Think how Jesus must have felt going back to His home town of Nazareth after performing many healing miracles elsewhere. Jesus must have especially wanted to heal the people He had known for so many years.

When Jesus began to teach in the synagogue in Nazareth the people questioned His authority. They knew Jesus as a local carpenter. His brothers and sisters still lived in Nazareth. They said, "Is not this the Carpenter, the son of Mary and the brother of James and Joses and Judas and Simon? And are not His sisters here among us? And they took offense at Him and were hurt [that is, they disapproved of Him, and it hindered them from acknowledging His authority] and they were caused to stumble and fall" (Mark 6:3).

Jesus explained why the people of Nazareth did not have faith in Him. He said, "...A prophet is not without honor (deference, reverence) except in his [own] country and among [his] relatives and in his [own] house. And He was not able to do even one work of power there, except that He laid His hands on a few sickly people [and] cured them. And He marveled because of their unbelief (their lack of faith in Him)..." (Mark 6:4-6).

This passage of Scripture does not say that Jesus did not want to heal the people in Nazareth. Mark 6:5 says that He "*was not able*" to do mighty healing miracles there. Jesus "marveled because of their unbelief." You must understand that there is no question that *human beings can block the mighty healing power of God because of doubt and unbelief.*

Your Father *will* do what He says He will do. If you are sick you must understand the vital importance of doing exactly what the Word of God instructs you to do to steadily increase your faith in God.

Some people say, "I know this is what the Bible says, but..." As soon as the word "but" is added to whatever God promises to do, this unbelief will *block* the power of God. There are *no* "buts" concerning the Word of God. Your Father's promises are definite and absolute. He will do what He says He will do according to your faith in Him.

In four different places in His Word your Father tells you that He wants you to *live by faith* (see Habakkuk 4:2-4, Romans 1:17, Galatians 3:11 and Hebrews 10:36). If God tells you the same thing four times, you can see by this repetition how much emphasis *He places* on the absolute importance of every aspect of your life being solidly anchored on your faith in Him.

If you know what the Word of God says about divine healing and you do not believe that your Father will do exactly what He says He will do, your doubt and unbelief actually indicate that you believe God is a liar. "…he who does not believe God [in this way] has made Him out to be and represented Him as a liar…" (I John 5:10).

You must not be like the Israelites many years ago who failed to receive blessings from God because they did not believe He would do what He said He would do. When Moses spoke to the Israelites after the exodus from Egypt he chastised them because of their unbelief. Moses said, "Yet in spite of this word you did not believe [trust, rely on and remain steadfast to] the Lord your God…" (Deuteronomy 1:32).

Some Christians today do not receive healing from God "in spite of" what the Word of God says about healing because they "do not believe, trust, rely on and remain steadfast to God." The disciples of Jesus Christ saw Him perform many miracles, but they showed their lack of faith in Him. "Even though He had done so many miracles before them (right before their eyes), yet they still did not trust in Him and failed to believe in Him" (John 12:37).

If the disciples who saw Jesus perform numerous miracles still "did not trust in Him and failed to believe in Him," you can clearly see why many Christians do not receive healing from God today. On one occasion the disciples were afraid when they were out in a boat in a very severe storm. Jesus was sleeping in the back of the boat. They woke Him up and He rebuked the storm and everything became calm. "He said to them, Why are you so timid and fearful? How is that you have no faith [no firmly relying trust]?..." (Mark 4:40).

Is Jesus asking *you* if you are "timid and fearful" and if "you have no faith?" On another occasion the disciples saw Jesus walking on the water toward their boat. "...they were terrified and said, It is a ghost! and they screamed out with fright. But instantly He spoke to them, saying, Take courage! I AM! Stop being afraid!" (Matthew 14:27).

Jesus also tells *you* to "stop being afraid." You must not allow fear, worry, doubt and unbelief to block your faith in your Healer. Shortly after that Peter stepped out in faith and actually walked on the water toward Jesus. Jesus must have been very pleased to see Peter step out in faith.

However, when a strong wind came up Peter took his eyes *off* Jesus and focused on the wind. "...when he perceived and felt the strong wind, he was frightened, and as he began to sink, he cried out, Lord, save me [from death]! Instantly Jesus reached out His hand and caught and held him, saying to him, O you of little faith, why did you doubt?" (Matthew 14:30-31).

Peter "was frightened" because he focused on "the strong wind." Jesus told Peter that he had "little faith." Some Christians are frightened because of the sickness in their bodies. They have "little faith." They "doubt" that they will receive healing from God. These Christians are frustrated by the seeming severity of the sickness in their bodies. They focus on the sickness in their bodies instead of focusing continually on God (see Isaiah 26:3).

On another occasion after Jesus was crucified and rose from the dead He expressed great concern about His disciples who refused to believe in His resurrection. "...He appeared to the Eleven [apostles themselves] as they reclined at table; and He reproved and reproached them for their unbelief (their lack of faith) and their hardness of heart, because they had refused to believe those who had seen Him and looked at Him attentively after He had risen [from death]" (Mark 16:14).

You have just seen three different occasions where the disciples of Jesus Christ showed doubt and unbelief. You must not allow doubt and unbelief to block *you* from receiving healing from God. Your Father wants you to have the same unwavering faith that Abraham had. "No unbelief or distrust made him waver (doubtingly question) concerning the promise of God…" (Romans 4:20).

This passage of Scripture refers to an instance that occurred when Abraham was one hundred years old and his wife was ninety years old. God told Abraham that his wife would give birth to a son. Human logic says that a one hundred year old male and a ninety year old female cannot conceive a child. Abraham did not allow the limitations of human logic to influence his faith in God. Abraham believed God wholeheartedly and his wife gave birth to a child. You must not allow sickness to block your faith in God, no matter how severe this sickness might seem to be.

The Israelites saw the waters of the Red Sea part. They saw many other miracles of God. Nevertheless, when they were in the wilderness, they took *forty years* to make a trip that should have taken only *eleven days*. "It is [only] eleven days' journey from Horeb by the way of Mount Seir to Kadesh-barnea [on Canaan's border; yet Israel took forty years to get beyond it]" (Deuteronomy 1:2).

Why did it take so long for the Israelites to get through the wilderness? *Why* did they walk in a gigantic circle in the wilderness for forty years? *They failed because of disobedience and unbelief.* You must not make this mistake. "…take care, lest there be in any one of you a wicked, unbelieving heart [which refuses to cleave to, trust in, and rely on Him], leading you to turn away and desert or stand aloof from the living God" (Hebrews 3:12).

This passage of Scripture refers to the unbelief of the Israelites in the wilderness. Shortly after that you are told that the Israelites were unable to rest in faith in God because of unbelief.

"...they were not able to enter [into His rest], because of their unwillingness to adhere to and trust in and rely on God [unbelief had shut them out]" (Hebrews 3:19).

Are *you* unable to "enter into God's rest" because you are so concerned about the sickness in your body? Are you "unwilling to adhere to and trust in and rely on God?" Is "unbelief shutting you out" from receiving the healing that already has been provided for you?

You must follow God's specific instructions to increase your faith in Him so that you will not make the same mistake the Israelites made in the wilderness. "Let us therefore be zealous and exert ourselves and strive diligently to enter that rest [of God, to know and experience it for ourselves], that no one may fall or perish by the same kind of unbelief and disobedience [into which those in the wilderness fell]" (Hebrews 4:11).

This passage of Scripture tells you how to enter into the rest of God and remain there. When you are sick or when you face any other problem, you *can* come into God's presence where healing is. You are instructed "to be zealous and exert yourself and strive diligently to enter that rest."

This book is filled with specific instructions for increasing your faith in God for healing. You must "be zealous and exert yourself." You must "strive diligently." *You will learn to rest in God* if you continually fill your eyes, your ears, your mind, your heart and your mouth with Scripture pertaining to divine healing and increased faith in God. You *will* learn to rest in God as you spend time with Him each day immersing yourself in His supernatural living Word, praying and listening, worshipping and loving.

God is much greater and much more powerful than *any* sickness. Do not block His mighty healing power through unbelief. Jesus said, "...Do not be faithless and incredulous, but [stop your unbelief and] believe!" (John 20:27).

Do not allow the sickness in your body to dominate your consciousness to the degree that you are "faithless and incredulous" regarding divine healing. Your Father is telling you to "stop your unbelief and believe."

In this chapter you have seen many scriptural examples of unbelief. You have learned the importance of faith in God. We now are ready to move forward to learn one step at a time *exactly* what your Father instructs you to do to develop deep, strong and unwavering faith that you *will* receive manifestation of the healing that *already* has been provided for you.

Chapter 17

Divine Healing, Obedience and Trust

You have learned that you cannot please God without faith (see Hebrews 11:6). In this chapter we will look into the Word of God to see exactly what it says about the relationship between your obedience to God's instructions, your faith in God and receiving manifestation of healing from God.

You have learned that your Father loves every person on earth with a love that is much greater than you can possibly comprehend. Your Father's love and compassion for you are beyond the limits of your human understanding.

If you are a loving parent you know how it feels when one of your children is very sick. I can still remember more than forty years ago when our children were very young. When they were sick I often wished that I could take the sickness upon myself for them. Your loving Father *has done this* through His beloved Son Jesus Christ.

Faith is required to believe that the Son of God came to earth, was born of a virgin, took the sins of the entire world upon Himself and died on a cross at Calvary. Because of His love for you and His grace God *gave you enough faith* to trust Jesus for your eternal salvation. The Bible speaks of "…each according to the degree of faith apportioned by God to him" (Romans 12:3).

Your Father has given you specific instructions telling you exactly what you should do to *increase* the faith He *already has given you* to receive Jesus as your Savior. You need to do two things if you want to receive healing from God – trust and obey. I believe that these two words contain the key to receiving healing from God and every other blessing your Father has provided.

God has filled His Word with numerous facts concerning the many blessings He has promised for those who trust Him and obey Him. Unfortunately, many Christians who are sick know little or nothing about these magnificent promises and instructions from God. They do not even know how to begin to increase their faith for healing.

Faith in God begins with humility. Your Father gives marvelous grace to His children who truly are humble and trusting. "…God sets Himself against the proud (the insolent, the overbearing, the disdainful, the presumptuous, the boastful) – [and He opposes, frustrates, and defeats them], but gives grace (favor, blessing) to the humble" (I Peter 5:5).

Would you like to have Almighty God "set Himself against" you? Would you like Almighty God to "oppose and frustrate" you? Sickness often is a great equalizer. Some people who were proud when they were healthy become much more humble when they are very sick. This humility can and should be the foundation for increased faith in God. Your Father *will* give you "grace, favor and blessing" if you truly are humble and obedient.

We now are ready to look into the Word of God to learn what it says about two things that are exactly opposite – blessings from God and the curse of the Law. In the Old Testament God imposed judgment through the curse of the Law. The Old Testament promises of divine healing were based on the Israelites obeying God's instructions. God said, "Behold, I set before you this day a blessing and a curse – the blessing if you obey the commandments of the Lord your God which I command you this day; and the curse if you will not obey the commandments of the Lord your God, but turn aside from the way which I command you this day to go after other gods, which you have not known" (Deuteronomy 11:26-28).

Deuteronomy 27:15-26 lists several curses the Israelites would suffer if they disobeyed God's law. The statements in these verses pertain to general curses, but the subject of sickness is not yet mentioned.

Deuteronomy 28:1-14 lists many blessings that the Israelites would receive from God *if* they obeyed His Law. Deuteronomy 28:15-60 then lists additional curses. Many of these curses include sickness. In addition to the specific sicknesses that are mentioned Deuteronomy 28:61 includes *all other sickness* that has not been mentioned in the preceding verses.

Jesus has *set you free* from the sickness and disease that were part of the curse of the Law. "Christ purchased our freedom [redeeming us] from the curse (doom) of the Law [and its condemnation] by [Himself] becoming a curse for us, for it is written [in the Scriptures], Cursed is everyone who hangs on a tree (is crucified)" (Galatians 3:13).

Jesus Christ, the Son of God, actually "became a curse for us." He became a curse for *you*. He paid the price you should have had to pay. Jesus has made many blessings available to you by His sacrifice. Healing is one of these blessings.

Each person who asks Jesus Christ to be his or her Savior is made righteous before God by the sacrifice of Jesus Christ. You should do your very best to live a righteous life at all times by learning and obeying the many instructions your Father has given you. "...the [uncompromisingly] righteous shall come out of trouble" (Proverbs 12:13).

Sickness certainly is trouble. "Uncompromising righteousness" should be a way of life for all Christians. You can "come out of trouble" by refusing to compromise on any of the instructions your Father has given you. If you want to see the glory of God manifested in your life you should do what Jesus instructed Martha to do after her brother Lazarus died. "Jesus said to her,

Did I not tell you and promise you that if you would believe and rely on Me, you would see the glory of God?" (John 11:40).

Martha obeyed these specific instructions. She believed in Jesus even though her brother was dead. She relied on Him. Because of her faith and obedience she was able to see God's glory as Jesus raised Lazarus from the dead. *You* will see the glory of God if you trust Him completely. Your Father has provided everything you will ever need if you will trust Him completely. "…the Lord is a Sun and Shield; the Lord bestows [present] grace and favor and [future] glory (honor, splendor, and heavenly bliss)! No good thing will He withhold from those who walk uprightly. O Lord of hosts, blessed (happy, fortunate, to be envied) is the man who trusts in You [leaning and believing on You, committing all and confidently looking to You, and that without fear or misgiving]!" (Psalm 84:11-12).

This passage of Scripture tells you that "no good thing will be withheld" from those who "walk uprightly." Healing is a "good thing." You have learned that Jesus already has provided healing for you. The amplification of this passage of Scripture says that you should "lean and believe on God." You are instructed to "commit all and confidently look to God" without any fear. "…What eye has not seen and ear has not heard and has not entered into the heart of man, [all that] God has prepared (made and keeps ready) for those who love Him [who hold Him in affectionate reverence, promptly obeying Him and gratefully recognizing the benefits He has bestowed]. Yet to us God has unveiled and revealed them by and through His Spirit…" (I Corinthians 2:9-10).

Do you want to receive "all that God has prepared (made and keeps ready) for those who love Him?" These words include healing. You will receive this wonderful blessing from God if you "love Him [hold Him in affectionate reverence, promptly obey Him and gratefully recognize the benefits He has bestowed]." The Holy Spirit will reveal this great spiritual truth to you if you obey these specific instructions from God.

Knowing God as your Father and Friend is His desire for you. Your Father wants you to love Him so much that you *yearn* to draw closer to Him. He wants you to have a deep desire to learn and obey every one of His specific instructions. "Blessed (happy, fortunate, to be envied) are they who keep His testimonies, and who seek, inquire for and of Him and crave Him with the whole heart" (Psalm 119:2).

Your Father created you to love Him. He wants you to seek Him wholeheartedly. You are instructed to "keep God's testimonies" (obey His instructions) and "seek, inquire for and of Him and crave Him with your whole heart."

Are you determined to learn and obey all of the instructions your Father has given to you to receive manifestation of the healing that already has been provided for you by Jesus Christ? This book is filled with these specific scriptural instructions.

Do you seek God with all of your heart? Do you crave a closer relationship with Him? This book is filled with many scriptural instructions that will help you to develop a close and intimate personal relationship with God.

The Word of God repeatedly explains the relationship between receiving manifestation of healing, receiving other blessings from God and obeying His specific instructions. Psalm 128:1, Proverbs 16:20, Proverbs 28:14, Luke 11:28 and John 11:40 are other passages of Scripture that promise blessings as a result of obedience to God's instructions.

You will not have feelings of guilt if you are doing your very best to live a righteous life according to God's instructions. You will have a clear conscience. The Bible explains that a definite relationship exists between a clear conscience and your ability to trust God. "...if our consciences (our hearts) do not accuse us [if they do not make us feel guilty and condemn us], we have confidence (complete assurance and boldness) before God, and we receive from Him whatever we ask, because we [watchfully] obey His orders [observe His suggestions and injunctions, follow His plan for us] and [habitually] practice what is pleasing to Him" (I John 3:21-22).

If you have a clear conscience you can "have confidence, complete assurance and boldness before God." You *will* "receive from Him whatever you ask" *if* you obey His specific instructions and "habitually practice what is pleasing to Him." The all-inclusive word "whatever" in this passage of Scripture includes healing. "You meet and spare him who joyfully works righteousness (uprightness and justice), [earnestly] remembering You in Your ways…" (Isaiah 64:5).

Your Father promises to "meet you and spare you" if you "joyfully work righteousness." He wants you to live an "upright" life. He wants you to "earnestly remember Him in His ways." "…he who trusts in, relies on, and confidently leans on the Lord shall be compassed about with mercy and with loving-kindness" (Psalm 32:10).

The words "compassed about" mean "to be surrounded by." Do you want to be surrounded by your Father's mercy and loving-kindness? You will receive God's mercy and loving-kindness *if* you "trust in, rely on and confidently lean on Him." "A faithful man shall abound with blessings…" (Proverbs 28:20).

The word "abound" means to receive greatly. You will receive tremendous blessings from God if you have unshakable and unwavering faith in Him. You will be blessed if you have learned exactly what His Word says about the healing He has provided for you and if you have unshakable and unwavering faith in Him. "…blessed (happy, fortunate, and to be envied) are all those who seek refuge and put their trust in Him!" (Psalm 2:12).

Please highlight or underline the words "all those." These words include *you*. Do you want to receive the blessing of divine healing? Be determined to "put your trust in Him" to give you manifestation of the healing Jesus already has provided for you.

In this chapter you have seen the relationship between obeying God's instructions, believing God's promises and receiving healing from God. We now are ready to look into God's Word for many additional *facts* that will tell you *exactly* how to increase your faith in God to the degree that you *will* be able to receive the healing that *already* has been provided for you.

Chapter 18

How Strong is Your Faith in God?

You have learned that it is *impossible* to please God without faith. You have learned of the many blessings your Father promises to His children who are trusting and obedient. The Word of God tells you that receiving God's promise of divine healing or any other promise is dependent on your faith in Him. "...[inheriting] the promise is the outcome of faith and depends [entirely] on faith..." (Romans 4:16).

This passage of Scripture explains how vitally important your faith in God is if you truly desire to receive manifestation of God's promises to heal you. Please highlight or underline the word "entirely." This word in the amplification of this passage of Scripture tells you how *vitally important* your faith in God is.

How deep and strong is *your* faith in God? Do you believe that your faith in God is strong enough to stand the test of severe illness? An "I hope so" attitude is not good enough. Many people who are sick need to work diligently to increase their faith in God so that their faith will become unshakable and unwavering. The Scripture in this book will help you to understand God better and to be absolutely certain that He already has provided healing for you.

Many people who are severely ill find that the sickness in their bodies drains them. You often can offset this physical fatigue if you energize yourself spiritually every day by immersing yourself in the energizing power of the supernatural living Word of God.

You can easily become discouraged when you are sick. Discouragement can take whatever courage you have out of you. Instead of allowing yourself to be constantly discouraged by sickness you can learn how to constantly be *encouraged* by the supernatural power of the living Word of God.

The prefix "en" means "in." When you are encouraged you put courage *into* yourself. When you are discouraged you lack courage; whatever courage you have is taken *out* of you. You must learn how to encourage yourself when you are sick. Your Father has provided His supernatural living Word as a constant source of encouragement to you. "Comfort and encourage your hearts and strengthen them [make them steadfast and keep them unswerving]..." (II Thessalonians 2:17).

Are you "comforting and encouraging" your heart every day? Are you "strengthening" your heart so that it will be "steadfast and unswerving?" Many Christians who are sick cannot answer these questions affirmatively. This book will show you exactly what your loving Father instructs you to do to constantly encourage yourself when you are sick. You will learn how to continually increase your faith in God through the power of God's supernatural Word coming alive deep down inside of your heart.

The Word of God is filled with energizing power. You can and will be energized and strengthened *if* you focus continually on your Father's supernatural Word instead of dwelling on the sickness in your body. You must understand the tremendous restorative power of the Word of God. Christians who are sick *must* invigorate themselves every day with a fresh supply of encouragement from the supernatural living Word of God.

The Bible tells you exactly why the Israelites in the wilderness failed to receive encouragement from God. "...the message they heard did not benefit them, because it was not mixed with faith (with the leaning of the entire personality on God in absolute trust and confidence in His power, wisdom, and goodness)…" (Hebrews 4:2).

This book is filled with good news from the holy Scriptures for Christians who are sick. You must *not* conclude that "this message you heard does not benefit you." You must continually increase your faith in God. The amplification of this passage of Scripture says that you should "lean your entire personality on God." You should have "absolute trust and confidence in His power, wisdom and goodness."

Many Christians who are very sick do *not* lean completely on God. They hear life-giving promises from the Word of God, but they do not receive manifestation of these promises because they do not have deep, strong and unwavering faith that their Father will do exactly what He promises to do. Two Christians can hear the *same* scriptural facts on divine healing. One person can persevere in faith to receive healing. The other person will remain sick because of insufficient faith in God.

I pray that you will learn and faithfully obey the specific scriptural instructions in this book to continually increase your faith in God. You must do more than just know what the Bible says about healing. Your Father wants you to add faith to your knowledge. He wants you to continually increase your faith in Him. He wants you to learn to live in the rest of God where you trust Him completely. "…we who have believed (adhered to and trusted in and relied on God) do enter that rest, in accordance with His declaration that those [who did not believe] should not enter…" (Hebrews 4:3).

Your loving Father has provided a place of rest for you. You enter into God's rest by *believing* God. You can fail to enter into God's rest if you do not believe God. All Christians who are sick continually make the decision whether they will trust God and enter into His rest or whether they will fail to enter into God's rest because they do not really trust Him.

Your Father wants you to rest in Him instead of laboring and struggling to receive what He already has provided for you. Your

Father knows exactly how much you trust Him. He wants you to be prepared for all adversity through your trust in Him. "The Lord is good, a Strength and Stronghold in the day of trouble; He knows (recognizes, has knowledge of, and understands) those who take refuge and trust in Him" (Nahum 1:7).

Christians who are sick can consistently increase their faith in God by following God's specific instructions to increase their faith in Him. The Bible explains that different people have differing degrees of faith in God. The following Scripture references will give you an indication of the different degrees of faith that Christians have in God:

- "no faith" (Mark 4:40).
- "little faith" (Matthew 6:30).
- "weak faith" (Romans 14:1).
- "steadfast faith" (Colossians 2:5).
- "rich in faith" (James 2:5).
- "exceedingly growing faith" (II Thessalonians 1:3).
- "full of faith" (Acts 6:5).
- "completed faith" (James 2:22).

If you are sick you should have a fervent desire to continually increase your faith in God. Your loving Father wants you to have *so much faith* in Him that you will persevere in this faith until you receive manifestation of the healing He has provided for you. Most Christians believe that God *can* heal. The question you must ask yourself when you are sick is, "How *certain* am I that God *already* has healed *me* through the completed work of Jesus Christ?"

· The Bible explains many different ways that God heals us. The Bible says that you can be healed by intercessory prayer of others, by the laying on of hands, by the anointing of oil, by anointed servants of God who have a gift of the miracles of healing and/or by the gift of working of miracles. You cannot know exactly how healing will come to you. You can be healed in any of these ways.

You have seen that it is impossible to please God without faith. If you have been a Christian for a long time and you have *not* done what God has instructed you to do to steadily increase your faith in Him, *now* is the time to do your very best to steadily increase *your* faith in God. Make the decision to devote every bit of energy you can each day to do exactly what your Father has instructed you to do to increase your faith in Him. "…How are people to call upon Him Whom they have not believed [in Whom they have no faith, on Whom they have no reliance]?…" (Romans 10:14).

Unfortunately, many Christians cry out to God asking Him for healing even though they do not have strong and unwavering faith that He will answer their prayer. Your Father wants you to come to Him with *full knowledge* of what His Word says about healing and *absolute confidence* that He stands completely behind every promise in the Bible.

Your Father has done His part. He has given you many promises and instructions pertaining to divine healing. He wants you to do your very best to do your part. He wants you to consistently fill your mind and your heart with Scripture. He wants you to draw closer to Him each day. This book will show you what the holy Scriptures instruct you to do to continually draw closer to God so that your faith in Him will steadily increase.

Is your Father asking too much to require you to believe Him totally, completely and absolutely? Think of the price God paid by sending His beloved Son to go to the whipping post and the cross to pay the price for *your* sickness and *your* sins. Think of the price that Jesus paid for *you* at the whipping post and on the cross at Calvary. The Word of God says that it is impossible to please God without faith. Do you believe you can please Him if you are not doing your best to steadily increase your faith in Him?

In this chapter you have learned many facts about the need to continually encourage yourself when you are sick. We now are ready to learn many additional facts about increasing your faith for divine healing.

INTENTIONALLY BLANK

Chapter 19

Deeply Rooted Faith in God

Your faith in God often is vitally important in determining whether or not you will receive manifestation of the healing that *already* has been provided for you. Jesus said, "…it shall be done for you as you have believed…" (Matthew 8:13).

Jesus spoke these words to a centurion who asked Him to heal one of his servants who was paralyzed and in great pain. The word "you" in this passage of Scripture also applies to *you*. Personalize and meditate on this great spiritual truth.

If you have trusted completely in Jesus Christ for your eternal salvation you have utilized the faith that God gave you to receive Jesus as your Savior. Your Father wants you to do what the apostle Paul prayed that the Thessalonians would do. Paul said, "…make good whatever may be imperfect and lacking in your faith…" (I Thessalonians 3:10).

Many Christians do *not know* how to increase their faith in God. This book is filled with specific instructions from the holy Scriptures telling you exactly what your loving Father wants you to do to increase your faith in Him. If you are sick you should be determined to consistently increase your faith in God. "…build yourselves up [founded] on your most holy faith [make progress, rise like an edifice higher and higher]…" (Jude 20).

Are you "building yourself up?" Is your faith in God increasing steadily? Is your faith in God "rising like an edifice higher and higher?" Are you familiar with the biblical account of a man who had never walked because he was crippled from birth who was miraculously healed *because of his faith*? "…a man sat who found it impossible to use his feet, for he was a cripple from birth and had never walked. He was listening to Paul as he talked, and [Paul] gazing intently at him and observing that he had faith to be healed, shouted at him, saying, Stand erect on your feet! And he leaped up and walked" (Acts 14:8-10).

Please focus on *why* this crippled man was healed. Paul looked at him "intently." When Paul saw that this man "had faith to be healed" *then* the faith of the crippled man was ignited by Paul shouting, "Stand erect on your feet!" The crippled man's action produced an instant healing miracle – "he leaped up and walked."

You must understand how important it is for you to have deep faith in God. If you are sick you cannot afford to allow your faith in God to regress. My personal experience has shown me that, if my faith in God is not increasing, it is decreasing. I do not believe that faith in God ever stands still.

Our Father has instructed us to renew our minds continually in His Word and to meditate on His Word throughout the day and night. If you ignore these specific instructions I believe that your faith in God will not remain strong.

You can see a good example of this principle when someone is injured and unable to exercise for a sustained period of time. When this person is able to start exercising again his or her strength usually has decreased. The same principle applies to your faith in God.

Many Christians have not paid the price to steadily increase their faith in God (see our book, *Unshakable Faith in Almighty God*, and our Scripture Meditation Cards and the accompanying cassette tape that each are titled *Continually Increasing Faith in God*). Many Christians do not understand what the Bible says about increasing their faith in God.

Increasing your faith in God each day is important at any time in your life, but increasing your faith in God is *especially impor-*

tant if you are sick. You will not be able to persevere in faith during the pain and discomfort of sickness unless your faith in God is deep, strong and unwavering.

I believe that faith in God can be compared to riding a bicycle. A bicycle can only stand upright when it is in motion or when it is leaning on something. If you do not continually increase your faith in God, your faith will fail just as a bicycle will fall down if it does not keep moving forward or if it is not held up by something.

Many Christians do not know how strong their faith in God is because they often go a long period of time without having their faith tested. Many of us go through periods in our lives when everything is going relatively well so we *do not do* each day what the Bible instructs us to do to continually increase our faith in God. If your faith in God was tested continually you could see the erosion.

I did not miss one day of increasing my faith in God during my first two years as a Christian. I was on the verge of bankruptcy, business failure and a nervous breakdown. I was in a state of panic. I was totally dedicated to increasing my faith in God. As I learned and applied God's principles and placed my trust in Him, I saw a turnaround in our business. The business that almost went bankrupt is still doing well today, thirty-one years later.

I cannot say the same thing about my faith in God. Over the years I have taught many classes on faith in God and written two books and co-authored with Judy a set of Scripture Meditation Cards on this subject. However, I can tell you in all honesty that I often have fallen into the trap of becoming too secure in my knowledge of God's Word.

I can tell you from personal experience that a great deal of difference exists between applying God's principles for finances and applying God's principles for healing. In my early years as a Christian I faced extreme financial problems. I worked diligently to understand and obey God's instructions pertaining to finances. I learned what the Bible said to do and I obeyed these instructions day after day, week after week and month after month. In 1983 I wrote a book titled *Trust God for Your Finances* that now is in its nineteenth printing and has been translated into eight languages.

However, when I became sick and I reached deep down inside of myself to see what I understood about God's principles for divine healing, I found that the faith I have consistently developed for finances was much stronger than the faith I needed to receive healing from God. The same principles of developing faith apply, but I learned through personal experience that I had to start all over again to study and meditate continually on what the Word of God says about *healing* just as I had done in the past regarding finances.

Several years ago when I was quite sick one Christian brother and one Christian sister came to me separately within a twenty-four hour period. Each person asked if I was studying what I really needed to study. These people knew that I had been a Bible student for many years, but when they each asked me the same question, I realized that I was *not* renewing my mind each day in Scripture pertaining to *healing*. I was not meditating day and night on what the Word of God says about *healing*.

I then focused my daily Bible study and Scripture meditation on healing. My health improved significantly as this process continued over a period of time. I learned then that all Christians who are sick should *continually* fill their eyes, their ears, their minds, their hearts and their mouths with healing Scripture.

I ask each person who is reading this book, "Have *you* studied and meditated continually on healing Scripture?" This book is *filled* with *facts* from the Word of God pertaining to divine healing. You cannot have faith that God will heal you *if you do not even know* what His Word says about healing. I urge you to steadily develop your faith for divine healing by continually studying and meditating on the Scripture in this book. This knowledge must be touched by the living God and activated by Him.

Increased or decreased faith in God can be compared to people who work out diligently by lifting weights to build their muscles.

If a person did these physical workouts consistently for a long period of time and then went several months without working out at all, the muscles that once were strong would become flabby. I can tell you from personal experience that this principle has applied to my faith in God.

I have been *too confident* in my faith on many occasions. The Word of God warns us against making this mistake. "…let anyone who thinks he stands [who feels sure that he has a steadfast mind and is standing firm], take heed lest he fall [into sin]" (I Corinthians 10:12).

You should not be confident in yesterday's faith in God. This principle is important at all times, but it is vitally important when you are sick. Most people who are sick faithfully obey their doctor's instructions for taking medicine. You must obey the Great Physician's instructions to steadily increase your faith in Jesus Christ as your Healer.

You must not be overconfident regarding your faith in God. Jesus was especially concerned about the faith of the apostle Peter shortly before He was about to go to the cross. Jesus said, "Simon, Simon (Peter), listen! Satan has asked excessively that [all of] you be given up to him [out of the power and keeping of God], that he might sift [all of] you like grain, but I have prayed especially for you [Peter], that your [own] faith may not fail…" (Luke 22:31-32).

Peter's response to Jesus showed the *overconfidence* he had in his faith in Jesus. "And [Simon Peter] said to Him, Lord, I am ready to go with You both to prison and to death. But Jesus said, I tell you, Peter, before a [single] cock shall crow this day, you will three times [utterly] deny that you know Me" (Luke 22:33-34).

Jesus knew that Peter's faith in Him was not as strong as Peter thought it was. You cannot afford to make this mistake if you are sick. I have learned over the years that I move forward *slowly* in increasing my faith in God. I have learned that I move backward *rapidly* if I do not consistently increase my faith in God.

Your faith in God is determined by your relationship to Him. If you faithfully obey the scriptural instructions in this book your relationship with God will continually become more intimate. You will love God and you will have more awareness of His love for you. Your faith in Him will increase.

You should have lived constantly in an atmosphere of faith *before* you became sick. All Christians should belong to a church that consistently teaches about increasing faith in God. You should attend that church regularly (see Hebrews 10:25).

You should associate often with other believers who have deep faith in God. You should continually observe leaders in your church and other Christian leaders who have successful ministries. "Remember your leaders and superiors in authority [for it was they] who brought to you the Word of God. Observe attentively and consider their manner of living (the outcome of their well-spent lives) and imitate their faith (their conviction that God exists and is the Creator and Ruler of all things, the Provider and Bestower of eternal salvation through Christ, and their leaning of the entire human personality on God in absolute trust and confidence in His power, wisdom, and goodness)" (Hebrews 13:7).

Are you "observing attentively" Christian leaders who have deep, strong and unwavering faith in God? Are you "imitating their faith?" Are you constantly learning how these Christian leaders have increased their faith? Are you applying these principles in your life? Do you *lean* on God with "absolute trust and confidence in His power, wisdom and goodness?" You should do these things before you are sick. If not, you must *accelerate* the faith-building process after you are sick.

If you do not continually feed and exercise your body it will atrophy. This same principle applies in the spiritual realm. You need to continually feed your spirit with God's Word. You need to continually exercise your faith in God by using it whenever you face any kind of adversity. If you do not feed and exercise your faith regularly it will atrophy just as your body will atrophy in the natural realm. Faith in God is like a muscle. Muscles grow stronger by being used. Your faith in God becomes stronger *when you use it.*

Christians who are sick should not allow one day to go by when they do not obey God's specific instructions to steadily increase their faith in Him. You should be relentless in your commitment to constantly increase your faith in God. If you are severely ill you must continually draw closer to God. Staying in His presence will keep you in His peace and you will receive clear direction. You will trust Him with your life.

You should commit to spend large amounts of time to learn everything the Word of God teaches about healing and increasing your faith in God. The more your faith in God increases, the more you will be in His presence where healing is. You cannot tap into God's mighty power without faith. Faith in God is the key that unlocks the manifestation of healing your Father has provided for you through Jesus Christ.

Have you ever tried to open a door with the wrong key? This mistake is similar to the mistake that some Christians make in their desire for healing. If you want to receive healing you must use the right spiritual key. You must do what God says, not what you think you should do (see Proverbs 14:12).

Your Father wants your faith in Him to be deep, strong and unwavering. He wants you to continually develop your faith in Him. "...continue to stay with and in the faith [in Christ], well-grounded and settled and steadfast, not shifting or moving away from the hope [which rests on and is inspired by] the glad tidings (the Gospel), which you heard and which has been preached [as being designed for and offered without restrictions] to every person under heaven..." (Colossians 1:23).

Your Father wants your faith in Him to be "well-grounded and settled and steadfast." He absolutely does not want your faith in Him to be "shifting or moving away." God has made His instructions concerning healing and many other blessings available "to every person under heaven."

A sickness consciousness often develops *rapidly* in people who are sick. A healing consciousness *takes time to develop*. The days should turn into weeks and the weeks into months where you *continually* fill your heart with Scripture on faith in God, divine health and divine healing. As this process continues over time your faith that God will give you manifestation of healing will become stronger and stronger.

You must not allow yourself to become careless about continually drawing closer to the Lord. "…beware lest you forget the Lord…" (Deuteronomy 6:12). Some Christians go day after day without drawing closer to the Lord. God, speaking of the Israelites, once said, "…My people have forgotten Me, days without number" (Jeremiah 2:32).

Our relationship with God deepens by time in His Word and by precious quiet time alone with Him. Each day as you praise Him, speak to Him, listen to Him, love Him and receive His love, you will trust Him more and more.

Your faith in God should be so deeply rooted that you *will* be able to persevere when your body aches with pain. Your faith in God can be compared to the roots of a tree during a hurricane. I have lived in Florida for the past eighteen years. I have seen the results of hurricanes and tropical storms.

After these hurricanes and storms I could see that many trees without deep roots were torn out of the ground by the force of the storm. The roots of your faith in God should be *so deep* and *so strong* that the storms of life cannot overcome you. Some Christians who are sick only persevere for a little while. They give in to the pain and discomfort in their bodies because their faith in God is not deeply rooted. Jesus said, "…they have no real root in themselves, and so they endure for a little while…" (Mark 4:17).

Every aspect of your life should revolve around Jesus Christ. Jesus lives in your heart if you are a Christian (see Galatians 2:20). Jesus wants you to be so close to Him that you are deeply rooted in your faith in Him. "…you must abide in (live in, never depart from) Him [being rooted in Him, knit to Him]…" (I John 2:27).

The *only* way to have deeply rooted faith in Jesus is to be "knit to Him" – to be extremely close to Him throughout every day of your life. "You must abide in Him, live in and never depart from Him." Every aspect of your life should revolve around your *absolute certainty* that Jesus Christ your Healer lives in your heart.

You must know Jesus intimately. If you set aside quality time each day to be alone with your precious Lord, you *will* draw closer and closer to Him. The roots of your faith in Him will grow deeper and deeper. Ultimately, these roots *will* be strong enough to receive manifestation of the healing He already has provided for you.

Chapter 20

Unwavering Faith Connects You with Divine Healing

God already has done everything to provide healing for you. Jesus Christ took upon Himself your sin and your sickness. God has provided you with faith to connect with His power to break the bonds of sin and sickness. Steadily increasing the faith that God already has given to you is *your* responsibility.

God and His supernatural living Word are the same (see John 1:1). The more you immerse yourself in God's Word and fill your heart with His Word, the better you will know Him. Your faith in God will grow stronger as you constantly fill your heart with His supernatural living Word.

You have learned some basic facts from the Bible about increasing your faith in God so that you will be able to receive the healing your loving Father has provided for you. We now are ready to look at additional facts from the Word of God that will clearly show you the absolute necessity of developing deep, strong, unwavering and unshakable faith in Jesus Christ your Healer.

Some Christians block God from healing them because their faith in Him wavers. When you pray to God, your Father wants you to be *so close* to Him and have *so much* trust in Him that you will not doubt Him. God always does exactly what His Word says He will do. Your faith in Him is the determining factor. "…it must be in faith that he asks with no wavering (no hesitating, no doubting). For the one who wavers (hesitates, doubts) is like the billowing surge out at sea that I blown hither and thither and tossed by the wind. For truly, let not such a person imagine that he will receive anything [he asks for] from the Lord" (James 1:6-7).

This passage of Scripture says that you "*must* ask in faith" when you pray. This statement excludes all begging, wishing and hoping prayers. Your Father wants you to come to Him with knowledge of exactly what He already has done in regard to divine healing and with *absolute certainty* that He *always* does exactly what He says He will do (see Numbers 23:19, Joshua 23:14, Isaiah 46:11, Jeremiah 1:12, Romans 10:11 and I Corinthians 1:9).

Your Father says that you must not "waver, hesitate or doubt" when you pray. If you waver in your faith when you pray you will be like a "billowing surge out at sea" that is "tossed by the wind." Divine healing is a *fact*. If your faith that God will do what He said He would do wavers you should "not imagine that you will receive anything you ask for from the Lord."

Would you be pleased if you made a definite promise to your children and your children showed by their words and actions that they did not believe you would do what you promised to you? Your loving Father is much more worthy of your trust than any human being. He wants you to know exactly what He has promised to do in regard to divine healing.

This book is filled with healing promises from God. Your Father does not want your faith in Him and His absolute promises to waver in the slightest, regardless of the symptoms of sickness in your body. "[For being as he is] a man of two minds (hesitating, dubious, irresolute), [he is] unstable and unreliable and uncertain about everything [he thinks, feel, decides]" (James 1:8).

Your Father does not want you to be double-minded. You will be "unstable and unreliable and uncertain" if you are "hesitating, dubious and irresolute." Your faith in God must be single-minded and unwavering. Your Father wants your faith in Him to be steady and constant.

Your Father wants you to react to His healing promises the same way you would react if He personally walked into the room where you are right now and spoke His healing promises to you audibly. How much faith would you have in God's healing power if He spoke to you audibly face to face? God's Word is supernaturally alive. God *is* speaking to you right now if you are meditating on His Word and listening in your heart.

You must know and believe that each of God's healing promises in the Bible is just as personal and just as authentic as if He approached you in person. You might be a casual Christian when everything is going well. You will find out what you *really believe* if you are very sick. You will see how much you *really* trust God when you are facing severe illness or any other significant adversity.

Unshakable faith is not intimidated by sickness. Unshakable faith is absolutely confident in God's integrity. Unshakable faith knows that God has provided healing. Unshakable faith does not waver. Unshakable faith refuses to dwell on sickness. Unshakable faith focuses continually on God (see Isaiah 26:3).

This book is filled with hundreds of specific promises and instructions pertaining to divine healing and increasing your faith in God. Your Father wants you to develop your faith for divine healing so that this faith will be "…firm (steadfast, immovable)…" (I Corinthians 15:58).

Is your faith in God "firm, steadfast and immovable?" Have you faithfully followed all of God's specific instructions that are contained in the Bible so that your faith in your loving Father is rock-solid? "Trust in, lean on, rely on and have confidence in Him at all times…" (Psalm 62:8).

Your Father wants you to trust Him "at all times." He makes this statement in the New Testament. He makes this statement in the Old Testament. He wants you to "lean on Him" when you are sick.

Your Father does not want you to focus on the pain and discomfort caused by sickness in your body. He wants you to focus constantly on Him. He wants you to focus continually on the healing promises He has given to you. "Let your eyes look right on [with fixed purpose], and let your gaze be straight before you" (Proverbs 4:25).

Your Father wants "your eyes to look right on." He wants you to *focus on Him continually*. He wants you to have a "fixed purpose" – absolute determination that you *will* see in your body manifestation of the healing Jesus already has provided for you. He wants your eyes to be "straight before you." The psalmist David said, "With God rests my salvation and my glory; He is my Rock of unyielding strength and impenetrable hardness, and my refuge is in God!" (Psalm 62:7).

David said that God was "his Rock of unyielding strength and impenetrable hardness." David refused to be moved no matter what he faced because he trusted completely in God. God was his "refuge." God wants to be *your refuge* when you are sick. Your loving Father wants you to be *so close* to Him that you come into the safety of His presence and remain there.

You have learned that the Word of God provides emphasis through repetition. If you will look in your Bible at the 62nd Psalm you will see that David *repeated* this statement in the sixth, seventh and eighth verses. David absolutely refused to waver in his faith in God. If you are tempted to waver in your faith in God, meditate on the Scripture in this book over and over again so that your faith in the completed work of Jesus Christ will be deep, strong and unwavering.

Your Father wants you to have unwavering faith in Him throughout the morning, throughout the afternoon and throughout the evening during every day of your life. He wants you to have unwavering faith in Him twenty-four hours a day, seven days a week and fifty-two weeks a year.

Your Father does not want your faith in Him to waver in the slightest, no matter how severe the pain and discomfort in your body might be. "Those who trust in, lean on, and confidently hope in the Lord are like Mount Zion, which cannot be moved but abides and stands fast forever. As the mountains are round about Jerusalem, so the Lord is round about His people from this time forth and forever" (Psalm 125:1-2).

Your faith in God will be "like Mount Zion" if you have paid the price of consistent daily Bible study and meditation on what the Word of God says about divine healing and increasing your faith in God. This heavenly mountain "cannot be moved." Mount Zion "stands fast forever." Your loving Father has promised to deliver you from every problem you face, no matter how difficult this problem might seem. "When the righteous cry for help, the Lord hears, and delivers them out of all their distress and troubles" (Psalm 34:17).

You are "righteous" before God if you have received Jesus Christ as your Savior. You can be absolutely certain that "the Lord hears" you when you "cry for help" because of the sickness in your body. He promises to "deliver you out of all distress and trouble."

Please focus on the word "all" in this passage of Scripture. *Know* that this word includes the distress and trouble you face at this time because of the sickness in your body. The psalmist emphasized this point when he said "Many evils confront the [consistently] righteous, but the Lord delivers him out of them all" (Psalm 34:19).

The words "consistently righteous" refer to a life of obedience to and commitment to God. Please highlight or underline the words "the Lord delivers him out of them all." The word "all" in this passage of Scripture *includes* the sickness in *your* body. Your Father wants you to be *absolutely certain* that *you* are included in the word "all" in both Psalm 34:17 and Psalm 34:19.

Your Father wants you to have *so much* faith in Him that you will not doubt Him regardless of the severity of the physical symptoms in your body. Jesus said, "…Have faith in God [constantly]. Truly I tell you, whoever says to this mountain, Be lifted up and thrown into the sea! and does not doubt at all in his heart but believes that what he says will take place, it will be done for him." (Mark 11:22-23).

Jesus emphasized that you should "have faith in God constantly." Sickness is a "mountain" in your life. Dr. Jesus has instructed you to *speak to* this sickness, telling it to be gone. The Divine Physician does not want you to "doubt at all in your heart" that this sickness *will* go away as you persevere in faith. You must believe that "what you say will take place."

When your body aches with pain you *must* focus continually on these magnificent promises from God. You must focus on God's faithfulness. Your Father has told you again and again that He does not want your faith in Him to waver. Some Christians say, "I know the Bible says that but…" *There are no "buts"* pertaining to *anything* that is promised in the Bible. You *cannot* allow any "buts" to enter into your eyes, your ears, your mind, your heart and your mouth.

You must be absolutely certain to do the "ifs" that are part of all of God's conditional promises in His Word. Manifestation of God's promises is *not* automatic. You must do your part to continually increase your faith in God so that you will be able to receive manifestation of the healing that already has been provided for you.

Your Father wants you to be a radical believer. He wants you to be *completely* sold out to Him. He wants you to place *all* of your hope, faith, trust and confidence in Him. Unwavering faith in God creates a spiritual bridge that will carry you from the pain and discomfort in your body into the outstretched arms of your loving Father. "…underneath are the everlasting arms…" (Deuteronomy 33:27).

This chapter is filled with *facts* from the holy Scriptures that will *encourage* you when you are going through a difficult time with the symptoms of sickness in your body. Go back over this Scripture Study it. Meditate on these magnificent promises from Almighty God. Speak them boldly. Personalize them. Put them

in the first person. Continually increase your faith for divine healing.

Chapter 21

Fight the Good Fight of Faith

Our Father's plan is for every one of us to have a close, vibrant and intimate relationship with Him. He will *not* be pleased if you show unbelief in His many promises that He will give *you* manifestation of healing. "…the just shall live by faith [My righteous servant shall live by his conviction respecting man's relationship to God and divine things, and holy fervor born of faith and conjoined with it]' and if he draws back and shrinks in fear, My soul has no delight or pleasure in Him" (Hebrews 10:38).

Your Father wants you to "live by faith." He wants every day of your life to be focused on Him. He wants your relationship with Him to be so strong that you will have a "holy fervor" at all times in spite of the sickness in your body. He will not be pleased if you "draw back and shrink in fear."

Your Father wants you to come to a point of total release to Him. He wants you to live in the Spirit instead of being controlled by your flesh and your emotions. He wants you to have absolute faith in the completed work His Son has done for you.

Most people who are sick hope they will be healed. Your Father wants you to hope, but He wants you to do more than hope. He wants you to be *absolutely assured* that He already has provided healing for you. "…faith is the assurance (the confirmation, the title deed) of the things [we] hope for, being the proof of things [we] do not see and the conviction of their reality [faith perceiving as real fact what is not revealed to the senses]" (Hebrews 11:1).

You *can* be certain that Jesus already has provided healing for you. God's Word is your "assurance" that He already has done what you hope He will do. The amplification in this passage of Scripture compares this assurance from your faith in God to a "title deed" that shows you have title to a specific piece of property.

A title to a piece of property gives you a claim to that property. The Bible gives you specific confirmation of your healing. The Word of God consists of an Old Testament and a New Testament. A testament is a legal covenant. The Bible is a legal agreement between God and man. The Bible gives you absolute assurance that your loving Father has provided healing as part of the atonement of Jesus Christ.

The Word of God is your "proof" from God Himself that the price for the healing you "do not see" already has been paid. Your Father wants you to have "absolute conviction" of the "reality" that healing is your inheritance. He wants you to "perceive" manifestation of this healing as "real fact" even though this healing has not yet been "revealed to your senses."

God created the world through visualization and speaking the world into existence (see Genesis 1:1-26). You are created in God's image (see Genesis 1:27). You create things the same way that God does. God created the world through speaking what He planned. He wants you to receive manifestation of healing in your body through constantly seeing yourself the way you will be when you are completely healed. He wants you to continually speak faith-filled words about the healing Jesus has provided for you.

Speak to your body in the Spirit of God. Spend a considerable amount of time each day drawing closer to God. Abide in the presence of God where wholeness and wellness are to be found.

Your loving Father wants you to hold tightly onto the healing promises He has given you. He wants you to focus on these great truths continually so that you *will* be able to *turn away* from focusing on the pain and discomfort in your body. "…My trust and assured reliance and confident hope shall be fixed in Him…" (Hebrews 2:13).

Your Father wants you to have absolute "trust and assured reliance and confident hope" in Him. He wants your mind and your heart to be "fixed on Him." Your faith in God should be strong, vibrant, relentless and unwavering.

Some Christians have weak, lazy and unexercised faith. They have not paid the price to strengthen their faith in God to the point of living in God's presence and understanding His healing nature. Your Father does not want your faith in Him to be tentative, hesitant and wishful. "…the [uncompromisingly] righteous are bold as a lion" (Proverbs 28:1).

Your faith in God should be as "bold as a lion." You should not back off if you face severe sickness. You should step out boldly on your faith in God. Your words and your actions should constantly indicate your absolute faith in God. "…because of our faith in Him, we dare to have the boldness (courage and confidence) of free access (an unreserved approach to God with freedom and without fear)" (Ephesians 3:12).

Once again you are told that you should "dare to" have boldness in your faith in God. The amplification of this passage of Scripture says that you should have "courage and confidence" when you approach the throne of God and partake of healing for your body. You *can* approach Almighty God "with freedom and without fear."

Your Father wants you to keep on fighting. He wants His children who are sick to absolutely refuse to give up. He wants you to "fight the good fight of the faith…" (I Timothy 6:12).

This passage of Scripture refers to eternal salvation. This principle of fighting the good fight also applies to divine healing. Your Father wants you to obey the specific instructions He has given you to continually strengthen your faith in Him so that *you* will fight the good fight of faith He wants you to fight.

This good fight takes place while you are waiting for manifestation of the healing that Jesus has provided for you. You may be required to fight this good fight when the symptoms of sickness are severe. Will you believe *more* in the power of the Word of God than you do in the power of the symptoms of sickness in your body?

Sickness can be enervating. Pain and physical discomfort can deplete your energy. Many people who are sick allow the sickness in their bodies to control their lives. Their lives are dominated by the symptoms of sickness in their bodies.

Satan's demons will whisper into your ears to tell you that you cannot possibly be healed because of the severe symptoms of sickness in your body. If you really trust in God you will trust *completely* in Him instead of believing the lies that Satan's demons whisper into your ears. You must be absolutely certain of the truth of God's Word that tells you that Jesus bore the sickness and infirmity in your body for you (see Isaiah 53:4 and Matthew 8:17).

Many people who are severely ill actually are fighting for their lives. The good fight of faith can be a life or death proposition. This book is filled with *facts* from the Bible to help *you* fight a good fight.

The good fight of faith can only be won in the spiritual realm. You must learn what the Word of God says about divine healing. You must constantly study and meditate on the instructions and promises in the holy Scriptures pertaining to divine healing and increasing your faith in God. You must "…wage the good warfare, holding fast to faith (that leaning of the entire human personality on God in absolute trust and confidence)…" (I Timothy 1:18-19).

This passage of Scripture says that you should "wage the good warfare." A *good* fight of faith is a fight that *you win.* Your Father wants you to "hold fast" to your faith in Him. The amplification of faith in this passage of Scripture says that you should "lean your entire human personality on God in absolute trust and confidence." No matter how you might feel, you must not give up. You must fight this good fight of faith throughout every day and night. What else can take priority in your life if you are very sick?

You are losing this fight if you allow your mind to be controlled by the symptoms of sickness in your body. You are fighting the good fight if you continually turn away from these symptoms to focus entirely on God.

Your Father does not want you to lose. He wants you to *win* this fight. He wants you to know exactly what He has instructed you to do to fight this fight. He wants you to *obey* His specific instructions. He wants you to know exactly what He has promised concerning divine healing. He wants you to *believe wholeheartedly* in every one of these promises.

The fight of faith is called a *good* fight because *you will win* if you will persevere in faith and absolutely refuse to give up. You fight the good fight of faith based on the victory Jesus won for you. You *can* fight the good fight of faith because of your absolute *certainty* that Jesus paid the total price for manifestation of healing in your body when He went through such a horrible ordeal for *you* at the whipping post and shed His blood for you on the cross (see Chapter Two).

Your Father wants you to *know* that you are victorious in Christ. He wants you to *know* that your loving Healer paid the complete price for your healing at the whipping post and on the cross. Jesus already won this fight. You do *not* have to fight it all over again. *You already have received* the healing you need. You must persevere in faith until this healing is manifested.

You fight the good fight of faith by the words you speak when the symptoms in your body are severe. Will you talk continually about how bad the pain and discomfort are or will you continually speak the Word of God with bold faith? Will you speak healing Scripture continually? Will you constantly speak of the magnificent victory that Jesus won for you at the whipping post and on the cross? Will you continually speak of your *absolute certainty* that healing already has been provided for you?

You must fight throughout every day and night if you are going to fight the good fight of faith and win this fight and regain your health. You *must obey* your Father's instructions to meditate on His Word continually throughout the day and night (see Joshua 1:8 and Psalm 1:2-3).

Your part is to love, obey and rest in God. Immerse yourself in God's Word. The worse the symptoms of sickness in your body are, the more you should fill your eyes, your ears, your mind, your heart and your mouth with the mighty power of the supernatural living Word of God.

You cannot fight the good fight of faith if Scripture about healing and Scripture about faith in God is *only* in your mind. You fight the good fight of faith when this mighty and powerful Scripture drops from your *mind* down into your *heart*. Your *mind* is filled with the Word of God by continually *studying* the Word of God. Your *heart* is filled with the Word of God when you continually *meditate* on the holy Scriptures.

You now are ready to learn many facts from the Bible that tell you exactly how to fight the good fight of faith. In the next chapter you will learn how to get the Word of God up off the printed pages of the Bible into your *mind*. Once you have learned how to get the supernatural power of the living Word of God into your mind, you then will learn how to get the Word of God to drop from your mind down into your *heart*.

Chapter 22

Understanding Divine Healing from God's Perspective

Now that you have learned why it is necessary for you to develop deep, strong and unwavering faith for divine healing, you are ready to look into the Word of God to learn exactly how to develop this faith. Faith in God for divine healing *begins* with renewing your *mind* in the Word of God. You cannot understand divine healing from God's perspective unless you first study to learn exactly what the Word of God says about divine healing.

An unrenewed mind thinks the way the world thinks. The only way you can understand divine healing or anything else from God's perspective is to renew your mind in the Word of God in that specific area. "…the natural, nonspiritual man does not accept or welcome or admit into his heart the gifts and teachings and revelations of the Spirit of God, for they are folly (meaningless nonsense) to him; and he is incapable of knowing them (of progressively recognizing, understanding, and becoming better acquainted with them) because they are spiritually discerned and estimated and appreciated" (I Corinthians 2:14).

Unbelievers who are unable to continually renew their minds in God's Word are "natural and unspiritual" in their thinking. Unfortunately, Christians who fail to obey their Father's instructions to continually renew their minds in His Word (see II Corinthians 4:16 and Ephesians 4:23) put themselves in the same position.

They will live eventually in heaven, but they still think the way unbelievers think about sickness and healing.

These Christians do *not* "accept or welcome or admit" into their minds the "revelations of the Spirit of God" regarding divine healing because they have not taken the first step of continually renewing their minds in the Word of God. These Christians are "incapable of progressively recognizing, understanding and becoming better acquainted" with the *facts* in the Word of God pertaining to divine healing. They do not understand the truth about divine healing because this truth must be "spiritually discerned and estimated and appreciated."

You must not make this mistake. Christians with an open mind are willing to look into the Word of God to learn exactly what it says about divine healing that is vastly different from the world's system of healing. "…the spiritual man tries all things [he examines, investigates, inquires into, questions, and discerns all things]…" (I Corinthians 2:15).

You must be willing to carefully "examine, investigate and inquire into" what the Word of God says about healing before you will be able to "discern" exactly what your Father is saying to you about this subject. You have seen that God's ways are much higher and very different from the ways of the world (see Isaiah 55:8-9). The only way you can even begin to understand divine healing from God's perspective is to carefully and thoroughly study this subject in the holy Scriptures. You cannot expect to develop a deep, strong and unwavering faith for divine healing without *first* renewing your *mind* in the Word of God on this subject.

Any Christian who is seriously ill should have a deep and strong desire to pay the price to learn exactly what the Word of God says about healing. Thousands of thoughts go through your mind each day. You must learn to *substitute* God's instructions and promises pertaining to divine healing for any thoughts you currently have about sickness

Your Father has given you the power to direct your thoughts just as He has given you the power to control your arms, your hands, your legs and your feet. You must not allow your thoughts to be controlled by sickness. Instead, you should continually bring your thoughts into alignment with God's thoughts in the area of divine healing.

You received a recreated spirit when you asked Jesus to be your Savior, *but you still have the same soul and the same body.* Your carnal mind still will be spiritually dead unless it constantly is being renewed and guided by the Holy Spirit. "...the mind of the flesh [which is sense and reason without the Holy Spirit] is death [death that comprises all the miseries arising from sin, both here and hereafter]. But the mind of the [Holy] Spirit is life and [soul] peace [both now and forever]" (Romans 8:6).

Unbelievers and Christians who have not renewed their minds in the Word of God think with "the mind of the flesh." They think thoughts of worldly "sense and reason without the Holy Spirit." They allow their body and their soul to rule their spirit. If you are sick you must learn how to tap into "the mind of the Holy Spirit that is life." You cannot afford to think the thoughts about sickness and healing that unbelievers and carnal Christians think.

An unrenewed mind cannot possibly comprehend divine healing or anything else from God's perspective. "[That is] because the mind of the flesh [with its carnal thoughts and purposes] is hostile to God, for it does not submit itself to God's Law; indeed it cannot" (Romans 8:7).

A carnal mind is "hostile to God." You "cannot submit" to God's instructions and promises pertaining to divine healing unless you faithfully renew your mind in God's Word each day. You must continually "...direct your mind in the way [of the Lord]" (Proverbs 23:19).

The more you renew your mind in God's Word about divine healing, the more reasonable the truth of the supernatural realm on this important subject will be to you. You will develop an increasing ability to grasp God's great spiritual truths about divine healing that seem totally unreasonable to an unrenewed mind. "Do not be conformed to this world (this age), [fashioned after and adapted to its external, superficial customs], but be transformed (changed) by the [entire] renewal of your mind [by its new ideals and its new attitude], so that you may prove [for yourselves] what is the good and acceptable and perfect will of God, even the thing which is good and acceptable and perfect [in His sight for you]" (Romans 12:2).

You must *not* be "conformed to the world" in regard to sickness and healing. The "external, superficial" ways of the world regarding sickness and healing often will *not* be sufficient to give you the manifestation of healing that only can come from God. You must be "transformed by the entire renewal of your mind" day after day, week after week and month after month.

The Greek word "metamarphoo" that is translated as "transform" in this passage of Scripture is the same Greek word that was used in Matthew 17:1-2 to describe the transfiguration of Jesus Christ when He went up on a mountain with two of His disciples and His countenance was completely changed. *Your mind will be transformed* if you will continually renew your mind with the scriptural facts pertaining to divine healing and increased faith in God that are contained in this book.

You will not block God in the area of divine healing by looking at healing from an ungodly, worldly perspective. If you continually renew your mind you will have "new ideals and a new attitude" regarding sickness and healing. You will learn what "the good and acceptable and perfect will of God" is in the area of divine healing. You will "...not become discouraged (utterly spiritless, exhausted, and wearied out through fear). Though our outer man is [progressively] decaying and wasting away, yet our inner self is being [progressively] renewed day after day" (II Corinthians 4:16).

Paul was encouraging the Corinthians to hold fast to their faith when they were being persecuted for their belief in Jesus Christ. The same principle applies to perseverance regarding sickness in your body. Your Father does *not* want you to "become discouraged" because of the enervating effect of sickness on your body.

Sick people who allow themselves to be discouraged often are "utterly spiritless, exhausted, and wearied out through fear." Their bodies are "progressively decaying and wasting away." You must *offset the decay in your body* by "progressively renewing your inner self day after day." As this process continues over a period of time you will think more and more the way your Father thinks in regard to sickness, divine healing and divine health.

Many sick people are worried, fearful and discouraged. Your Father does not want you to give in to these negative emotions. He wants you to constantly renew your mind in His Word so that you will be able to maintain His supernatural peace even though you are sick. "…the incorruptible and unfading charm of a gentle spirit, which [is not anxious or wrought up, but] is very precious in the sight of God" (I Peter 3:4).

Paul was telling women to adorn themselves with grace and gentleness for their husbands. Your Father wants you to have this same "gentle spirit" when you are sick. He does not want you to be "anxious or wrought up" because of the sickness in your body. Your Father wants you to be calm, quiet and peaceful deep down inside of yourself because you have faithfully obeyed His instructions to renew your mind in His Word day after day.

The word "progressively" in II Corinthians 4:16 is very important. When you do something progressively you move forward in successive stages. This book is filled with *facts* from the Bible about divine healing and increasing your faith in God. If you study these scriptural facts *each day* you will *progressively* turn away from focusing on the symptoms of sickness in your body to focus instead on what the Word of God says about healing.

Your mind *will* be transformed *if* you renew your mind in the Word of God continually. You will be able to see yourself healed as God sees you instead of seeing yourself sick because you have been focusing on the physical pain and discomfort in your body.

Many people who have been Christians for several years have not learned of God's provision of healing. They have not renewed their minds in the Word of God pertaining to divine healing. All of these instructions sound like a lot of hard work to them. They do not understand that they should have been renewing their minds daily every day since Jesus Christ became their Savior.

You cannot expect to develop faith that God will give you manifestation of healing from sickness unless your faith is solidly anchored on scriptural *facts* about divine healing. "Strip yourselves of your former nature [put off and discard your old unrenewed self] which characterized your previous manner of life and becomes corrupt through lusts and desires that spring from delusion; and be constantly renewed in the spirit of your mind [having a fresh mental and spiritual attitude]" (Ephesians 4:22-23).

You must "strip yourself of your former nature." You must not think the way you used to think about sickness and healing. You must "put off and discard your old unrenewed self." You must not be deluded by the world's ways pertaining to sickness and healing. Instead, you must be "constantly renewed in the spirit of your mind."

Please highlight or underline the word "constantly" in this passage of Scripture. You *must renew your mind continually* day after day, week after week and month after month to develop a "fresh mental and spiritual attitude" concerning divine healing.

Most doctors agree that a great deal of sickness is caused by our minds. If your mind is powerful enough to cause you to be sick doesn't it make sense that a renewed mind can be used by God to enable you to receive the healing He has provided for you? "...you have stripped off the old (unregenerate) self with its evil practices, and have clothed yourselves with the new [spiritual self], which is [ever in the process of being] renewed and remolded into [fuller and more perfect knowledge upon] knowledge after the image (the likeness) of Him Who created it" (Colossians 3:9-10).

Your Father wants you to "strip off your old unregenerate self." He does not want you to think about sickness and healing the way that people whose minds have not been renewed think. He wants you to "clothe yourself with your new spiritual self."

When you "clothe yourself" you cover yourself. Your Father wants your mind to constantly be "renewed and remolded." He wants you to "be in the image of Him Who created you." Your Father does *not* want your thoughts to be dominated by sickness. He wants every one of His children to "...lead every thought and purpose away captive into the obedience of Christ (the Messiah, the Anointed One)..." (II Corinthians 10:5).

God would not have told you to "lead every thought and purpose away" from sickness unless you are able to change *all* of your thoughts pertaining to sickness. Your Father wants your thoughts pertaining to sickness to be brought "captive into the obedience of Christ." Jesus Christ is your Healer.

God created us with the ability to direct our thoughts. Christians who are very sick cannot possibly direct their thoughts through sheer willpower. You can only direct your thoughts and your beliefs by constantly filling your mind and your heart with the power of the supernatural living Word of God. I believe that you should have such a strong desire to learn everything you can about divine healing that you will have an "...inclination of mind and eagerness, searching and examining the Scriptures daily..." (Acts 17:11).

This passage of Scripture refers to the Jewish people in a synagogue who were open to the message of eternal salvation through Jesus Christ that Paul and Silas preached. This same "eagerness" to learn from God can apply to divine healing. You must be "inclined" to want to think the way that God thinks about divine healing. You must "search and examine the Scriptures daily" as you continually renew your mind in the Word of God. Your Father wants you to strengthen your mind each and every day when you are sick. His Word tells us to "...brace up your minds..." (I Peter 1:13).

A "brace" is something that holds something else up and strengthens it. You must faithfully obey God's instructions to renew your mind on a daily basis so that you will establish a solid scriptural foundation for faith in divine healing.

Renewing your mind in the Word of God is merely the starting point to developing strong faith for divine healing. You must learn how to get the printed words up off the pages of the Bible into your mind *before* you can learn how to get these scriptural principles to drop from your mind down into your heart. We now are ready to look into the Word of God to learn exactly what your Father instructs you to do to get scriptural principles of divine healing to drop from your mind down into your heart.

Chapter 23

Wholehearted Belief in Divine Healing

You have learned the relationship between renewing your mind in God's Word and divine healing. Renewing your mind is the starting point to increasing your faith for divine healing. However, faith in God does not work in your mind alone. You *think* with your *mind*. You *believe* with your *heart*. "…with the heart a person believes (adheres to, trusts in, and relies on Christ)…" (Romans 10:10).

You have seen previously that this passage of Scripture refers to trusting Jesus Christ for eternal salvation. You also have seen that divine healing is part of the redemption Jesus has provided for you. This passage of Scripture definitely applies to divine healing as well as eternal salvation.

What does the Bible refer to when it refers to your heart? The Bible does not refer to the organ in your body that pumps blood. When the Bible refers to your heart it refers to what you really are deep down inside of yourself. The Bible defines this inner person as "…the hidden person of the heart." (I Peter 3:4).

The "hidden person of the heart" is the real you. This person is what you are when you face a severe crisis and you spontaneously react based upon your inner core beliefs. This same hidden person is vitally important if you are very sick. You must believe deep down in your heart that Jesus Christ is your Savior and that He also is your Healer.

You need *more* than knowledge in your *mind* about divine healing. You must have deep, strong and unwavering faith in God in your *heart*. If you constantly renew your mind in the Scripture contained in this book you will increase your factual knowledge pertaining to divine healing. However, you must learn how to get these facts about divine healing from the Word of God to drop from your mind down into your heart. Your heart is the key to your life. "…as he thinks in his heart, so is he…" (Proverbs 23:7).

You usually connect the word "thinking" with your mind. This passage of Scripture does *not* say "as he thinks in his *mind*, so is he." The key to your life is what you really believe deep down in your heart. This heartfelt belief is the key to healing and every other area of your life.

This book shows you exactly what to do to get Scripture pertaining to divine healing up off the printed pages of the Bible into your mind and then down into your heart. Your heart should be *so full* of Scripture that this overflow of Scripture will constantly override any thoughts in your mind that you will not be healed.

Your Bible will not do you any good when it is sitting on a desk or a shelf. Your Father has told you exactly where His Word should make its home. "…let the word [spoken by] Christ (the Messiah) have its home [in your hearts and minds] and dwell in you in [all its] richness" (Colossians 3:16).

We are studying divine healing in this book. You absolutely must get every possible Scripture reference pertaining to receiving manifestation of healing from God and increased faith in God up off the printed pages of the Bible into its home in your mind and your heart. This Scripture should "dwell in you in all its richness."

If you are sick I believe that your Father wants your heart to be filled with *truth* pertaining to divine healing. Jesus said, "…Your Word is Truth" (John 17:17). Your Father wants the truth of His Word to come alive deep down inside of you. "You desire truth in the inner being…" (Psalm 51:6).

You now are ready to learn marvelous spiritual truths from a vitally important passage of Scripture about divine healing living in your heart. "My son, attend to my words; consent and submit to my sayings. Let them not depart from your sight; keep them in the center of your heart. For they are life to those who find them, healing and health to all their flesh. Keep and guard your heart with all vigilance and above all that you guard, for out of it flow the springs of life" (Proverbs 4:20-23).

We looked briefly at this passage of Scripture in a chapter on divine health because Proverbs 4:22 contains the words "health to all their flesh." We now will look at this passage of Scripture in regard to divine healing.

These anointed words that King Solomon spoke to his son also are anointed words from your Father in heaven to *you*. Your Father wants you to "attend to His Word" – to pay close attention to His Word at all times. He wants you to "consent and submit" to the instructions He has given you. He wants you to be determined to learn and obey each of His instructions carefully and exactly.

Please highlight or underline the words "let them not depart from your sight." Your Father wants His Word to *fill your eyes* continually throughout every day and night of your life. In the next five chapters you will learn many facts from the Word of God about meditating on the Word of God throughout the day and night. I believe that Scripture meditation is the best way to keep the Word of God in front of your eyes continually.

As you meditate continually on God's Word you will know God better. As you know God better His Word will come alive more and more deep down inside of you. The Word of God is "life to those who find it, healing and health to all their flesh." *Please highlight or underline these important words*. This passage of Scripture clearly shows you the relationship between continually keeping the Word of God in front of your eyes, filling your heart with the Word of God, receiving manifestation of healing and enjoying good health.

You must understand the *vital importance* of this passage of Scripture. You are instructed to "keep and guard your heart with all vigilance." You have seen that your heart is the real you. Your heart is the center of your innermost being. You *must* vigilantly guard whatever you allow to enter into your heart. *Nothing is more important because the "springs of life" flow out of your heart.*

This scriptural principle applies to every area of life. If you are sick you absolutely must guard what you allow to enter into your heart pertaining to sickness and healing. Your heart should be so filled with God's supernatural Word pertaining to divine healing, divine health and faith in God that negative thoughts pertaining to the sickness in your body will *not* be able to get a foothold in your mind and your heart.

Many people who are sick are worried about the sickness in their bodies and what this sickness could lead to in the future. Their hearts are heavy because of the fearful thoughts they have allowed to enter into their hearts. Your Father tells you exactly what to do when you face this predicament. "Anxiety in a man's heart weighs it down, but an encouraging word makes it glad" (Proverbs 12:25).

You have just seen in Proverbs 4:23 that you should guard your heart vigilantly. You must not allow fear, worry and anxiety to get into your heart. This anxiety in your heart will "weigh it down." Your heart will be heavy if you allow anxiety to obtain a foothold.

Instead of having a heavy and anxious heart you should fill your heart continually with supernatural *encouragement* from the living Word of God. These "encouraging words" will create a "glad heart." Your heart will *sing with joy* in spite of the sickness because you will be focusing entirely on what God says about divine healing and about your faith in Him. Jesus said, "...Do not let your heart be troubled, neither let them be afraid. [Stop allowing yourselves to be agitated and disturbed; and do not permit yourselves to be fearful and intimidated and cowardly and un-settled.]" (John 14:27).

Please highlight or underline the words "let," "allowing" and "permit." These words clearly show that *you decide* what will enter into your heart. You must not "*let* your heart be troubled." You must not "*let* your heart be afraid." You must not "*allow* yourself to be agitated and disturbed" by the sickness in your body. You must not "*permit* yourself to be unsettled." If you allow these negative thoughts to come into your heart the cumulative result of this thinking will make the sickness in your body worse.

Your heart should be so full of God's Word that the mighty power of the supernatural living Word of God in your heart is *much more* real and meaningful to you than the symptoms of sickness in your body. The sickness is there, but you do not have to accept it. Christians who are sick must fight a constant battle between faith in God in their hearts and the symptoms of sickness in their bodies. You fight this battle by continually filling your heart to overflowing with the Word of God.

Christians who are sick will make the situation *much worse* if they allow worry, fear and anxiety to enter their hearts. Satan is able to obtain a foothold in your mind and your heart if you worry. "All the days of the desponding and afflicted are made evil [by anxious thoughts and forebodings], but he who has a glad heart has a continual feast [regardless of circumstances]" (Proverbs 15:15).

Some people are "despondent" because of the "affliction" of sickness in their bodies. All of their days are "made evil" by constant preoccupation with sickness. Satan's demons are able to get into their minds with "anxious thoughts and forebodings." You must not allow yourself to become despondent because of the sickness in your body. You will give Satan a foothold if you do this. Instead, the Word of God instructs you to "have a glad heart" regardless of the circumstances in your life relating to sickness.

You will have "a continuous feast *regardless of circumstances*" if you constantly feed your heart with the vitally important spiritual food of the supernatural living Word of God. You will *not* allow the circumstance of sickness to control your life. Your "glad heart" will sing with joy because it is filled to overflowing with the mighty power of the supernatural living Word of God. Sickness will *not* be able to pull you down.

We now are ready to look at a passage of Scripture that we studied previously from a different perspective. "A happy heart is good medicine and a cheerful mind works healing, but a broken spirit dries up the bones" (Proverbs 17:22).

You learned previously that the Word of God is your Father's "medicine" for you. You will have a "happy heart" if you continually fill your heart with the spiritual medicine of the Word of God. A "happy heart" and a "cheerful mind" will "work healing." Your happy heart creates a healing atmosphere. Many tests have shown that a continual positive attitude creates positive chemicals in the body and a continual negative attitude creates negative chemicals in the body.

You must *not* allow "a broken spirit to dry up your bones." You must not make the mistake of allowing the sickness in your body to override your happy heart and your cheerful mind. You must keep healing Scripture and Scripture about faith in God alive in your mind and your heart on a *daily basis*. You cannot afford to allow the supply of this Scripture to dwindle. The Scripture in your mind and your heart should increase continually.

If you continually obey your Father's instructions to meditate on His Word throughout the day and night, your heart *will* be filled to overflowing with the mighty healing power of the supernatural living Word of God. In the next several chapters you will learn exactly what to do to meditate continually on the Word of God throughout the day and night.

Chapter 24

Plant Healing Seeds from God's Word into Your Heart

If you are sick you must understand that divine healing is a spiritual *harvest* you will receive *if* you learn how to continually plant *seeds* from God's Word in your heart. Jesus said, "…the seed is the Word of God" (Luke 8:11).

Shortly after explaining that the Word of God is a spiritual seed Jesus went on to explain that you should continually plant these marvelous supernatural spiritual seeds in the spiritual soil of your heart. Jesus said, "…as for that [seed] in the good soil, these are [the people] who, hearing the Word, hold it fast in a just (noble, virtuous) and worthy heart, and steadily bring forth fruit with patience" (Luke 8:15).

Please highlight or underline the words "good soil." Successful farmers are very careful to plant the best seeds they can obtain in the best soil that is available. There is no better spiritual seed than the Word of God. There is no better spiritual soil than your heart. Jesus said that you should plant the spiritual seeds of God's Word in the fertile soil of your "just, noble, virtuous and worthy heart."

You should consistently plant these seeds in your heart over a period of time so that you will "steadily bring forth fruit with patience." If you want to receive a harvest of carrots what kind of seeds would you plant? Carrot seeds. If you want to receive a harvest of corn what kind of seeds would you plant? Corn seeds. If you want to receive a harvest of healing what kind of seeds should you plant? *Healing seeds.*

You plant these seeds in your heart throughout every day and night by continually meditating on the supernatural living Word of God. You must persevere for as long as your Father requires you to persevere until you receive the harvest of manifestation of healing from the sickness in your body.

Farmers do not have to understand everything that takes place chemically when they plant seeds in the ground. They know from experience what will happen when they plant good seeds in good soil. They plant these seeds and wait patiently to receive a harvest.

You should do the same in the spiritual realm. Do not attempt to intellectualize this process. Continually plant these magnificent spiritual seeds with unwavering faith in Almighty God. If Jesus told you that His Word is a seed and that the good soil to plant these seeds is your heart, that is all you need to know. You should be *determined* to plant as *many* healing seeds as you possibly can into the fertile spiritual soil of your heart.

No farmer would attempt to go into a field to receive a harvest if he had *not* planted seeds in that field. Even though it does not make sense to attempt to receive a harvest without planting seeds, *this is exactly what many Christians do.* Many Christians attempt to receive a harvest of healing without faithfully planting healing seeds in the good soil of their hearts.

Your Father has told you exactly what you should expect to reap at harvest time. You will receive a harvest based on whatever seeds you sow. "…whatever a man sows, that and that only is what he will reap" (Galatians 6:7).

Please highlight or underline the words "that and that only." You should continually plant an abundance of God's healing seeds in your heart. "For as the rain and snow come down from the heavens, and return not there again, but water the earth and make it bring forth and sprout, that it may give seed to the sower and bread to the eater, so shall My word be that goes forth out of My mouth: it shall not return to Me void [without producing any effect, useless], but it shall accomplish that which I please and purpose, and it shall prosper in the thing for which I sent it" (Isaiah 55:10-11).

God explains that His Word is a "seed." He says that His Word "shall not return to Him void." Your Father promises that His Word always will "accomplish that which He pleases and purposes." God says that His Word "shall prosper in the thing for which He sent it."

These words mean that your Father has provided you with specific seeds for specific purposes. Christians who have financial challenges should plant financial seeds from God's Word in their hearts. If you have severe sickness in your body you should continually plant healing seeds in your heart. You cannot plant these seeds continually "without producing any effect."

God has completed His part. He *already has provided* everything you will need in every area of your life, including healing (see Psalm 34:10, Matthew 6:25-33, Romans 8:32, II Corinthians 9:6-8 and Philippians 4:19). Your part is to learn and obey all of the scriptural instructions your Father has given you pertaining to divine healing and increasing your faith in Him. Your part is to learn and believe wholeheartedly all of the scriptural healing promises your Father has given you. Your part is to continually plant healing seeds from these promises and instructions in your heart.

God's laws of sowing and reaping apply to every area of your life. God's laws of sowing and reaping work for all of us, whether or not we realize that this process is taking place. We *all* reap whatever we sow in many different areas of our lives. "While the earth remains, seedtime and harvest, cold and heat, summer and winter, and day and night shall not cease" (Genesis 8:22).

God's laws of "seedtime and harvest" have existed since God created the earth. God's laws of sowing and reaping "shall not cease." Your Father tells you that you should meditate day and night on His Word because He wants you to continually plant spiritual seeds from His Word in your heart throughout every day and night of your life.

Many people cannot understand that words that are printed on a piece of paper can be and are *much more powerful* than any severe illness. "...when you received the message of God [which you heard] from us, you welcomed it not as the word of [mere] men, but as it truly is, the Word of God, which is effectually at work in you who believe [exercising its superhuman power in those who adhere to and trust in and rely on it]" (I Thessalonians 2:13).

You must *not* look at the words from God that are printed on the pages of your Bible as the words "of mere men." You must understand that all of the Scripture you have been studying in this book "truly is the Word of God."

What does your Father tell you that His supernatural living Word will *do for you* if you continually plant it in the fertile soil of your heart? Please highlight or underline the words "effectually at work in you who believe." God's Word *will* work effectively in you to the degree that *you believe it will.*

The amplification of this passage of Scripture tells you that the Word of God has "superhuman power." You *cannot even begin to understand* with your limited human understanding the immense power of the Word of God that you are planting in your heart. The supernatural power of the Word of God *will* produce a harvest of healing in your life *if* you "adhere to and trust in and rely on it."

Please go back and meditate on I Thessalonians 2:13. Personalize it. Believe that God is speaking to *you* about the sickness in *your* body. *Know* that the superhuman power of the Word of God is *much more powerful* than *any* sickness, no matter how devastating that sickness may seem to be.

The supernaturally powerful Word of God brings understanding of God. Your Father wants you to know what His Word says about healing. He wants you to trust Him completely. Jesus said,

"…you are wrong because you know neither the Scriptures nor God's power" (Matthew 22:29).

Jesus spoke these words to a group of Sadducees who questioned Him. He told these Sadducees that they were "wrong" because they did not "know the Scriptures or God's power." You must not make this mistake. *Your life could depend on* your knowledge and understanding of what the holy Scriptures say about the power of God in regard to healing your body and increasing your faith in God.

You must not overestimate the power of the sickness in your body, no matter what a doctor may have told you about the severity of this sickness. The Word of God is a powerful spiritual sword that is able to perform spiritual surgery on the sickness in your body. You must not underestimate the supernatural power of the living Word of God. "…the Word that God speaks is alive and full of power [making it active, operative, energizing, and effective]…" (Hebrews 4:12).

Please highlight or underline the words "alive and full of power." You must understand that the healing Scripture you are meditating on is *alive* – it has a spiritual life of its own. You must know that the healing Scripture you are meditating on is "full of power" from God.

The amplification of this passage of Scripture tells you that the Word of God is "active." The Word of God will be active in *your* life if you will continually meditate on it. God's Word will "energize" you – it will build you up. God's Word is "effective" – it *will* produce results in your body.

The Word of God is infinitely above anything on this earth. The Word of God is filled with precious supernatural spiritual seeds that are filled with the living power of God Himself. If you continually plant these precious seeds from God's Word in your heart *you actually are planting the power of Almighty God* deep down inside of yourself.

God is an awesome God. He is holy. He is mighty. His supernatural Word is ignited with His mighty power. Your Father wants you to have tremendous awe and respect for His Word. "Hear the word of the Lord, you who tremble at His word..." (Isaiah 66:5).

If you "tremble" because of your awe of the supernatural power of the living Word of God you will clearly hear what God is saying to you. The supernatural power of the Word of God is more than sufficient to overcome the sickness in your body. "...we possess this precious treasure [the divine Light of the Gospel] in [frail, human] vessels of earth, that the grandeur and exceeding greatness of the power may be shown to be from God and not from ourselves." (II Corinthians 4:7).

The Word of God is a "precious treasure." It is "divine Light." Your Father wants the supernatural power of His living Word to *come alive* in your "frail human body." If you continually plant supernatural healing seeds from God's Word into your heart your frail body will be filled with "the grandeur and exceeding greatness of the power" of God. The Word of God is *so powerful* that the world we live in and all of the planets, stars and galaxies in the entire universe are controlled by it. "...upholding and maintaining and guiding and propelling the universe by His mighty word of power..." (Hebrews 1:3).

You must understand that the supernatural living Word of God is *much more powerful* than *any* sickness anyone has ever had. This passage of Scripture says that the universe is "maintained" by the Word of God. When something is maintained it is kept in working order so that it will operate efficiently. The Word of God is *so powerful* that it is able to keep the universe in perfect working order at all times. If God's Word has enough power to hold up *the entire universe* you can be *certain* that God's Word is *much more powerful* than the sickness in your body.

You also are told that the Word of God "guides" the universe. When you are guided, you are directed and kept on course. The Word of God is so powerful that it is able to keep everything in the universe on course and headed in the right direction.

You are told that the universe is "propelled" by the Word of God. The word "propelled" means "to drive forward." The Word of God is so powerful that it is able to keep everything in the universe moving forward at all times.

Once you begin to understand that all of your thoughts, words and actions actually are spiritual seeds, you will focus on continually planting the seeds your Father instructs you to plant with your thoughts, words and actions. Jesus explained the mighty power of spiritual seeds when He said, "…The kingdom of heaven is like a grain of mustard seed, which a man took and sowed in his field. Of all the seeds it is the smallest, but when it has grown it is the largest of the garden herbs and becomes a tree, so that the birds of the air come and find shelter in its branches" (Matthew 13:31-32).

Jesus used the example of a mustard seed for a specific reason. Jesus said that this seed is the "smallest of all seeds" yet it grows into a tree that is large enough so that "the birds of the air come and find shelter in its branches." Jesus used this analogy to show you how much *your* faith in God can *grow and increase.* All Christians start out with the same amount of faith that we each are given by God's grace to enable us to trust Jesus Christ for eternal salvation. What you do with this original amount of faith is *up to you.*

Your faith in God starts out small like a mustard seed. However, these seeds can and will grow … and grow … and grow *if* you continually plant these seeds from the Word of God into your heart. When His disciples were unable to rebuke a demon and they came to Jesus and He instantly rebuked the demon, the disciples asked Jesus why they could not do what He did. "He said to them, Because of the littleness of your faith [that is, your lack of firmly relying trust]. For truly I say to you, if you have faith [that is living] like a grain of mustard seed, you can say to this mountain, Move from here to yonder place, and it will move; and nothing will be impossible to you" (Matthew 17:20).

Jesus told the disciples that they could not do what He did "because of the littleness of their faith." Once again Jesus compares faith in God to a mustard seed. He said that your faith in

God can become *so strong* that you will be able to tell a *mountain* to move from one place to another and "it *will* move." Jesus said that "nothing will impossible to you" if you trust God completely.

These words include the sickness in your body. Sickness is a tremendous "mountain" in the life of a very sick person. No matter how severe the sickness may seem, you must stand on God's Word.

Unbelievers cannot sow the seeds of God's Word in their hearts. Christians *are* given the privilege and ability to sow these seeds. Are you sick? Are you utilizing the precious privilege you have been given to continually plant healing seeds from God's Word in your heart?

Satan and his demons are fully aware that the Word of God is a mighty supernatural seed. The last thing Satan and his demons want Christians who are sick to do is to continually plant healing seeds from the Word of God into their hearts. Satan and his demons will try to *steal* the seed of God's Word out of your heart. Jesus said, "The sower sows the Word. The ones along the path are those who have the Word sown [in their hearts], but when they hear, Satan comes at once and [by force] takes away the message which is sown in them" (Mark 4:14-15).

Your job is to "sow the Word." You will be on the path your Father wants you to be on if you continually sow seeds from the Word of God into your heart. It is much easier to dig up a seed immediately after it is planted than it is to dig up the same seed after it has put down roots and started to grow. This same principle applies in the spiritual realm.

You must *not* allow Satan, the pain and discomfort in your body or anyone or anything to *stop you* from continually planting supernatural seeds from God's Word into your heart. This chapter is filled with *facts* from the holy Scriptures about the mighty supernatural power of the seed of God's living Word.

If you understand this great spiritual truth, you must not allow anything to dissuade you from continually meditating on the healing Scripture and on Scripture that explains how to increase your faith in God. Jesus said, "As for what was sown on good soil, this is he who hears the Word and grasps and comprehends it; he indeed bears fruit and yields in one case a hundred times as much as was sown, in another sixty times as much, and in another thirty" (Matthew 13:23).

In this passage of Scripture Jesus explained how *you* can receive thirty, sixty or even a hundred times as much as you sow. You must learn how to sow healing seeds from the Bible into the "good soil" of your heart. If you "grasp" what the Word of God says about divine healing and "comprehend" and understand these great spiritual truths, you will persevere because of your faith in God. Your faith, patience and perseverance ultimately will be honored when all of the seeds you have planted "bear fruit" and produce a marvelous harvest of healing from God.

Jesus finished the work of healing more than two thousand years ago. Your healing is complete. You must learn how to partake of the completed work of healing that has been provided for you by Jesus Christ.

Now that you have learned the spiritual importance of the contents of your heart and the absolute necessity of planting spiritual seeds in your heart, you are ready to look into the Word of God to learn exactly *how* to plant these seeds in your heart. You are ready to learn what the holy Scriptures teach you about constantly planting the supernatural seeds of God's Word in *your heart* as a result of *continual Scripture meditation.*

Chapter 25

Scripture Meditation and Divine Healing

You have learned how important it is to renew your *mind* in God's Word so that you can *study* divine healing from God's perspective. You have learned that the Word of God is a mighty and powerful supernatural seed. You have learned that you need to cause these powerful *seeds* from God's Word to drop from your mind down into your *heart*. In the next four chapters you will learn exactly what to do to cause the supernatural seeds in God's Word in your mind to drop down into your heart as a result of continual Scripture meditation.

We will begin these chapters by carefully studying two passages of Scripture that are vitally important to all Christians – Joshua 1:8 and Psalm 1:2-3. Scripture meditation is the heart of everything we teach in Lamplight Ministries. Surveys at our seminars have shown us that *only a very small percentage* of God's children faithfully obey their Father's specific instructions to meditate on His Word continually throughout the day and night.

When Moses reached the age of 120 and was unable to continue all of his duties as the leader of Israel, God appointed a young man named Joshua as his successor (see Deuteronomy 1:30). Joshua had served as an assistant to Moses when he was a captain in Israel's army. Even though Joshua had served with distinction in his assistance to Moses, he undoubtedly was apprehensive about the awesome responsibility he would be given when he became the leader of Israel.

God spoke directly to Joshua to encourage him. He said, "This Book of the Law shall not depart out of your mouth, but you shall meditate on it day and night, that you may observe and do according to all that is written in it. For then you shall make your way prosperous, and then you shall deal wisely and have good success" (Joshua 1:8).

Please look at the *last* part of this passage of Scripture first. The words that God spoke to Joshua apply to you. God says that *you* can "make your way prosperous, deal wisely and have good success." This prosperity, wisdom and success applies to *every* area of your life. Since we are studying healing in this book we will apply this promise from God to healing.

The word "prosperous" does not mean the same as this word means in the English language today. The Hebrew word "tsalach" that is translated as "prosperous" in this passage of Scripture does refer to having the financial wherewithal you need, but it *also* means to "push forward, break out and go over." You absolutely *must* be able to push forward, break out and go over to receive manifestation of healing from God.

When God speaks of "dealing wisely" He refers to receiving His wisdom. You must learn how to receive God's wisdom so that you will be able to receive the healing He has provided for you. The final benefit that God has promised in this passage of Scripture is "good success." This passage of Scripture tells *you* how to be successful in *any* area of your life *including* success in receiving the healing from God that already has been provided for you. You should not expect to be successful in receiving healing from God unless you follow the specific instructions your Father has given you in the first part of this passage of Scripture.

We have examined the last part of this passage of Scripture to see the three blessings that God promises to you. Now we are ready to go back to the first part of this passage of Scripture to see exactly what your Father *instructs you to do* to receive these blessings.

Your Father gives you *three* specific instructions to follow if you sincerely desire to receive the three blessings of spiritual prosperity, wisdom and success. Your Father has told you that you should *speak* His Word continually, *meditate* on His Word throughout the day and night and *do* everything His Word instructs you to do.

Are you sick in your body? If so, could I ask without attempting to be critical *if you are doing all three of these things* God has instructed you to do? Most Christians who are healthy do *not* obey these specific instructions. Christians who are sick *must understand* the vital importance of obeying these specific instructions from God.

The first part of this passage of Scripture says "This Book of Law shall not depart out of your mouth." Your Father wants you to *speak* His Word continually. If you want your faith for healing to grow, one of the most important things to do is to open your mouth to continually speak Scripture pertaining to healing and increasing your faith in God. We will carefully study the scriptural instructions in this area in subsequent chapters.

The second instruction in the first part of Joshua 1:8 is to *meditate* on the Word of God throughout the day and night. The Hebrew word "hagah" that is translated "meditate" in this passage of Scripture means to "mutter, speak, study, talk and utter." You can clearly see that meditating day and night means that *you* need to *speak* the Word of God *throughout the day and night*. In subsequent chapters you will learn exactly what to do to meditate on Scripture. Before you learn *how* to meditate on God's Word you must understand the *absolute necessity* of meditating on the Word of God throughout the day and night.

The third instruction in this passage of Scripture is to "observe and do according to all that is written" in the Word of God. If you sincerely desire to receive healing in your body, you must learn everything you can about what the Word of God says concerning divine healing and increasing your faith in God. You then must *do what God instructs you to do*. This book is filled to over-flowing with specific scriptural instructions pertaining to divine healing.

I learned some interesting facts by surveying many audiences when I used to give seminars in the United States and Canada on the subject of Scripture meditation. I learned that *less than five percent* of the Christians I surveyed actually were doing the three things that Joshua 1:8 instructs all of us to do.

Your Father has told you in one other place in the Bible about the tremendous blessings *you* will receive *if* you consistently meditate on His Word throughout the day and night. "...his delight and desire are in the law of the Lord, and on His law (the precepts, the instructions, the teachings of God) he habitually meditates (ponders and studies) by day and by night. And he shall be like a tree firmly planted [and tended] by the stream of water, ready to bring forth its fruit in its season; its leaf also shall not fade or wither; and everything he does shall prosper [and come to maturity]" (Psalm 1:2-3).

We also will look at this passage of Scripture from the per-spective of healing. First you are told that you should have "great delight and desire" for the Word of God. You are told that you should "habitually meditate, ponder and study the Word of God by day and by night." If you continually meditate on God's Word you are told that you will "be like a tree that is planted next to a stream of water that will bring forth its fruit in its season." You then are told that the leaves on this tree "will not fade or wither."

Please visualize several rows of trees in an orchard next to a stream of water. Imagine that a long season of drought caused the leaves on these trees to fade and wither. Please visualize that ev-ery row of trees in this orchard is brown, faded and withered *except the one row of trees that is next to the stream of water.*

Psalm 1:3 tells you that the leaves on these trees will *not* fade or wither. These trees *will* bring forth fruit in the proper season. *Why* will this one row of trees be green and lush and continue to produce fruit in the midst of a drought? The answer is that these trees next to a stream of water are able to reach their roots down into the stream to bring up water from the stream even though no rain is coming down from the sky.

This passage of Scripture is directly applicable to divine healing. The same Hebrew word "tsalach" that is translated as "prosperous" in Joshua 1:8 also is translated as "prosper" in Psalm 1:3. Once again, this word refers to more than financial prosperity. This Hebrew word means "to push forward, break out and go over." The amplification in Psalm 1:3 says that you must "come to maturity."

Do you want to "push forward, break out and go over" the sickness in your body? Do you want to "come to maturity" in regard to understanding healing from God's perspective? You must understand the *absolute importance* of meditating throughout the day and night on the Word of God.

I have spent thousands of hours over a period of more than thirty years studying and meditating on the Bible. I have found hundreds of Scripture references that reveal God's nature, how He heals and what He requires of us. You do not have to spend hundreds of hours trying to dig all of this Scripture out of your Bible because I already have devoted many years to accomplishing this goal. All of this Scripture is included in this book.

I recommend that you *read* this book *once*, *study* it the *second* time through and *then meditate* on its scriptural contents *continually*. Some readers of our books have told us that they have gone through our books so many times that pages have fallen out.

We could print our books in hard covers so that pages would stay intact. We have not done this yet. Only a very small percentage of our readers currently study and meditate on the scriptural contents of our books enough to cause pages to fall out. We give thousands of free copies of our books to needy people in Third World countries and to inmates in prisons and jails. At this time we must publish these books in soft cover so that we can continue to give away large numbers of books.

I hope *you* will go through this book *so many times* that you also will find that pages are falling out. I want to share with you specific facts that I have learned about how to read, study and meditate on the scriptural contents of this book.

Perhaps you are just *reading* this book the first time through. Reading this book can be very beneficial because you will be exposed to marvelous scriptural facts about divine healing and increasing your faith in God. You can *study* this book by highlighting key passages of Scripture, underlining specific scriptural instructions and promises and by writing notes in the margins at the top and bottom of each page.

If you do not do these things the first time you go through this book, we urge you to *study* the scriptural contents of this book with a highlighter or a pen the second time you go through it. Please highlight or underline everything *you* would like to retain for future Scripture meditation. You are *renewing* your mind when you *study* the Word of God this way. You are obeying the instructions that we gave you explaining how to continually renew your mind in the Word of God.

Once you have highlighted or underlined the scriptural facts that are important to you and written notes at the top and bottom of several pages, you are ready to begin *meditating* on the scriptural contents of this book. If your body aches and you are very uncomfortable a constant infusion of healing Scripture will *encourage* you. If you obey God's instructions to meditate on His Word throughout the day and night you will have healing Scripture at the forefront of your consciousness at all times. You will know God more intimately. You will come into His presence.

You must understand the power of repetition. Water that drips on a rock over a long period of time eventually can wear away the rock. Your faith in God will deepen as you continually feed the supernatural healing power of God's Word into your heart. Many sick people allow sickness in their bodies to dominate their consciousness. *Your spirit will control your soul and your body* if you meditate continually on the Scripture in this book.

This chapter has given you a basic foundation pertaining to Scripture meditation on divine healing. Now that you have this basic foundation you are ready to learn exactly what you should do to meditate continually throughout the day and night on God's Word so that you will obey God's instructions regarding health and healing.

Chapter 26

How to Meditate on the Word of God

In this chapter I will give you examples of Scripture meditation on several passages of healing Scripture. You will be able to see for yourself the way that I have found is most beneficial to meditate on the Word of God. These examples will give you a sample for your own personal Scripture meditation.

This book is filled with hundreds of passages of Scripture that you can meditate on. The examples in this chapter are only a few of the passages of healing Scripture that are contained in *Receive Healing from the Lord.* This book also is filled with many additional passages of Scripture for meditation to help you increase your faith in God.

You can learn a great deal when other people teach you the Word of God. There is no question that other people can help you to get the Word of God into your mind. However, you must realize that the words that are most effective in bringing divine healing into your body are words from your *heart* that you speak with your *mouth. No one else* can meditate on the Word of God for you.

I cannot personalize the following passages of Scripture too much because I would be putting my name and myself in them. I will do this to some degree, but you should personalize *every* passage of Scripture you choose for meditation. You should look at each passage of Scripture as a promise or instruction from God *directly to you.*

When you meditate *visualize* God appearing to you personally to give you this specific promise or instruction. Release your imagination. Refuse to be bound by the limitations of traditional intellectual thinking. The Bible says that all Scripture is inspired by God (see II Timothy 3:16). Since all Scripture is inspired by God you can believe that your Father is coming personally to you in each passage of Scripture.

I do not believe that people who are seriously ill can *spend their time more profitably* than to continually meditate on the promises of God in this book pertaining to divine healing and increased faith in God. Go through this book again and again and meditate on the Scripture you have highlighted or underlined. Speak this Scripture. Put these Scripture references in the first person. Insert your name. Personalize every one of these promises and instructions from God. When you do this you are communing with God. You are in His presence talking with Him. He is the Healer.

There is no one way to meditate on Scripture. Sometimes I walk back and forth and meditate on a particular passage of Scripture. Many times I have put a specific Scripture card on the dashboard of my automobile and meditated on it as I drove from one place to another. You can put Scripture on your desk, workbench, counter or any other place you occupy during the day. If you are sick in bed you can keep Scripture with you and meditate on it continually.

You have seen that Joshua 1:8 says that God's Word should not depart from your mouth. You have seen that your Father wants you to meditate on His Word throughout the day and night. Once again, the Hebrew word "hagah" that is translated "meditate" means "to ponder, mutter, speak, study, talk and utter." If you deeply desire to receive the healing from sickness that Jesus already has provided for you, you should *say what God says* about divine healing and your absolute faith in Him throughout every day and every night.

You *release* the supernatural power of Almighty God when you continually personalize Scripture, speaking it boldly. The cumulative effect of this meditation is enormous. As this process continues over days, weeks and months the Scripture you are meditating on will rise up inside of you. This Scripture will become more and more real to you. You will become certain that you *will* receive the healing Jesus has provided for you.

You should speak with conviction and expectation when you meditate on Scripture. You can be certain that the words from God you are meditating on are the absolute truth. The words you speak should constantly show the unwavering expectancy you have that you will receive manifestation of the healing from God that already has been provided for you by Jesus Christ.

You release enormous spiritual power when you speak the Word of God with faith as you meditate on it. The cumulative effect of speaking these words from God again and again definitely will increase your faith in God. I now will list several promises from the Word of God that pertain directly to divine healing. We have covered some of the Scripture references previously. This time we will look at each of them from the perspective of Scripture meditation.

Healing Scripture "Bless (affectionately, gratefully praise) the Lord, O my soul, and forget not [one of] all His benefits – Who forgives [every one of] all your iniquities, Who heals [each one of] all your diseases" (Psalm 103:2-3).

Example of meditation: "Dear Father, I know that I will live eternally in heaven. I will not live eternally in heaven because of anything I have done. I will live in heaven because Jesus has paid the price for all of my sins. I have come to You, Father, repenting of my sins and asking You to forgive my sins. I am absolutely certain You have forgiven me.

"The Bible goes one step further. I am urged not to forget any of the benefits You have provided for me. This passage of

Scripture says that You have forgiven me of every one of my sins, but it *does not stop there*. I also am told that You, dear Father, heal *all* of my diseases.

"The word 'all' includes the sickness in my body at this time. Your Word does not leave any doubt whatsoever as to how many diseases You have provided healing for. I praise You and I thank You, dear Father. I receive by faith manifestation of the healing that Jesus already has provided for me."

Healing Scripture: "…I am the Lord Who heals you" (Exodus 15:26).

Example of meditation: "Dear Lord, I thank You that You are my Physician. I thank You that You are my Healer, Jehovah Rapha. I thank You for this wonderful promise. I receive the word 'you' as applying to me personally. Thank You so much for *healing me*, dear Lord.

"I know that You have provided healing for me through the tremendous sacrifice that You have made for *me*. Jesus, I *receive* healing from the sickness in my body because of Your wonderful sacrifice. Thank You for healing me. Thank You. Thank You. Thank You."

Healing Scripture: "…it was the will of the Lord to bruise Him; He has put Him to grief and made Him sick…" (Isaiah 53:10).

Example of meditation: "Dear Father, this passage of Scripture says that it was Your will to bruise Your beloved Son Jesus Christ. It says that You have put Jesus to grief and that You have made Him sick. Jesus, You took upon Yourself all of the sins of every person in the world by becoming sin for us. You also took upon Yourself all of the sickness in the entire world by becoming sick.

"Thank You, dear Jesus, for taking upon Yourself the sickness that I have in my body. I praise You and I thank You for the tremendous sacrifice You have made on my behalf. I receive complete manifestation of healing from the sickness in my body because You already have taken this sickness on Yourself."

Healing Scripture: "He was despised and rejected and forsaken by men, a Man of sorrows and pains, and acquainted with grief and sickness; and like One from Whom men hide their faces He was despised, and we did not appreciate His worth or have any esteem for Him. Surely He has borne our griefs (sicknesses, weaknesses, and distresses)..." (Isaiah 53:3-4).

Example of meditation: "Jesus, Isaiah prophesied about the tremendous price that You have paid for me at that whipping post. The whipping You received from the Roman soldiers was *so bad* that people hid their faces from You. You went through a horrible physical ordeal to pay the price for the sickness in my body. I thank You from the bottom of my heart, dear Jesus. I receive by faith the healing You have provided for me.

"Isaiah 53:4 says that You *surely* have borne my sicknesses. If You already bore this sickness I do not need to bear it again. I refuse to bear this sickness. I have absolute faith that You have paid the complete price for healing in my body. Thank You, dear Jesus."

Healing Scripture: "...with the stripes [that wounded] Him we are healed and made whole" (Isaiah 53:5).

Example of meditation: "Jesus, I thank You so much for doing what the prophet Isaiah prophesied You would do. Because of the stripes on Your body from the whips of the Roman soldiers I am healed and made whole. You took sickness upon Yourself. You also went through horrible physical punishment. Thank You, dear Jesus, for paying the complete price for healing my sickness."

Healing Scripture: "...He fulfilled what was spoken by the prophet Isaiah, He Himself took [in order to carry away] our weaknesses and infirmities and bore away our diseases" (Matthew 8:17).

Example of meditation: "Jesus, You did exactly what Isaiah prophesied You would do. You carried away the sickness in my body. You bore this sickness upon Yourself. Because You have carried it away and because You already bore this sickness, I do not have to bear it again. I already am healed in the spiritual realm. By faith I receive in the natural realm complete manifestation of the healing You have provided for me. Thank You. Thank You. Thank You. Thank You, dear Jesus."

Healing Scripture: "…by His wounds you have been healed" (I Peter 2:24).

Example of meditation: "Jesus, this inspired writing by the apostle Peter tells me that I *already* have been healed. The prophecy from Isaiah was in the future tense. These anointed words from Peter are in the *past tense.*

"My healing is an accomplished fact. You already have provided healing for me in the spiritual realm. I will receive manifestation of this healing in the natural realm because I believe wholeheartedly in the tremendous price You paid so that I am healed. Thank You, dear Jesus."

Healing Scripture: "…He sends forth His word and heals them…" (Psalm 107:20).

Example of meditation: "Father, the Word of God is filled with supernatural healing power. I receive the healing that Jesus has provided for me as I meditate over and over and over again on the mighty power of Your living Word. This passage of Scripture tells me that You heal me with *Your Word.*

"As I meditate on Your Word continually throughout the day and night week after week and month after month, my faith that I already have been healed grows and grows. You live inside of me, dear Healer. As I fill my eyes, my ears, my mind, my mouth and my heart continually with Your supernatural living Word, Your Word *rises up* on the inside of me. My faith for manifestation of healing grows and grows and grows. Thank You, dear Lord, for healing me."

These seven examples will give you just a brief example of what I believe Scripture meditation should be like. The examples of Scripture meditation I have given are *much briefer* than they would be if I actually spoke this meditation with my mouth. I have meditated for *more than an hour* on one passage of Scripture.

These passages of Scripture are just a few of the 464 passages of Scripture in this book pertaining to divine health, divine healing and increasing your faith in God. If you have highlighted or underlined a large number of the passages of Scripture in this book, you can go back and meditate on each of these Scripture references again and again, seeking God with all of your heart. You have been provided with a tremendous amount of Scripture for meditation throughout the day and night.

When you meditate constantly on the Word of God this process actually downloads Scripture from heaven. When you meditate on the Word of God you program yourself continually in a manner that is similar to programming a computer except that you are invoking the power of God. You never should neglect the precious opportunity you have been given to program yourself throughout every day and night with words from God that will help *you* to receive manifestation of the healing Jesus already has provided for you.

The amplification of the word "meditate" in Psalm 1:2 says that you should "ponder and study by day and night." When you ponder God's Word you think deeply about what your loving Father is saying to you. You continually fill your eyes, your ears, your mind, your heart and your mouth with specific words that come from God Himself.

The sickness that may seem so severe to you is *not* an area of concern to God. Jesus already has provided healing for cancer as well as for any minor illness. Your Father wants you to look at sickness from His perspective, not from the world's perspective. As you meditate continually on God's Word instead of thinking continually about the sickness in your body, you are focusing on your Father.

When you meditate on a promise from God you visualize this specific promise as being fulfilled in your life. If you faithfully obey your Father's instructions to meditate on His Word throughout the day and night you are constantly visualizing manifestation of healing in your body. Your mouth is opening continually to speak words of faith based on these supernatural promises from Almighty God.

As you meditate on the Word of God you change "logos" which is the written Word of God into "rhema" which is the spoken Word of God that is quickened and made alive and active. When you study the Word of God you focus entirely on logos. Logos is a spiritual seed. Your spoken words become rhema as you continually speak the Word of God while you meditate.

If you meditate continually on the Scripture in this book you soon will find that you are meditating on the same passages of Scripture. Perhaps you will have highlighted or underlined several hundred passages of Scripture. Nevertheless, if you continue to meditate over a period of time you will come back to Scripture you have previously covered.

Do *not* think that, just because you have meditated on specific passages of Scripture on faith in God and divine healing in the past, you do not need to meditate on these *same* passages of Scripture again and again and again. I can tell you from personal experience that I often have meditated on passages of Scripture that I knew by heart. I could open my mouth and speak these words from my heart. Nevertheless, the Holy Spirit often has given me *fresh new revelation* as I continued to meditate on God's supernatural living Word.

Meditating on the Word of God is a full time endeavor. This is why your Father instructs you to meditate on His Word throughout the day and night. This chapter has given you some brief illustrations of how you can meditate on God's Word. Let yourself go. Ask the Holy Spirit to anoint your mind and your words as you meditate.

Now that you have received specific instructions on Scripture meditation you are ready to learn many additional facts pertaining to this subject. I believe that the facts in the next two chapters will help *you* to partake of the healing that Jesus already has provided for you.

Chapter 27

Store Up the Word of God in Your Mind and Your Heart

You must understand the importance of meditating continually on the Word of God. Your Father has instructed you to meditate on His Word *throughout every day and night* because you must *remain strong* in your faith when you are sick or when you face other challenges. You cannot rely on Scripture you have meditated on in the past. Your Father wants you to keep a *fresh supply* of His supernatural Word going into your eyes, your ears, your mind and your heart throughout every day and night.

Christians who are sick cannot afford to allow one day to go by where they disobey God's specific instructions to meditate on His Word throughout the day and night. As this process continues over a period of time you will develop a deeply ingrained habit of meditating continually on the holy Scriptures. *Good habits are just as hard to break as bad habits.*

Your Father wants you to follow the example of the psalmist who began his daily meditation very early in the morning. He said "...I am awake before the cry of the watchman, that I may meditate on Your Word." (Psalm 119:148). The psalmist loved the Word of God so much that he meditated on God's Word throughout the day. He said "Oh, how love I Your law! It is my meditation all the day" (Psalm 119:97).

Do you "love" the Word of God so much that "it is *your meditation* all the day?" Do you love the Word of God so much that you cannot get enough of it? Do you find that you have an insatiable hunger for the supernatural living Word of God?

You have learned that the Word of God is the spiritual medicine the Great Physician has provided for you. If a doctor gives you a prescription you are instructed to take this prescription at prescribed times throughout each day and night. The Great Physician also has given you a prescription. He has instructed you to begin meditating on the medicine of His Word early in the morning and to continue partaking of His magnificent medicine throughout every day and night.

You should have this healing Scripture at the forefront of your consciousness so that it will be working inside of you while you sleep. As you speak God's healing promises and personalize them while you are meditating on them, the seeds of these promises will be planted in your mind and in your heart to work on your behalf throughout the night. You should follow the example of the psalmist David who said "...I remember You upon my bed and meditate on You in the night watches" (Psalm 63:6).

Some people who are sick often are awake during the night. I can tell you from personal experience that I have spent many hours when I was awake during the night filling my eyes, my ears, my mind, my heart and my mouth with the supernatural living Word of God. If you cannot sleep you should make the most constructive use you can of this time. The psalmist said, "I will meditate on Your precepts and have respect to Your ways [the paths of life marked out by Your law]. I will delight myself in Your statutes; I will not forget Your word" (Psalm 119:15-16)

The psalmist meditated on the Word of God to imprint God's instructions in his heart. He had a deep desire to follow "the paths of life marked out" by the Word of God. The psalmist "delighted himself" in God's Word. He meditated on the Word of God continually so that he "would not forget" God's Word.

Your Father does not want you to give in to the sickness in your body. *You must not give up hope.* You should follow the example of the psalmist who explained the encouragement he received from meditating on God's Word. He said, "My hands also will I lift up [in fervent supplication] to Your commandments, which I love, and I will meditate on Your statutes. Remember [fervently] the word and promise to Your servant, in which You have caused me to hope. This is my comfort and consolation in my affliction: that Your word has revived me and given me life" (Psalm 119:48-50).

The psalmist was so enthusiastic about God's Word that he "lifted up" his hands toward heaven "in fervent supplication" because he loved the Word of God so much. He "fervently re-membered" God's promises to him. He received "hope, comfort and consolation" from God's Word that "revived him and gave him life."

Your Father will provide these same wonderful blessings for *you* if you will meditate continually on healing Scripture and Scrip-ture explaining how to increase your faith in Him. Hope will rise up inside of you when you fervently meditate on God's super-natural Word. You will receive comfort and consolation from your Father. God's Word will revive you and give you life.

When God created you He gave you your eyes and your ears as the gateways to your mind and your heart. You should guard these precious gateways at all times (see Proverbs 4:20-23). You will not allow the sickness in your body to pull you down *if* you *constantly* fill your eyes and your ears with the mighty power of the supernatural living Word of God.

You will be able to tap into God's supernatural power if you continually fill your eyes and your ears with His Word. Have you had the experience of hearing a song and being unable to get this song out of your mind for several hours? Your Father wants His Word to be like this throughout every day and night of your life. You will receive significant revelation from the Holy Spirit if you meditate consistently on the Word of God. Your eyes, your ears, your heart, your mind and your mouth will be *so full* of God's Word that it will dominate every aspect of your life.

You saw in the fourth chapter of Proverbs that your Father does not want you to allow His Word to depart from your eyes. God, speaking through the anointed words of King Solomon, gave you similar information when He said, "My hands also will I lift up [in fervent supplication] to Your commandments, which I love, and I will meditate on Your statutes. Remember [fervently] the word and promise to Your servant, in which You have caused me to hope. This is my comfort and consolation in my affliction: that Your word has revived me and given me life. My son, let them not escape from your sight, but keep sound and godly Wisdom and discretion, and they will be life to your inner self, and a gracious ornament to your neck (your outer self)" (Proverbs 3: 21-22).

You must *not* allow the Word of God to "escape from your sight." You should pour the supernatural medicine of God's Word into your eyes and your ears continually. If you obey these instructions the Word of God will come alive deep down in your heart. The precious holy Scriptures will be "life to your inner self."

Every aspect of your life should revolve around your mind and your heart being filled continually with the supernatural power of the living Word of God. You will focus on God's promises and instructions continually if your eyes and your ears are constantly being filled with God's Word. You will be encouraged if you saturate yourself in the Word of God.

There is *only one thing* in this world that comes from God that you can make contact with through your senses. You can *see* God's Word with your eyes. You can *hear* the Word of God with your ears. Jesus said, "The eye is the lamp of the body. So if your eye is sound, your entire body will be full of light. But if your eye is unsound, your whole body will be full of darkness…" (Matthew 6:22-23).

Your eyes are the "lamp of your body." "Your entire body will be full of light" if you continually fill your eyes with the Word of God. The "darkness" of sickness ultimately will be forced out of your body.

You determine whether you will allow your eyes to be filled with the light of God or the darkness of Satan. Satan wants to get into your eyes and your ears with anxious and foreboding thoughts pertaining to the pain and discomfort in your body. Jesus wants you to resist these thoughts (see James 4:7 and II Corinthians 10:5). Continual infusion of thoughts from Satan's demons will cause you to walk in Satan's darkness. Continual infusion of thoughts from God's supernatural Word will cause you to walk in God's light.

Christians who are sick should constantly fight a battle between the pain and discomfort in their bodies and encouragement from the supernatural living Word of God. Your Father wants you to win this battle. He instructs you to continually store up His Word in your mind and your heart.

Many people store up money and other financial assets in an attempt to give themselves security. Your Father wants you to store up His Word in your mind and your heart so that you will have the spiritual sustenance you must have to resist the pain and discomfort in your body. "…you shall lay up these My words in your [minds and] hearts and in your [entire] being" (Deuteronomy 11:18).

Please highlight or underline the words "lay up." There is no question that your loving Father wants you to continually store up His Word in your mind and in your heart. Your Father wants His supernatural living Word to pervade your innermost self.

You will be able to reach deep down inside of yourself to draw upon the supernatural power of God's living Word. When pain and discomfort from sickness threaten to overcome you, you must encourage yourself with the Word of God. "Receive, I pray you, the law and instruction from His mouth and lay up His words in your heart. If you return to the Almighty [and submit and humble yourself before Him], you will be built up..." (Job 22:22-23).

Please highlight or underline the words "lay up" in this passage of Scripture. Your loving Father repeatedly emphasizes that He wants you to constantly store up His Word in your mind and your heart. When you constantly "receive instruction" from God you will "submit" to God and "humble yourself" before God. Your faith in God will be "built up" continually if you faithfully obey these instructions from God.

Your Father wants you to learn everything you possibly can about the instructions and promises in His Word pertaining to divine healing. He repeatedly instructs you to store up His Word in your mind and your heart. "My son, keep my words; lay up within you my commandments [for use when needed] and treasure them" (Proverbs 7:1)

These instructions that King Solomon gave to his son also are God's instructions to *you* today. God emphasizes through repetition. Please highlight or underline the words "lay up." Your Father definitely wants you to "lay up" His Word deep down inside of yourself. Are you doing this? The amplification of this passage of Scripture says that you should have God's Word living inside of you "for use when needed." The Word of God is a marvelous spiritual "treasure." "Wise men store up knowledge [in mind and heart]..." (Proverbs 10:14)

Please highlight or underline the words "store up" in this passage of Scripture. You have just seen four specific instructions from your Father telling you to "lay up" or "store up" His Word in your mind and your heart. *Can there be any doubt* that your loving Father wants *you* to constantly fill your mind and your heart with the mighty power of His supernatural living Word?

You saw in Joshua 1:8 that you will "deal wisely" if you meditate continually on God's Word. Proverbs 10:14 confirms this great spiritual truth by saying that "wise men store up knowledge." Do you want to receive wisdom from God regarding the sickness in your body? If you do you should continually store up God's supernatural Word in your mind and your heart.

Your Father has not placed any limit on the amount of His living Word that you can store up in your mind and your heart. *There is no limit except any limit you set.* If you are very sick you should be *determined* to constantly fill *your* mind and *your* heart with the mighty healing power of the Word of God.

When pain and discomfort threaten to dominate your thoughts and your emotions you must have something to offset this pain and discomfort. The "something" you must have is an abundance of the Word of God living in your mind and your heart. If you are struggling with your health, you *must* have an ample supply of God's Word living in your mind and your heart so that you will be able to reach deep down inside of yourself to receive powerful spiritual sustenance.

Your mind and your heart are spiritual reservoirs. Your Father has made it possible for you to be able to fill your mind and your heart with a tremendous amount of Scripture. Have you *ever* heard any Christian say that he or she had *too much* of the Word of God inside of himself or herself? You *cannot* have too much of God's Word in your mind and in your heart. "The strong spirit of a man sustains him in bodily pain or trouble, but a weak and broken spirit who can raise up or bear?" (Proverbs 18:14).

In this chapter we have been talking about "bodily pain." *How* do you "sustain" yourself when the pain and discomfort in your body threaten to overcome you? You do this with a "strong spirit" – a heart that is filled with an abundance of God's supernatural Word.

Does your body ache with pain? Does the discomfort seem to be more than you can bear? *You can be assured that your loving Father has made provision for you to sustain yourself* through this discomfort one day at a time. Your loving Father has made provision for you to be able to strengthen yourself spiritually throughout every day and night. From early in the morning throughout the day and evening hours He wants *you* to be *en-*

couraged because you are faithfully *obeying* His instructions to meditate on His supernatural Word throughout the day and night.

Chapter 28

Increase Your Faith for Divine Healing

You must do much more than just pay mental assent to the Word of God. You must learn how to *continually* move God's Word from your mind down into your *heart*. You must believe totally, completely and absolutely in Jesus Christ Who is your Healer. You must constantly replenish your faith that your Father will give you manifestation of the healing that Jesus already has provided for you.

Severe illness can drain you physically, mentally and emotionally. Many sick people become extremely discouraged. Instead of giving in to discouragement your Father wants you to pour constant encouragement into your heart. Discouragement means lack of courage. Encouragement means receiving courage. "…whatever was thus written in former days was written for our instruction, that by [our steadfast and patient] endurance and the encouragement [drawn] from the Scriptures you might hold fast to and cherish hope" (Romans 15:4)

Your loving Father made provision in His Word many years ago "in former days" to give you the scriptural "instruction" you must have when you face adversity, including sickness. He has made provision for the "steadfast and patient endurance" you will need if you are very sick. He has given you exactly what you need to encourage yourself *today*. This passage of Scripture says that you *can* "hold fast to and cherish hope" because of "the encouragement drawn from the Scriptures."

Your Father does not want the pain and discomfort of sickness to cause you to give up. He wants you to endure steadfastly and patiently. He wants you to be so encouraged because your mind and your heart are filled with His Word that you will *not* allow discouragement to overcome you.

You *will* build yourself up spiritually if you meditate continually on the Word of God throughout every day and night over a period of weeks and months. You *will* receive the blessings that the apostle Paul told the elders of the church at Ephesus about when he said, "...I commend you to the Word of His grace [to the commands and counsels and promises of His unmerited favor]. It is able to build you up and to give you [your rightful] inheritance among all God's set-apart ones (those consecrated, purified, and transformed of soul)" (Acts 20:32)

You are able to receive the supernatural, mighty and powerful living Word of God only because of your Father's grace. You did not earn the Word of God. You do not deserve the Word of God. You are able to receive the magnificent instructions and promises in the Word of God because of the "unmerited favor" that has been given to you by God.

You will make a big mistake if you do not fully avail yourself of the mighty power of God's supernatural living Word. Please highlight or underline the words "build you up" in this passage of Scripture. Personalize this promise. Highlight or underline the word "you." Know that your loving Father has made complete provision for *you* to steadily increase your faith that He will give you manifestation of healing in your body. You can receive your "rightful inheritance" of divine healing. The amplification of this passage of Scripture says that you can be "consecrated, purified and transformed of soul."

Every aspect of your life should revolve around the Lord Jesus Christ Who paid such an enormous price for your salvation and your healing. "Have the roots [of your being] firmly and deeply planted [in Him, fixed and founded in Him], being continually built up in Him, becoming increasingly more confirmed and established in the faith… " (Colossians 2:7).

This passage of Scripture also uses the words "built up." If "the roots of your being" are "firmly and deeply planted" in Jesus Christ, your faith for manifestation of healing from the sickness in your body will be "fixed and founded in Him." Your faith in Jesus will be "continually built up." You will become "increasingly more confirmed and established in your faith" so that you will understand that God is love and that He is Healing and Health.

Jesus Christ and the Word of God are the same. When you continually fill your mind and your heart with the Word of God you continually fill your mind and your heart with Jesus Christ Who is your Healer. "In the beginning [before all time] was the Word (Christ), and the Word was with God, and the Word was God Himself" (John 1:1).

There is no question that the Word of God is "God Himself." As you meditate continually on the Word of God your faith in Jesus will increase because "…the title by which He is called is the Word of God" (Revelation 19:13).

Notice the consistency of your Father's instructions to you in each of the areas you have been studying. Your Father does *not* just give you instruction in *one* passage of Scripture. He *emphasizes* what He wants you to do through continual repetition.

The effect of filling your mind and your heart with the Word of God is cumulative. Meditating on God's Word for a few days or a few weeks may not produce appreciable results. However, *continuing* this meditation indefinitely for as long as your Father requires you to continue definitely *will* produce specific results.

If you want to keep your faith in God strong, your eyes and your ears should be filled with God's Word day after day, week after week, month after month and year after year. Your faith in God can only remain strong when a *continual flow* of God's Word *pours into* your eyes and your ears on a daily basis. Faith in God is cumulative. You must not back off in the slightest from your determination to meditate on the living Word of God throughout every day and night of your life.

You will grow in your understanding of the healing nature of God as you continually study and meditate on His Word. Every book in the Bible reveals the coming and the victory of the Messiah, the Lord Jesus Christ. As you continually study and meditate Jesus will become more and more real to you. Jesus said, "...These [very Scriptures] testify about Me" (John 5:39).

You *will* know Jesus much more intimately if you consistently meditate on the holy Scriptures. Jesus will come alive to you as you saturate yourself in His holy Word. As you meditate continually on the Word of God you will draw closer to Jesus Who makes His home in *your* heart (see Galatians 2:20).

Jesus wants you to partake of the privilege you have been given to meditate on His Word. When you ask Jesus to be your Savior you are given the opportunity to partake of the blessings of God. Continual meditation *unlocks* the Word of God. Jesus said, "...To you it has been given to know the secrets and mysteries of the kingdom of heaven, but to them it has not been given. For whoever has [spiritual knowledge], to him will more be given and he will be furnished richly so that he will have abundance; but from him who has not, even what he has will be taken away" (Matthew 13:11-12).

All Christians should avail themselves of the opportunity to learn more and more about "the secrets and mysteries of the kingdom of heaven." Unbelievers have "not been given" this privilege, but *you* have been given this privilege if you are a Christian. *Are you* taking full advantage of this magnificent privilege?

Your spiritual knowledge and understanding will increase as you continually meditate on God's supernatural Word. Jesus said, "For whoever has spiritual knowledge, to him will more be given." Your faith in God will be "furnished richly so that you will have abundance." If your faith in God is not constantly increasing, it will decrease because Jesus said, "…even what he has will be taken away."

You should meditate often on passages of Scripture you have meditated on previously. If you do not keep these passages of Scripture at the forefront of your consciousness they can easily depart from you. "…we ought to pay much closer attention than ever to the truths that we have heard, lest in any way we drift past [them] and slip away" (Hebrews 2:1).

You should pay "much closer attention to the truths that you have heard." You *cannot get too much* of the Word of God. You must not "drift past" the great spiritual truths your Father wants you to learn. You must not allow these magnificent truths to "slip away."

I believe that constant meditation on the Word of God can be compared to putting a plug into an electrical socket. The plug connects the room you are in with the power of electricity. Continual meditation on the holy Word of God *plugs you into the kingdom of heaven*. You are in the realm of the Spirit.

As you faithfully obey your Father's instructions to meditate continually on His Word, the Holy Spirit will honor your obedience by giving you increased revelation on the Scripture you are meditating on. The Word of God is vastly different from books written by human beings. The Holy Spirit can and will illuminate the holy Scriptures and cause them to come alive in a fresh and new way, no matter how many times you have meditated on the same passage of Scripture.

Each time you meditate on healing Scripture you are incrementally increasing your faith in God. You will grow in your understanding of God's healing nature. The more you meditate on the Word of God, the more revelation you will receive from the Holy Spirit. The psalmist said, "…the meditation of my heart shall be understanding" (Psalm 49:3).

Do you want to understand more and more of God's Word? The psalmist said that he received "understanding" from the "meditation of his heart." As you meditate continually on the Word of God you will draw back the spiritual veil that may have blocked you from understanding the Holy Spirit's revelation pertaining to the healing that has been provided for you.

Can you say that you *love* the Word of God? You should be like the psalmist who said, "Oh, how love I Your law! It is my meditation all the day. You, through Your commandments, make me wiser than my enemies, for [Your words] are ever before me. I have better understanding and deeper insight than all my teachers, because Your testimonies are my meditation" (Psalm 119:97-99).

You have seen previously that the psalmist loved the Word of God. He meditated on God's Word "all the day." He received "better understanding and deeper insight" than his teachers had because the Word of God was "ever before him." You *must understand* the vital importance of saturating yourself in the Word of God.

If you truly love the Word of God you will *not* begrudge the time you spend meditating on the holy Scriptures. As you faithfully meditate on God's Word I believe that you will receive the continual revelation from the Holy Spirit that you often are required to have to receive manifestation of healing in your body. "The entrance and unfolding of Your words give light; their unfolding gives understanding (discernment and comprehension) to the simple" (Psalm 119:130).

When you continually meditate on God's Word it "enters" into your heart. It "unfolds" inside of you. This process is very similar to a "light" being turned on in a dark room. This continual unfolding gives you constantly increasing "understanding, discernment and comprehension."

Your Father wants you to be humble and teachable (see I Peter 5:5-6). You should yearn to understand healing more and more from God's perspective. You should have a deep desire to turn away from human logic and intellectual understanding to comprehend healing (or any other subject you are meditating on) from God's perspective.

As the Word of God fills your heart you will be able to understand divine concepts that you could not possibly understand without this continual meditation. You will be able to turn away from the darkness of Satan to come more and more into God's light. God's Word cannot unfold when it is outside of you. God's Word can only unfold when it is inside of you.

You *will* experience a tremendous spiritual breakthrough if you will continue to meditate on the Scripture in this book. You will come to the point where your understanding of healing will cause you to be absolutely certain deep down inside of yourself that you have been healed. The scriptural promises that were in your mind will have dropped down into your heart and taken root. Your faith in God will increase significantly. Your faith in God will increase even more as you continue this meditation.

You may be very learned and capable in the natural realm, but this natural knowledge *does not mean anything* in the spiritual realm. As you humbly realize your spiritual ignorance and you begin to comprehend how much you need to learn about divine healing, you will gladly meditate on God's Word continually. "...receive my words and treasure up my commandments within you, making your ear attentive to skillful and godly Wisdom and inclining and directing your heart and mind to understanding [applying all your powers to the quest for it]" (Proverbs 2:1-2)

You are instructed to "receive" God's Word and to "treasure up" God's Word within yourself. You will be "attentive to skillful and godly Wisdom" if you continually fill your heart with God's Word. You will "incline and direct your heart to understanding." You should have a constant "quest" to learn more from God.

Many Christians who are seriously ill who have never before obeyed God's instructions to meditate on His Word throughout the day and night will find that their perspective changes *completely*. Christians who are fighting for their lives will be *highly motivated* to be obedient to God.

Christians who are seriously ill will find that everything else fades into insignificance. Things that used to be very important to them when they were healthy are no longer a priority. Christians who are extremely ill are not spending forty or fifty hours a week on their vocation. They probably are not spending large amounts of time on the other things they were preoccupied with before they became extremely sick. These Christians have large amounts of discretionary time to spend immersing themselves in the Word of God. Christians who are very sick have all day and all night throughout every day and night of their lives to focus on God and His Word.

Christians who are very sick *need to* abide in a constant atmosphere of healing. Your consciousness should be pervaded with scriptural concepts pertaining to divine healing throughout every day and night of your life. I believe the continual healing consciousness you should have if you are very sick can be compared to previous events in your life.

Think back to the last time you purchased an automobile. Did you read automobile advertisements in the newspapers daily? Were you especially conscious during that period of time of different kinds of automobiles and the price of these automobiles?

The same principle applies to buying a home. I had a constant consciousness pertaining to real estate before we bought our present home. I thought about homes many times during a period of several months. I read the real estate advertisements regularly. I visited several open houses.

The focus on automobiles and real estate that you may have had at certain times in the past *cannot even remotely compare* with the focus you should have on divine healing. Many people who have been Christians for a long time have had many years to learn what the Word of God says about divine health and divine healing.

You have two openings in your ears and two openings in your eyes. Christians who are extremely sick should *flood* these four openings with healing Scripture and Scripture on increasing their faith in God.

Christians who are very sick should not focus on anything except the Lord. You must take your attention off the sickness in your body and keep your eyes on the Lord at all times. You should be like the psalmist who said, "My eyes are ever toward the Lord…" (Psalm 25:15).

Jesus Christ lives in your heart (see Galatians 2:20). You should focus on the indwelling presence of your Healer through-out every hour of every day and night in your life. "I saw the Lord constantly before me, for He is at my right hand that I may not be shaken or overthrown or cast down [from my secure and happy state]" (Acts 2:25).

If you "see the Lord constantly before you," you will be close to Him. You will "not be shaken" by the sickness in your body. You will not be "overthrown" by the severity of this sickness.

Now that you have learned all of these scriptural facts about getting the Word of God up off the printed pages of the Bible into your mind and then down into your heart, you are ready to take the next step. We will look carefully into the Word of God to learn *facts* from God about the enormous healing power that is contained in the words that continually flow out of your mouth.

Chapter 29

Divine Healing and the Words You Speak

In the next two chapters we will look into the Word of God to learn some interesting scriptural facts about the relationship between the words you speak and receiving healing from God. You have seen that Joshua 1:8 says, "This Book of the Law shall *not* depart out of your *mouth*..." You also saw in Proverbs 4:21 where God told you that His Word should *not* depart from your *sight*. Your Father wants your *eyes* to focus on His Word throughout every day and night. He wants His Word to pour out of your *mouth* throughout every day and night.

You soon will see that a definite relationship exists between the words you speak and receiving healing from God. How can you control the words you speak if you are very sick and do not feel well? The Bible says that you *cannot* control your tongue through sheer willpower. "...the human tongue can be tamed by no man. It is a restless (undisciplined, irreconcilable) evil, full of deadly poison" (James 3:8).

When this passage of Scripture says that "the human tongue can be tamed by no man" the words "no man" include you. Since you cannot direct your tongue through your own volition you must learn *how* God instructs you to direct the words you speak. Satan wants your tongue to be controlled by the pain and discomfort in your body. Your Father wants your tongue to be controlled by the Holy Spirit and by His Word that lives in your heart.

Jesus explained the *only* way to control your tongue when your body aches with pain. He said, "...out of the fullness (the overflow, the superabundance) of the heart the mouth speaks. The good man from his inner good treasure flings forth good things, and the evil man out of his inner evil storehouse flings forth evil things" (Matthew 12:34-35).

This passage of Scripture applies to every area of your life. Since we are talking about healing we will look at these words from the perspective of divine healing. If your body aches with pain and discomfort, you can only speak what the Bible says about healing from sickness in your body out of the "fullness of your heart." You have seen that your Father wants you to meditate on His Word continually throughout every day and night. If you faithfully obey God's instructions to meditate on His Word throughout the day and night, your *heart* will be filled to overflowing with "inner good treasure."

Whenever you face severe problems with your health or anything else you always will speak words that are based on *whatever you truly believe* deep down in your heart. If your heart is filled with the Word of God, you will worship Him and thank Him for the healing He has provided for you. You will know that Jesus is your Healer. You will rest in Him.

Christians who have *not* paid the price of continually filling their minds and their hearts with the Word of God inevitably will find themselves speaking words pertaining to the pain and discomfort in their bodies and their anxiety about what the future holds. Their mouths will be controlled by the symptoms of sickness in their bodies instead of being controlled by the Holy Spirit and the supernatural living Word of God.

The amplification in this passage of Scripture says that your mouth will speak based on the "overflow" and "superabundance" of your heart. Meditating continually on God's Word day after day, week after week and month after month will fill your heart to overflowing with the supernatural living Word of God. You absolutely cannot allow symptoms of sickness to control the words you speak. "…he who has My word, let him speak My word faithfully…" (Jeremiah 23:28).

You will "speak God's Word faithfully" if your heart is filled to overflowing with the Word of God. The psalmist said, "I believed (trusted in, relied on, and clung to my God), and therefore have I spoken [even when I said], I am greatly afflicted" (Psalm 116:10).

This passage of Scripture shows the relationship between "believing in God, trusting in God, relying on God and clinging to God" and the words you *speak*. The psalmist spoke these words of faith when he was "greatly afflicted." We are not told that the psalmist's affliction was caused by sickness, but this scriptural principle *does* apply when you are sick.

The apostle Paul emphasized the same principle many years later. Paul quoted the psalmist when he said, "…we have the same spirit of faith as he had who wrote, I have believed, and therefore have I spoken. We too believe, and therefore we speak" (II Corinthians 4:13)

Both Psalm 116:10 and II Corinthians 4:13 explain the relationship between your faith in God and the words you speak. When your body aches with pain *you* can have the "same spirit of faith" that the psalmist had and the apostle Paul had. *If* you continually fill your heart with God's Word "You too will believe and therefore you will speak." Jesus repeated this principle in a passage of Scripture we have looked at before when He said that whoever "…does not doubt at all in his heart but believes that what he says will take place, it will be done for him" (Mark 11:23).

You will *not* doubt in your heart *if* you have faithfully obeyed your Father's instructions to meditate on His Word continually throughout the day and night. Your heart will be so filled with God's Word that you will spontaneously open your mouth to speak words of faith regarding healing, regardless of the symptoms of sickness in your body. God's power will permeate every cell in your body.

If you are sick you should focus on two parts of your body every day of your life – your heart and your mouth. Is *your heart* filled to overflowing with the Word of God pertaining to divine healing, divine health and increased faith in God? Does this abundance from your heart continually pour out of *your mouth*? When you are sick you should open your mouth continually throughout the day and night to boldly and confidently *say what God says*. You should say that you *are* healed even if you do not feel healed or look healed.

You cannot afford to allow the symptoms in your body to control the words you speak. Your words should be controlled entirely by the abundance of God's Word living in your heart, no matter what you look like or how you feel. God says that you were healed, so you are healed.

God created the earth and everything and everyone on this earth by *speaking words*. If you are not familiar with these facts from the first chapter in the Bible, please turn to the first chapter of Genesis to see for yourself how many times it says "God said" and "God called."

Your Father wants you to continually open your mouth to speak Scripture that pertains to the healing Jesus has provided for you. Your Father wants you to "follow His example" and do the same thing with your mouth that He did when He spoke things into existence. "…Be imitators of God [copy Him and follow His example], as well-beloved children [imitate their father]." (Ephesians 5:1)

Some Christians have a difficult time saying they are healed when symptoms of sickness are still present in their bodies. They feel like they are lying. The Word of God instructs you to *say what you believe*. If you follow your Father's specific instructions, you will *not* feel that you are lying when you speak these words even though symptoms of sickness may be very prevalent in your body. You must speak in the realm of the Spirit and expect the natural realm to agree with the realm of the Spirit. "He who guards his mouth keeps his life, but he who opens wide his lips comes to ruin." (Proverbs 13:3).

If you are sick you *must* understand the importance of "guarding your mouth" if you want to "keep your life." The words that you consistently speak when you are sick often will determine whether you will die prematurely or whether you will live. "Death and life are in the power of the tongue…" (Proverbs 18:21)

This passage of Scripture definitely shows you that the words you consistently speak *can mean the difference between life and death*. Christians who are sick must understand the "power of the tongue." Many Christians do not even begin to comprehend the enormous power of the words they speak.

In addition to speaking words of faith you must understand that other words you speak also can have a great influence on whether or not you will receive manifestation of healing. A definite relationship exists between loving, forgiving and receiving healing from sickness. You must not speak harsh words to other people. "A gentle tongue [with its healing power] is a tree of life, but willful contrariness in it breaks down the spirit" (Proverbs 15:4).

The amplification of this passage of Scripture shows you the relationship between "a gentle tongue" and the "healing power" of your tongue. If you are "contrary" and consistently speak words that do not line up with God's Word, your words will "break down your spirit." "Pleasant words are as a honeycomb, sweet to the mind and healing to the body" (Proverbs 16:24).

See how the Word of God connects "pleasant words" and "healing to the body." There is no question that the words you speak to others and about others have a definite relationship to your body's sickness and wellness. "The words of a whisperer or talebearer are as dainty morsels; they go down into the innermost parts of the body" (Proverbs 18:8).

This passage of Scripture refers to gossip. Sometimes people hear "dainty morsels" about another person and they cannot wait to "whisper" these "dainty morsels" to others. If you consistently make this mistake the consequences will "go down into the innermost parts of your body." People who constantly gossip and are critical of others can bring sickness upon themselves or fail to receive healing from the sickness they already have.

The chapter is filled with very interesting scriptural facts about the words you speak and receiving healing from sickness. In the next chapter we will study this subject in more detail. We will carefully study passages of Scripture that will give you additional valuable information on the relationship between the words you speak and placing yourself in God's healing presence.

Chapter 30

Speak to the Sickness in Your Body

You have learned that Jesus Christ has given you authority over the sickness in your body because of the price He paid on the cross at Calvary and at the whipping post. We now will return to Mark 11:23. This time we will look at this passage of Scripture from the perspective of the *spiritual power of the words you speak*. Jesus told you exactly what you should do to the sickness in your body when He said, "...whoever says to this mountain, Be lifted up and thrown into the sea! and does not doubt at all in his heart but believes that what he says will take place, it will be done for him." (Mark 11:23).

Sickness is a "mountain" in the lives of people who are very sick. Please highlight or underline the two times the word "says" is used in this passage of Scripture. Jesus told you to *speak* to the mountains in your life with *absolute faith* that they *will* be removed. You should speak continually to the sickness in your body in the name of Jesus Christ and tell it to be gone. When you speak to this sickness you must "*not* doubt at all in your heart." You must "believe that what you say *will* take place."

These positive, faith-filled words are vitally important to all Christians who are sick. An example of speaking to the sickness in your body could be to say something like the following: "I *know* that I will live eternally in heaven because Jesus Christ paid the full price on the cross at Calvary for all of my sins. I *know* that

I have received healing in my body because Jesus paid the full price at the whipping post for my healing. Sickness, you are in my body where the Holy Spirit lives. You are *not* welcome there. You will not continue to exist in my body. *Get out. Go away*, sickness. I *command you* to leave in the mighty and supernatural power of the name of the Lord Jesus Christ."

If you have cancer, diabetes or any other specific disease, speak directly to that particular disease instead of just speaking generally to sickness. Many Christians fail to utilize the authority they have been given to *speak* to sickness. Jesus has given *you* the power and authority to remove sickness from your body with your mouth. You may have to speak to the sickness in your body day after day, week after week and month after month. The cumulative spiritual power of the bold faith-filled words you speak to this sickness is enormous.

If the symptoms of sickness become worse and the pain is severe you should open your mouth and speak healing Scripture again and again and again. You fight spiritual battles with *your mouth*, not with your fists, knives or guns. When the going is tough you must continually *say what God says* about divine healing. You must not back down. "…let us seize and hold fast and retain without wavering the hope we cherish and confess and our acknowledgement of it, for He Who promised is reliable (sure) and faithful to His word" (Hebrews 10:23).

All of your hope should be anchored on Jesus. You can depend on Him completely. Do not give up hope. Do not allow your faith in Him to waver. You should "seize and *hold fast* and retain *without wavering* the hope you cherish and confess and your acknowledgement of it." God always does what He says He will do. Your loving Father "is reliable and sure and faithful to His Word."

You must not sabotage the healing Jesus has given you by what you really believe deep down in your heart and by the words that come out of your mouth. This book is filled with powerful supernatural healing Scripture. The words that you speak *will* make a difference if you continually meditate on the Word of God pertaining to healing and increasing your faith in God. "There are those who speak rashly, like the piercing of the sword, but the tongue of the wise brings healing" (Proverbs 12:18).

People who "speak rashly" hurt other people with their words. Harsh words can be as detrimental in the spiritual realm as a "sword" is in the natural realm. You actually are *hurting yourself* if you speak this way to other people. When this passage of Scripture speaks of "the tongue of the wise" it refers to words that come out of your heart being filled with the Word of God. These words *will* "bring healing" into your body.

Healing Scripture should pour out of your mouth throughout every day and every night. Romans 10:17 says that faith comes from *hearing* the Word of God. As you meditate continually on the Word of God *your ears* will hear *your mouth* constantly speaking words of faith. You are creating an atmosphere of healing and health.

The more you confess the Word of God, the more real it will become to you. The Word of God will settle and put down roots in your heart. You must understand the vital importance of continually increasing your faith for healing by boldly speaking God's Word throughout every day and night of your life.

You should be *excited* about healing Scripture. This book is filled with promises from God telling you that healing already has been provided for you by Jesus Christ. Sickness has no place in your life. Hold fast to what you know to be the truth. Speak God's Word continually. Persevere in faith for as long as your Father requires you to persevere. You must fight the good fight of faith. You fight the good fight of faith when you say what God says with absolute faith, regardless of the symptoms of sickness in your body.

The Word of God tells you again and again that you will receive what you believe you will receive. You should follow the example of Abraham. God said that Abraham "...speaks of the nonexistent things that [He has foretold and promised] as if they [already] existed" (Romans 4:17).

Abraham believed wholeheartedly that God does exactly what He says He will do. You should follow his example with the sickness in your body. You should "speak of the nonexistent things that God has promised you as if they already existed." You should speak continually of the healing that God has promised you just as you would speak if you already had received this healing. You should see yourself more and more from God's point of view.

You do *not* need to feel healed to say that you are healed. Faith says what the Word of God says regardless of external circumstances. Your Father wants you to continually confess that you are healed regardless of the symptoms of sickness in your body.

Are you sick? What kind of words does God hear coming out of your mouth day after day, week after week and month after month? Does He continually hear words complaining about the symptoms of sickness in your body and the pain and discomfort as a result of this sickness? Does God continually hear words of faith pouring out of your mouth?

Christians who are *sense oriented* confess how they *feel*. Christians who are *Word of God oriented* confess what *God's Word says* regardless of how they feel. There is *no* place in the Word of God where you are instructed to talk about the sickness in your body. You should do what your Father has instructed you to do. You should speak continually of the healing He has provided for you through His beloved Son Jesus Christ.

You cannot expect to live a long and healthy life if you continually speak death. You must speak life. You have seen that the Word of God is alive and filled with the power of God (see Hebrews 4:12). You must not block God by talking about sickness. The more you talk about sickness, the more power you give to sickness. The easiest thing to do is to talk about the pain and discomfort in your body. The most difficult thing to do is to speak the Word of God instead, boldly proclaiming that you have been healed.

Some people talk about the sickness in their bodies because they want to receive sympathy from other people. *The price of sympathy is much too great.* Receiving a few words of sympathy from other people and blocking God from healing you is *not* what the Word of God instructs you to do.

Tell other people that you have been healed by the stripes of Jesus Christ. If your faith is not yet strong enough to speak this way, you should do the next best thing and say *nothing.* If you feel so badly that you do not feel you can speak the Word of God boldly at any given moment, you should close your mouth and say nothing. You are much better off saying nothing than to speak negative words about the sickness in your body.

When you speak this way you will be speaking the way your Father wants you to speak. You know very well that you have symptoms of sickness in your body. You are not denying this fact. You are choosing to look at your health from God's perspective. You are choosing to rest in His healing power and nature. The cumulative words that you speak over a period of years determine what will happen in your marriage, in your family, in your finances, in your ministry and in every other area of your life.

I often go to God and ask Him for forgiveness when I realize I have spoken words that do not line up with His Word. Your Father *will* forgive you whenever you confess your sins and repent of these sins. "If we [freely] admit that we have sinned and confess our sins, He is faithful and just (true to His own nature and promises) and will forgive our sins [dismiss our lawlessness] and [continuously] cleanse us from all unrighteousness [everything not in conformity to His will in purpose, thought, and action]" (I John 1:9).

If you speak negative words about the sickness in your body that you later realize you should not have spoken, you should go to God and "freely admit that you have sinned." You should "confess your sins." You should repent of what you have said.

Your Father is "faithful and just." He "will forgive your sin." He will "cleanse you from all unrighteousness." You are an imperfect human being. You will make mistakes with the words you speak. Your Father will give you a fresh start if you admit your sin and ask for forgiveness. He is willing to forgive and forget these words and treat them as if they were never spoken.

I have spoken briefly of the power of the name of Jesus Christ. In the next chapter we will look into the holy Scriptures to learn *tremendous facts* about the magnificent power of opening your mouth continually to speak the mighty and awesome name of the Lord Jesus Christ.

Chapter 31

The Healing Power of the Name of the Lord

In these chapters we will study some Scripture from the Old Testament that refers to the name of the Lord instead of the name of Jesus Christ because Jesus had not yet come to earth. The New Testament refers continually to the name of Jesus Christ instead of using the Old Testament wording of the name of the Lord.

We will begin this chapter by learning exactly what the name "Jesus" means and exactly what the name "Christ" means. The name of Jesus Christ was not a name that Joseph and Mary chose. An angel came to Joseph to tell him about Mary being pregnant from the Holy Spirit. The angel also told Joseph that they should name their new son Jesus. "…an angel of the Lord appeared to him in a dream, saying, Joseph, descendant of David, do not be afraid to take Mary [as] your wife, for that which is conceived in her is of (from, out of) the Holy Spirit. She will bear a Son, and you shall call His name Jesus [the Greek form of the Hebrew Joshua, which means Savior]…" (Matthew 1:20-21).

The name of Jesus comes from God. The amplification in this passage of Scripture explains that the Hebrew meaning of this name is "Savior." The name "Christ" is a Greek name meaning "the Anointed One" – the one Person God anointed above everyone else. Jesus is the Christ. The name of Jesus Christ means your Savior – the Anointed One.

Now that you have learned what this precious name means, you are ready to learn how God wants you to use this magnificent name toward receiving manifestation of healing in your body. The name of Jesus Christ is *much more powerful* than any human being can possibly comprehend with the limitations of our human understanding.

Jesus sits at the right hand of God. The Bible compares this elevated position of power to the supernatural power of the name of Jesus Christ. "...He sat down at the right hand of the divine Majesty on high, [taking a place and rank by which] He Himself became as much superior to angels as the glorious Name (title) which He has inherited is different from and more excellent than theirs" (Hebrews 1:3-4).

This passage of Scripture explains the great superiority of the position that Jesus has as He sits at the right hand of God. You then are told that this *same spiritual superiority* is given to "the glorious Name (title) which He has inherited." Do not ever underestimate the importance of opening your mouth continually to boldly speak the awesome and magnificent name of Jesus Christ.

As you study Scripture you will see again and again that the name of the Lord contains incredible spiritual power. "...You have exalted above all else Your name and Your word and You have magnified Your word above all Your name!" (Psalm 138:2).

You have learned in previous chapters about the incredible power of the supernatural living Word of God. This passage of Scripture tells you that the name of the Lord is second in spiritual power only to the mighty power of God's Word. Once you understand this great spiritual truth you will understand that Christians who are sick should open their mouths continually to speak *both* the Word of God and the name of the Lord with deep, strong and unwavering faith in God.

In Chapter One you learned that receiving eternal salvation through Jesus Christ and receiving healing in your body through Jesus Christ both are part of the Atonement. All people who have been born again receive their salvation through the precious name of the Lord Jesus Christ. "...there is salvation in and through no one else, for there is no other name under heaven given among men by and in which we must be saved" (Acts 4:12).

There is "no other name" that will enable people to be saved. There is no question that the name of Jesus Christ is a saving name. The name of Jesus Christ also is a healing name. You have learned that you can *speak* to the sickness in your body and command it to go. When you speak to the sickness in your body you always should speak to this sickness in the mighty name of Jesus Christ. When you speak boldly in the name of Jesus you are treating this sickness *just as if Jesus Himself was speaking these words.* You must understand that the mighty name of Jesus Christ contains the power to restore health to your body. Jesus has imparted this power to you.

The name of Jesus Christ is much greater than any other name. God has exalted the power of His name because of the tremendous sacrifice that Jesus made by leaving heaven and coming to earth to pay the price for your sins. "...[because He stooped so low] God has highly exalted Him and has freely bestowed on Him the name that is above every name, that in (at) the name of Jesus every knee should (must) bow, in heaven and on earth and under the earth, and every tongue [frankly and openly] confess and acknowledge that Jesus Christ is Lord, to the glory of God the Father" (Philippians 2:9-11).

The amplification of this passage of scripture says that God gave the name of Jesus Christ mighty supernatural power "because He stooped so low." Because Jesus humbled Himself to pay the horrible price that He paid at the whipping post and on the cross at Calvary, God has exalted His name to a position of supreme spiritual importance.

This passage of Scripture says that God has "highly exalted" His Son Jesus Christ. God has "freely bestowed on Him the name that is above every name." The name of Jesus is *much greater* than the name of whatever sickness is in your body. You can and should speak boldly to the sickness in your body throughout every day and night of your life commanding this sickness to *go* in the mighty supernatural power of the name of Jesus Christ.

The name of Jesus Christ is *so powerful* that "every knee in heaven and on earth and under the earth" ultimately must bow to it. The name of Jesus is *so powerful* that "every tongue" ultimately will "frankly and openly confess and acknowledge that Jesus Christ is Lord." The day *will* come when *all* of the people who rejected Jesus Christ during their lives on earth *will* bow down before His mighty name. Every person ultimately will "frankly and openly acknowledge that Jesus Christ is Lord."

Those who rejected the Messiah will spend eternity in torment and separated from God. Those who received the Messiah and chose to repent of their sins and follow Him will never be separated from Him. Death will take us instantly into His presence. If you have not made the decision to recognize Jesus Christ as the Messiah we invite you to do so now before it is too late (see the Appendix at the end of the book for specific scriptural instructions).

Jesus received mighty spiritual power when He rose victoriously from death. Jesus said, "...All authority (all power of rule) in heaven and on earth has been given to Me..." (Matthew 28:18).

This passage of Scripture says that Jesus has "*all* authority" over *everything* "in heaven and on earth." This broad and all-encompassing statement *includes* the sickness in your body. You soon will see that Jesus in His great might and power definitely instructs you to invoke His supernatural name for the purpose of healing. All Christians have been given the opportunity to release the tremendous power and authority that Jesus won when He won the greatest victory of all time. You should continually speak the name of Jesus Christ with deep, strong and unwavering faith.

When Jesus ascended into heaven the power of His name was *left behind* to be used on earth. His disciples had absolute faith in Him. They had seen Him perform many miracles. They knew how much power there is in His name.

In the Book of Acts we see many examples of these men performing great miracles by boldly speaking the name of Jesus Christ. Tremendous results will be received in *your life today* if you comprehend the immense power of the name of Jesus Christ and boldly speak His magnificent name throughout every day and night of your life.

The third chapter of Acts explains the first recorded instance of the disciples releasing the mighty power of the name of Jesus Christ. Peter and John went to the temple to pray. They came across a man there who had been crippled from birth. Each day this cripple was laid at the gate to the temple where he asked people for money.

When the crippled man asked Peter for money he received something that was much greater than anything money can buy. "...Peter said, Silver and gold (money) I do not have; but what I do have, that I give to you: in [the use of] the name of Jesus Christ of Nazareth, walk! Then he took hold of the man's right hand with a firm grip and raised him up. And at once his feet and ankle bones became strong and steady, and leaping forth he stood and began to walk, and he went into the temple with them, walking and leaping and praising God" (Acts 3:6-8).

Peter dared to step out on his faith in the name of Jesus Christ. Not only did Peter speak with faith in the name of Jesus, but he *acted* on his faith in that mighty and powerful name. Peter reached out and "took hold of the man's right hand with a firm grip and raised him up." The crippled man immediately found that "his feet and ankle bones became strong and steady." He was able to leap and walk. This man who once was severely crippled walked and leaped throughout the temple praising God continually.

Peter told people who observed this miracle that *faith in the name of Jesus Christ* was the reason why this crippled man was miraculously healed. Peter said, "...His name, through and by faith in His name, has made this man whom you see and recognize well and strong. [Yes] the faith which is through and by Him

[Jesus] has given the man this perfect soundness [of body] before all of you" (Acts 3:16).

There is no question that this crippled man was "made well and strong by faith in His name." Absolute faith in the mighty power of the name of Jesus Christ gave the man "perfect soundness of body." This mighty name can and should be used to bring about manifestation of healing in *your* body. Christians who are sick should speak the name of Jesus continually with deep, strong and unwavering faith.

You have learned about the mighty power of the name of Jesus Christ. You have learned that the Old Testament also teaches about the mighty power of the name of the Lord. The name of the Lord will protect you. "The name of the Lord is a strong tower; the [consistently] righteous man [upright and in right standing with God] runs into it and is safe, high [above evil] and strong." (Proverbs 18:10).

The name of the Lord "is a strong tower." "Consistently righteous" men (and women) should "run into it." Each person who has received Jesus Christ as his or her Savior and constantly attempts to yield to the Holy Spirit and obey the Word of God is "consistently righteous." When these people who are righteous before God boldly speak the name of the Lord they *will* be "safe, high above evil and strong."

Your Father did not *suggest* that you believe in the name of Jesus Christ. He has *commanded* you to believe in the name of Jesus. "...And this is His order (His command, His injunction): that we should believe in (put our faith and trust in and adhere to and rely on) the name of His Son Jesus Christ (the Messiah)" (I John 3:23).

Please highlight or underline the words "this is His order." Your Father in heaven has commanded you to "believe in, put your faith and trust in and adhere to and rely on the name of His Son Jesus Christ the Messiah." You must not ignore this vitally important command from God.

Some Christians use the name of Jesus routinely as part of their daily prayers because they have heard their pastor or other Christians praying in the name of Jesus. You *should* pray in the name of Jesus Christ, but you should *not* pray routinely in the name of Jesus Christ. Once you begin to comprehend *how much power* His name contains, your prayers will change tremendously as you release mighty spiritual power with bold faith as you continually speak the name of Jesus.

The name of Jesus Christ is a supernatural phenomenon that God has provided for *you*. His name is a major key to unlocking heaven's blessings which include healing. The name of Jesus contains authority and power that will help you immensely throughout your life on earth. God in heaven *will* honor the name of His Son Jesus Christ when you continually speak His name with deep faith.

Your understanding of the mighty power of the name of Jesus Christ will increase tremendously if you will spend a great deal of time meditating on the *facts* from the Word of God in this chapter. In the next chapter you will learn many additional facts about the mighty power of the name of Jesus Christ. Study this chapter carefully. Then go back and meditate on the scriptural facts in these two chapters.

Chapter 32

Speak the Name of Jesus Christ

Your loving Father in heaven has provided tremendous blessings for each of His children who will come to Him consistently with absolute faith in His Son Jesus and in the supernatural power of His name. "….Blessed (to be celebrated with praises) is He Who comes in the name of the Lord" (Luke 13:35).

These words that were spoken by Jesus confirm Psalm 118:26 that says, "Blessed is he who comes in the name of the Lord." When Jesus rose from the dead He gave you the privilege of receiving blessings from heaven because you come to God with absolute faith in His mighty and powerful name. Every person who has asked Jesus Christ to be his or her Savior has a legal right to come to God continually in the name of His beloved Son.

When someone on earth gives power of attorney to another person, this person gives the other person the legal right to perform actions in his or her name. Jesus has given *you* the legal right in the spiritual realm to perform actions with the *same* power that these actions would receive if they were performed by Him. You will receive manifestation of this supernatural power if you consistently come to God with absolute faith in His name.

You should boldly speak the name of Jesus Christ whenever you face sickness in your body or any other problem. Your words should clearly indicate that you depend completely on Jesus to give you healing and to bring you safely through every other challenge you face. "…And whatever you do [no matter what it is] in word or deed, do everything in the name of the Lord Jesus and in [dependence upon] His Person, giving praise to God the Father through Him" (Colossians 3:17).

"Whatever you do" should be done in the name of Jesus. You should "do everything in the name of the Lord Jesus." The words "whatever" and "everything" *include* seeking manifestation of the healing that Jesus already has provided for you. You will show your complete "dependence on Him" when you speak His mighty name with absolute faith. You should "praise God the Father through Him."

I believe that I speak the name of Jesus Christ at least twenty times each day and often much more than that. When you are conscious of the mighty power of His name you will not forego the magnificent privilege you have been given to speak His name constantly with deep, strong and unwavering faith. You should revere the name of the Lord. "O Lord, our Lord, how excellent (majestic and glorious) is Your name in all the earth!" (Psalm 8:9).

When this passage of Scripture mentions the words "in all the earth" this statement includes where *you* are right now. It includes the sickness in your body that you know Jesus already has healed. Speak this "excellent, majestic and glorious" name continually throughout every day and night of your life.

The name of Jesus Christ is treated with absolute reverence and awe throughout the kingdom of heaven. No matter how severe any physician may have told you the sickness in your body is, you must understand that you can be healed by continually speaking with absolute faith the incredibly powerful name of the Lord Jesus Christ.

Be conscious at all times that your Healer, Jesus Christ, lives in your heart. Know that Jesus is interceding for you when you pray to God for healing. "…He is always living to make petition to God and intercede with Him and intervene with Him" (Hebrews 7:25).

Please highlight or underline the words "always living." The word "always" means exactly what it says. Jesus is continually speaking to His Father on your behalf. He is praying for all of us all the time. As you become more aware of what Jesus is doing for you, you will develop an increasing awareness of His presence in your life. Jesus wants to "make petition to God and intercede with Him and intervene with Him" on your behalf when you pray in His name with absolute faith.

Do not limit Jesus. He is not limited to listening to just one prayer at a time. Jesus is omniscient. He can hear billions of prayers at the same time and intercede for every one of these people with His Father. "...we have an Advocate (One Who will intercede for us) with the Father—[it is] Jesus Christ [the all] righteous [upright, just, Who conforms to the Father's will in every purpose, thought, and action]" (I John 2:1).

Jesus is your "Advocate." He "*will* intercede for *you* with the Father." When Jesus intercedes on your behalf His intercession releases great spiritual power because Jesus is "all righteous, upright and just." His intercession on your behalf releases great power because Jesus "conforms to the Father's will in every purpose, thought and action."

Jesus tells us to come to Him in His name. The name of Jesus is everything that He is. You will partake of the nature of Jesus for what you need. You should be so at one with Jesus that you will partake of His nature to receive victory over the challenges you face.

You have seen that Jesus is your Healer. Jesus promises to answer when you pray in His name. He said, "...I will grant [I Myself will do for you] whatever you shall ask in My name..." (John 14:14).

Jesus said that He "will grant *whatever* you shall ask in His name." Please highlight or underline the word "whatever" in this wonderful promise from Jesus. Know that this all-inclusive word *includes* healing from the sickness in your body.

When you pray consistently with absolute faith in the name of Jesus Christ, your prayers will be answered because Jesus said they would be answered. When Jesus spoke to His disciples during the Last Supper He said, "…I assure you, most solemnly I tell you, that My Father will grant you whatever you ask in My Name [as presenting all that I AM]. Up to this time you have not asked a [single] thing in My Name [as presenting all that I AM]; but now ask and keep on asking and you will receive, so that your joy (gladness, delight) may be full and complete" (John 16:23-24).

Jesus "solemnly assured" His disciples that His Father would give them "whatever they asked in His name." Jesus emphasized that the disciples had not prayed up until that time in His name. Jesus told them to "ask and keep on asking." He emphasized the need of persevering in prayer with absolute faith in the mighty power of His name. These words apply to you today. Jesus said that you "will receive" and that "your joy, gladness and delight" will be "full and complete" *if* you will pray continually with absolute faith in the mighty supernatural power of His name.

When you pray to God for manifestation of healing in your body you should stand with unwavering faith on this wonderful promise from Jesus. The words "whatever you ask" include the sickness in your body. Release your faith that God will give you manifestation of healing because you persevere in prayer and pray each time with absolute faith in the mighty power of the name of Jesus Christ.

You saw in Psalm 138:2 that the Lord exalts two things above everything else – His Word and His Name. When you are sick you cannot open your mouth to say anything that is more important than to continually speak the Word of God and to continually speak the name of Jesus Christ.

Nothing can stand against the name of Jesus Christ. No sickness is more powerful than His name. Repeat His mighty name with unwavering faith over and over again. Know that you are releasing magnificent spiritual power as you continually speak the name of Jesus Christ with unwavering faith and reverence.

Open your mouth many times during each day and night to thank Jesus for healing you. Say, "Thank You so much, dear Jesus, for healing me." Continue to thank Jesus constantly. Speak His wonderful name with love, affection and gratitude each time you thank Him.

Open your mouth several times each day and say again and again, "In the name of Jesus Christ I have been healed…" In the name of Jesus Christ I have been healed.… In the name of Jesus Christ I have been healed. … In the name of Jesus Christ I have been healed. … In the name of Jesus Christ I have been healed." Say, "Jesus Christ took the sickness in my body on Himself. I am healed."

You are saying what the Word of God says when you speak these great spiritual truths. The cumulative effect of continually thanking Jesus for healing you, stating that you have been healed and doing all of this in His name places you in the presence of Jesus Christ the Healer.

Although this chapter deals primarily with healing in the name of Jesus Christ, you must understand that you can and should speak His mighty name whenever you face a crisis of any kind. Many times when you face a severe crisis you will not have time to carefully analyze the challenge you face or to pray a long prayer. Out of the depth of your heart the name that is more powerful than any other name should instantly and spontaneously pour out of your lips.

If you suddenly face a severe automobile accident, a plane crash or any other sign of impending disaster, open your mouth and speak the name of Jesus Christ with bold faith. Jesus comes on the scene when you speak His name with strong faith. Do not think that Jesus can only be in one place at one time. He is omnipresent. He can be in an infinite number of places at the same time. Jesus is with you when you are sick. He is with you when you face any other crisis. He is with you at all times.

You can be certain that Jesus will come to your assistance when you continually speak His name with bold faith. You place a spiritual hedge of protection around yourself when you speak the name of Jesus with absolute faith. Angels of God will move on your behalf when you speak the name of Jesus with faith.

I have found that continually repeating the name of Jesus has a great calming effect on me. Whenever I face a crisis situation I often say, "Jesus... Jesus... Jesus... Jesus... Jesus... Jesus... Jesus... Jesus...."

Whenever someone comes to me for prayer with a severe problem that I do not know the answer to I hold that person's hand and pray briefly. I then repeat the name of Jesus again and again and again. Time after time I have seen the great calming effect that takes place in other people when I pray in the name of Jesus.

Are you severely ill? Instead of focusing on the symptoms in your body and the pain and discomfort, open your mouth and say the name of Jesus again and again. Do this for five minutes the first time you try it. Try again a short time later and do this for ten minutes. Then do this again for fifteen minutes or more. As you do this constantly you place yourself in the presence of Jesus Christ the Healer.

You soon will see the tremendous faith that will rise up inside of you when you reverently speak His mighty and powerful name. You must not be timid about speaking the name of Jesus Christ. You should boldly speak His name, knowing that you walk in His victory when you *continually* speak His name with faith.

You have direct access to the throne of God when you boldly speak the name of Jesus. You do not have to scream the name of Jesus when you speak His name boldly. You can speak this marvelous name calmly with absolute certainty of the indisputable authority that is contained in the name of Jesus Christ.

You will not receive results in the spiritual realm based on how loudly you holler the name of Jesus. You will receive results in the spiritual realm based upon how much certainty you have in the supernatural power of the name of Jesus Christ. If your mouth is constantly speaking this marvelous name and if you are meditating on the Word of God continually throughout the day and night, you will be using the two most powerful spiritual weapons your Father has provided for you.

The Bible warns you to be very careful how you use the name of the Lord. "You shall not use or repeat the name of the Lord your God in vain [that is, lightly or frivolously, in false affirmations or profanely]; for the Lord will not hold him guiltless who takes His name in vain" (Exodus 20:7).

The amplification of this passage of Scripture says that people who use this marvelous name "lightly, frivolously, in false affirmations or profanely" use the name of the Lord "in vain." Too many Christians use the Lord's name casually. They speak His name by saying, "for God's sake," "Oh God" or "Good Lord." These and similar expressions have become relatively common-place today. You should have so much reverence for the name of the Lord that you will never use His mighty name lightly or casually.

I cannot think of anything that pains me more than to hear the name of my precious Savior Jesus Christ used "profanely." People who speak this magnificent name in a profane manner have *no* conception whatsoever of how much they are *hurting themselves* whenever they speak His name in this way.

You must not take this matter lightly. God does not take this matter lightly. He tells you one of the Ten Commandments when He tells you not to use His name in vain. These are not God's ten requests or God's ten suggestions. These are God's ten *commandments*.

Some religious people talk about God, but they do not boldly speak the name of Jesus Christ. Religious people who do not have a personal relationship with Jesus as their Lord and Savior often feel uncomfortable if they speak His name. Committed Christians should understand the mighty power of the name of Jesus Christ. His name should be on your lips constantly.

How often do *your lips* open to speak the name of Jesus Christ? How many times have *you* spoken the name of Jesus Christ *today*? Are you utilizing the precious privilege you have been given to consistently speak the mighty and powerful name of Jesus Christ?

The last two chapters have been filled with *facts* from the holy Scriptures pertaining to the supernatural power of the name of Jesus Christ. Although these chapters primarily deal with using this precious name with faith to receive manifestation of healing, they also contain many other facts about using the name of Jesus throughout every day of your life.

Go back and carefully study and then meditate on each passage of Scripture in these two chapters. Meditate on this Scripture again and again and again until *your heart is filled* with facts from God about the magnificent power of the name of Jesus Christ that is far above every other name.

Chapter 33

Praise the Lord Instead of Complaining

In the last four chapters you have learned about the immense spiritual power of continually speaking words of faith and continually speaking the name of Jesus Christ. We now are ready to look into the Word of God to see exactly what Christians who are sick are instructed to do in regard to praising God, worshiping God and thanking God.

If you are very sick and you see no indication of receiving healing, you may be tempted to be discouraged. When your body aches with pain and everything seems to be going wrong, *this is the time* when you should open your mouth to say exactly what your Father instructs you to say. You have learned that you should speak the Word of God continually and speak the name of Jesus continually. Now you will see that you are instructed to praise the Lord continually and thank Him continually even though the last thing you may feel like doing is praising the Lord and thanking Him.

God's angels and Satan's demons inhabit the atmosphere around you. Satan's demons want you to be depressed and discouraged when you are sick. Instead of giving in to a spirit of depression the Bible instructs you to cover yourself with "…the garment [expressive] of praise instead of a heavy, burdened, and failing spirit…" (Isaiah 61:3)

We will look at the last part of this passage of Scripture first. When this verse of Scripture speaks of "a heavy, burdened, and failing spirit" it refers to Satan and his demons. Satan's demons want to put a spirit of heaviness on you. They want the sickness in your body to be a heavy burden. They want you to believe that there is no hope for the future.

Your Father in heaven wants you to do just the opposite. The word "garment" in this passage of Scripture is similar to a piece of clothing. Your Father wants you to put on "the garment expressive of praise." He wants you to praise Him continually when you are sick and the future does not look good. The worse you feel, the more you should praise Him.

You must not allow the discouraging thoughts that Satan's demons attempt to put into your mind to pull you down. You should be like the psalmist who said, "Why are you cast down, O my inner self? And why should you moan over me and be disquieted within me? Hope in God and wait expectantly for Him, for I shall yet praise Him, my Help and my God" (Psalm 42:5).

The psalmist was speaking to himself in this passage of Scripture. He told himself not to be "cast down." He told himself not to "moan." Instead, under the anointing of the Holy Spirit you are instructed through the psalmist to "hope in God and wait expectantly for Him." You are instructed to "praise Him, your Help and your God."

You cannot allow yourself to be pulled down by the sickness in your body. Some people become extremely discouraged when they are sick. They moan, groan, gripe, grumble and complain. The psalmist asked himself *why* he did these things.

Your Father does *not* want you to give up hope. He wants you to persevere in faith. He wants you to praise Him continually while you wait patiently and faithfully to get well. The psalmist said "…I will hope continually and will praise You yet more and more" (Psalm 71:14).

Are you sick? Does the future look bleak? Your Father instructs you to "hope continually" in spite of the circumstances you face. He wants you to be absolutely certain that you already have been healed just as His Word says. He wants you to "praise Him more and more" regardless of the pain and discomfort in your body.

Praising God and thanking Him when your body aches with pain *does not make any sense* to an unrenewed mind. Your Father wants you to grow and mature in your faith in Him so that you will learn to live in His healing presence. Jesus is the Healer. Praise Him and thank Him continually for Who He is and how much He loves you even though your body may ache with pain and you see no sign whatsoever of the healing He already has provided for you.

You must understand the vast difference between God's ways and the ways of the world when logical thinking says that it makes no sense whatsoever to praise God when you are sick. (see Isaiah 55:8-9). When you are sick you absolutely cannot afford to think the way the world thinks. You must think the way that God thinks. Constant praise should be a way of life to you whether you are sick or in the best of health.

Praise is not an option. Praising God is a command of God. Your Father wants you to show your obedience to Him by boldly praising Him and continually thanking Him regardless of the condition of your health.

Your Father wants you to focus your attention *on Him* instead of focusing on how you feel. You can change the emphasis in your life from the self-centered life that many sick people have to a God-centered life. You will do this if you praise the Lord continually even though you do not feel like praising Him. "Let the peoples praise You [turn away from their idols] and give thanks to You, O God; let all the peoples praise and give thanks to You! The earth has yielded its harvest [in evidence of God's approval]; God, even our own God, will bless us" (Psalm 67:5-6).

This passage of Scripture says that "all the peoples" should praise God and thank Him. This word "all" includes *you*. You are placing yourself in God's healing presence when you praise God and thank Him even though you are sick.

You are making what the Bible calls "a sacrifice of praise" when you praise God continually in spite of the discomfort of sickness. "...let us constantly and at all times offer up to God a sacrifice of praise, which is the fruit of lips that thankfully acknowledge and confess and glorify His name" (Hebrews 13:15).

How often does your Father want you to make this sacrifice of praise? He says that you should make this sacrifice "constantly and at all times." Praise would *not* be a *sacrifice* if praising God was easy. Your Father wants your mouth to "thankfully acknowledge and confess and glorify His name" throughout every day and night regardless of how you feel.

Your Father wants you to praise Him and thank Him because of *Who He is*. If you constantly make this sacrifice and praise God and thank Him when you do not feel like praising Him and thanking Him, you are choosing to live in the realm of the Spirit where healing is. "Offer to God the sacrifice of thanksgiving, and pay your vows to the Most High, and call on Me in the day of trouble; I will deliver you, and you shall honor and glorify Me" (Psalm 50:14-15).

Once again the word "sacrifice" is used in this passage of Scripture. God tells *you* to "call on Him in the day of trouble." You face "days of trouble" when you are very sick. God promises to "deliver" you when you call on Him by praying faithfully and thanking Him and praising Him continually. Persevere in faith, praising God and thanking Him, believing that He already has delivered you from the sickness in your body. You should honor and glorify your Father when He delivers you.

Once again you must understand how different God's ways are from the ways of the world. When you praise God and thank Him continually, you make a continual "offering" to Him just as you make an offering to Him when you put your tithe into the collection at church. You give the Lord the "honor and glory" He deserves when you praise Him and thank Him continually. "He who brings an offering of praise and thanksgiving honors and glorifies Me…" (Psalm 50:23).

Sometimes you will have to praise God through your tears. Your praise and thanksgiving should not be based on how you feel. Your praise and thanksgiving should be solidly anchored on the Word of God. The worse you feel, the *more* you need to praise the Lord. You should praise Him and thank Him in advance for the healing He already has provided for you.

When you are sick and your body aches with pain, you should say something like the following: "Dear Father, I praise You and I thank You. I trust You completely. I glorify You. I exalt You. I worship You. I adore You. I magnify You. I praise You and thank You from the bottom of my heart. I have absolute faith in You despite the sickness in my body. Thank You, dear Father, that Jesus took this sickness upon Himself. Thank You so much, dear Father. I trust You completely. I praise You continually."

If you find that praising God in front of other people is difficult, you should develop the habit of praising God continually when you are alone. If the scriptural information in this chapter sounds somewhat strange to you and you have not praised the Lord very often, try an experiment when the sickness in your body is extreme. Find a place where you have complete privacy. When you are alone and you are not concerned about what other people might think, open your mouth and boldly praise the Lord.

Thank Jesus for the enormous sacrifice He made for you at the whipping post. Thank Him for the tremendous sacrifice He made for you on the cross at Calvary. Thank Him for the wonderful victory He has given you. Tell Him that you love Him. Tell Him again. Tell Him again. Keep on praising Him and thanking Him over and over and over.

Do this in privacy for several consecutive days. *See for yourself* if your faith in God does not increase as you faithfully obey these scriptural instructions. You soon will get over your hesitancy to praise the Lord publicly. You will be able to praise Him boldly in public as well as in private. You invite others into God's presence when you praise Him publicly. Jesus will become your focus. He will become everything to you.

When you praise God continually you actually will be living more in the Spirit than in the flesh. You will begin to see life more from God's perspective. You will rest in Him as you hold fast to your healing, praising God and thanking Him throughout each day and night.

You will see in the subsequent chapters on prayer that your Father instructs you to pray to Him continually. Your prayers should be prayers of thanksgiving. When you pray you should praise God and thank Him for Who He is, for His love for you, for His mercy, His grace and His faithfulness.

Jesus is worthy of your praise. He has earned your praise. You withhold from Him a blessing that is very important if you fail to praise Him continually regardless of how you feel. You should have a constant attitude of gratitude toward Jesus. Words of praise will not flow out of your mouth spontaneously unless your heart is filled to overflowing with deep and sincere gratitude toward Jesus.

You have learned that the words that flow out of your mouth in a crisis situation always will come from the abundance of whatever you truly believe in your heart (see Matthew 12:34). If your heart is filled with gratitude toward Jesus, you *will* praise Him continually. You have many reasons to thank Jesus. You saw many facts in Chapter Two about the tremendous price Jesus paid for *you* on the cross at Mount Calvary and at the whipping post. There is no question that you should be grateful to Jesus for paying this great price for your eternal salvation and your healing.

When you are in heaven you will understand the magnitude of the tremendous price that Jesus paid for you on the cross at Mount Calvary and at the whipping post. Jesus "…was betrayed and put to death because of our misdeeds and was raised to secure our justification (our acquittal, [making our account balance and absolving us from all guilt before God]" (Romans 4:25).

This passage of Scripture tells you that Jesus Who was completely innocent "was betrayed and put to death because of your misdeeds." Jesus paid the price for *your* sins and "absolved *you* from all guilt." If you can even begin to comprehend the price that Jesus paid for your healing at the whipping post and the price that He paid for your salvation on the cross at Calvary, you will praise Him and thank Him continually regardless of the symptoms of sickness in your body.

If you can even begin to comprehend what Jesus has done for you, *you will not be able to stop* praising Him and thanking Him. Pain and discomfort in your body or any other circumstance in your life should not have any effect on your desire to praise Jesus and thank Him continually. As you comprehend more about what Jesus actually has done for you, you will praise Him even more.

Do you want to bless Your Father in heaven? Do you want to bless Jesus? The Bible tells you exactly what you should do if you want to bless the Lord continually. You should be like the psalmist who said, "I will bless the Lord at all times; His praise shall continually be in my mouth" (Psalm 34:1).

You "bless the Lord" when His praise is "continually" in your mouth. Your praise is very important to God. Your Father created you to praise Him. "The people I formed for Myself that they may set forth My praise [and they shall do it]" (Isaiah 43:21).

Your Father "formed you for Himself." When you praise Him continually you are doing exactly what He created you to do. You must not ignore this specific instruction from God. Your Father is worthy of your praise. Jesus is worthy of your praise.

In this chapter we have established a scriptural foundation for praising the Lord regardless of the circumstances you face. There is no question that your Father in heaven has instructed you to praise Him at all times regardless of how you feel or what circumstances you face. In the next chapter you will learn more facts from the Word of God about the relationship between praising and thanking God continually and releasing your faith in God.

INTENTIONALLY BLANK

Chapter 34

Praise Releases the Power of God

The Word of God is filled with thousands of promises from your Father to you. You will have many of these promises living in your heart if you have faithfully obeyed your Father's instructions to renew your mind in His Word each day and to meditate on His Word continually throughout each day and night. *Why wouldn't you* praise the Lord and thank Him continually if you *really believe* all of the scriptural promises that are included in this book?

You should not beg and plead and try to cajole the Lord when you are sick. Instead, all of the words you speak should clearly express your absolute faith in His mighty healing power. You should praise Him and thank Him because you know that Jesus Christ has given you victory. I believe that you can block your faith in God from working if you do not praise Him and thank Him continually. "Great is the Lord and highly to be praised; and His greatness is [so vast and deep as to be] unsearchable" (Psalm 145:3).

The greatness of the Lord "is so vast and deep as to be unsearchable." No one can begin to comprehend how great our precious Lord is. You *must* focus on Him instead of focusing on the sickness in your body. He is "highly to be praised" because of His "vast, deep and unsearchable greatness."

Your Father has given you His Word to provide a solid foundation for your faith in Him. The psalmist loved the Word of God so much that he actually praised it. "In God, Whose word I praise, in the Lord, Whose word I praise, in God have I put my trust and confident reliance, I will not be afraid..." (Psalm 56:10-11).

You should approach the Word of God each day with absolute awe and reverence. God and His Word are the *same* (see John 1:1). The words "Whose word I praise" are repeated twice in this passage of Scripture for emphasis. Your Father wants you to praise Him and thank Him continually for His supernatural, magnificent living Word. The mystery of God's residence in His Word is a phenomenon. It is beyond human explanation.

You must "not be afraid" when you are sick. Because you know God and you know what God's Word says about healing, you should praise Him and thank Him. When you are not feeling well you should focus on God's love for you instead of focusing on the pain and discomfort in your body. The more you focus on God's love, the more you will praise Him just as the psalmist did. "Because Your loving-kindness is better than life, my lips shall praise You" (Psalm 63:3).

Chapter Fourteen is filled with many marvelous facts from the holy Scriptures about God's great love for you. You should place all of your trust in His love. If you know that your Father loves you unconditionally and if you trust Him completely, you *will* praise Him regardless of how you feel. "...give praise and thanks to the Lord of hosts, for the Lord is good; for His mercy and kindness and steadfast love endure forever..." (Jeremiah 33:11).

You should praise the Lord and thank Him continually because "He is good." His "mercy and kindness and steadfast love endure forever." Your Father never stops loving *you*. He always is kind and merciful to *you*. Your mouth will continually speak words of thanksgiving if you *really* trust Him.

Christians who have not renewed their minds in the Word of God and steadily increased their faith in God cannot understand why they should praise Him and thank Him when their bodies ache with pain. Your praise and thanksgiving should be *unconditional.* "Thank [God] in everything [no matter what the circumstances may be, be thankful and give thanks], for this is the will of God for you [who are] in Christ Jesus [the Revealer and Mediator of that will]" (I Thessalonians 5:18).

This passage of Scripture tells you to "thank God in everything no matter what the circumstances may be." There is no question that this specific instruction from God includes the sickness in your body. You are not thanking God *for* the sickness. You are thanking God *in* sickness for the healing that His Word says already has been provided for you. You must understand that thanking God and praising Him when you are sick is the will of God for you.

Chapter Two tells you that Jesus has given you a total, complete and absolute victory over the sickness in your body. Jesus is your Healer. He is the Master over all sickness and disease. You must not allow sickness to pull you down. If your body aches with pain, you should open your mouth and thank God for the marvelous victory He has given you over sickness because of the price Jesus paid for you. "...thanks be to God, Who gives us the victory [making us conquerors] through our Lord Jesus Christ" (I Corinthians 15:57).

You are fighting a spiritual battle when you are very sick. You are fighting a battle between giving in to pain and discomfort or absolutely believing what the Word of God says about the healing that has been provided for you by Jesus Christ. You *will* thank God continually if you are *certain* He has "given you the victory." You must not give up. Your loving Father has "made *you* a conqueror through the Lord Jesus Christ."

You have learned the importance of speaking the name of Jesus continually. We now will look again at a passage of Scripture we studied previously. You can see from the Word of God that you should praise God at the same time you speak the name of Jesus. "...whatever you do [no matter what it is] in word or deed, do everything in the name of the Lord Jesus and in [dependence upon] His Person, giving praise to God the Father through Him." (Colossians 3:17).

The sickness in your body *is included* in the words "whatever you do no matter what it is." When you are sick *"everything"* you do should be done "in the name of the Lord Jesus" because of your complete "dependence" on Him. You should praise God continually because you trust Him completely.

You may be tempted to give up if your faith in God is weak. Your Father wants your faith for healing to be deeply rooted because you have obeyed His instructions to study and meditate continually on His healing promises and on scriptural instructions for increasing your faith in Him.

As you praise God and thank Him while you wait for manifestation of healing, your faith in God will grow just as Abraham's faith grew when he praised God and glorified Him in the face of adversity. We looked at a portion of the following passage of Scripture in a previous chapter. We now are ready to expand our study by explaining the scriptural relationship between faith in God and praising God continually. "No unbelief or distrust made him waver (doubtingly question) concerning the promise of God, but he grew strong and was empowered by faith as he gave praise and glory to God, fully satisfied and assured that God was able and mighty to keep His word and to do what He had promised" (Romans 4:20-21).

Your faith in God must not "waver" because of unbelief or distrust. You must not "doubtingly question" God's healing promises. You will "grow strong and be empowered by faith" if you praise the Lord continually This passage of Scripture clearly shows you the relationship between increasing your faith in God and praising God continually. *Why wouldn't you* praise God continually *if* you are "fully satisfied and assured that God is able and mighty to keep His word and to do what He has promised?"

Praise takes your attention off the problem and focuses your attention on the Problem Solver. The more you turn away from the pain and discomfort in your body and focus instead on the One Who can and will solve all problems, the stronger your faith will become.

Faith and praise are closely related. Deep faith in God will cause you to praise Him continually. This continual praise will strengthen your faith in God even more. The more you praise God, the stronger your faith will become. The stronger your faith becomes, the more you will want to praise God.

Christians who do not have deep, strong and unwavering faith in God have a difficult time praising Him when their bodies ache with pain. Christians who have obeyed God's specific instructions to increase their faith in Him (see our book *Unshakable Faith in Almighty God*) will praise Him regardless of the challenges they face. You should be like the psalmist who said, "My lips pour forth praise [with thanksgiving and renewed trust] when You teach me Your statutes" (Psalm 119:171).

The psalmist said that "his lips poured forth praise with thanksgiving" because of "renewed trust." He was constantly renewing his faith in God because God taught him from His Word.

Praise is the language of heaven. If you praise the Lord and worship Him continually you will experience a preview of heaven while you are on earth. When you are in heaven you will observe the angels who surround the throne of God. "…day and night they never stop saying, Holy, holy, holy is the Lord God Almighty (Omnipotent), Who was and Who is and Who is to come" (Revelation 4:8).

All angels and all of the inhabitants of heaven praise God continually. Everyone in heaven sees God *as He really is.* They hold Him in absolute awe. They show their awe and reverence by worshiping and praising Him continually. Continual worship and praise will bring you deeply into God's anointing that brings supernatural results, including healing.

Some Christians have a distorted view of God because of the pull of the world, the influence of Satan and their failure to obey their Father's instructions to continually fill their minds and their hearts with His supernatural living Word. These Christians will find that their perspective will be much different when they are in heaven. When John received his revelation of heaven he said, "…I heard what sounded like a mighty shout of a great crowd in heaven, exclaiming, Hallelujah (praise the Lord)!..." (Revelation 19:1).

The praise in heaven was *so great* that John compared this overwhelming praise with pounding waves in the ocean and roars of thunder. John said, "…I heard what sounded like the shout of a vast throng, like the boom of many pounding waves, and like the roar of terrific and mighty peals of thunder, exclaiming, Hallelujah (praise the Lord)! For now the Lord our God the Omnipotent (the All-Ruler) reigns!" (Revelation 19:6).

There is no question that everyone in heaven worships and praises God continually. Power from God will be released to you, in you and through you if you praise God continually regardless of sickness or any other adversity you face.

You should praise the Lord continually because you should be absolutely certain that "the Lord your God the Omnipotent (the All-Ruler) reigns." God's mighty and awesome power reigns over everything including the sickness in your body. Praise Him and thank Him continually.

Chapter 35

Come into the Presence of the Lord

The Bible gives us an excellent example of God honoring praise in the face of adversity in the biblical account of what the apostle Paul and his friend Silas did when they were put into a prison in Philippi because they had told the people of Philippi that Jesus is the Messiah. "The crowd [also] joined in the attack upon them, and the rulers tore the clothes off of them and commanded that they be beaten with rods. And when they had struck them with many blows, they threw them into prison, charging the jailer to keep them safely. He, having received [so strict a] charge, put them into the inner prison (the dungeon) and fastened their feet in the stocks" (Acts 16:22-24).

How did Paul and Silas react to being attacked by a crowd of people, having their clothes torn off, being beaten with rods and being put into a dungeon with their feet fastened in stocks? This passage of Scripture goes on to explain that Paul and Silas *prayed and sang words of praise to God*. A great miracle occurred as a result of their prayer and praise. "...about midnight, as Paul and Silas were praying and singing hymns of praise to God, and the [other] prisoners were listening to them, suddenly there was a great earthquake, so that the very foundations of the prison were shaken; and at once all the doors were opened and everyone's shackles were unfastened" (Acts 16:25-26).

Paul and Silas refused to feel sorry for themselves because of the adversity they faced. Instead of complaining, they praised God continually. Their faith in God was shown by their praise in the face of extremely adverse circumstances. They released their faith in God by "praying and singing hymns of praises to Him."

Your Father wants you to follow the example of Paul and Silas. If you are sick and tired He wants you to speak His Word boldly with absolute faith. He wants you to speak the name of Jesus again and again. He wants you to praise Him and thank Him. He wants you to sing songs of praise even though singing praise may be the last thing you feel like doing.

The Bible gives us another explanation of the enormous power of praising the Lord in the face of adversity in the account of what took place when King Jehosaphat and the Israelites faced overwhelming opposition from the Moabites, the Ammonites and the Meunites. The Israelites heard from God as they prepared to face their mighty opponents. God said, "…Be not afraid or dismayed at this great multitude; for the battle is not yours, but God's" (II Chronicles 20:15).

God instructed King Jehosaphat and his followers to "be not afraid of this great multitude." God told them that *He* would fight the battle. He said, "You shall not need to fight in this battle; take your positions, stand still, and see the deliverance of the Lord [Who is] with you, O Judah and Jerusalem. Fear not nor be dismayed. Tomorrow go out against them, for the Lord is with you" (II Chronicles 20:17).

You can learn from these instructions. When you are fighting sickness you should not be afraid because of your absolute certainty that "the Lord is with you." "And Jehoshaphat bowed his head with his face to the ground, and all Judah and the inhabitants of Jerusalem fell down before the Lord, worshiping Him" (II Chronicles 20:18).

The Israelites did what your Father *wants you to do* when you face severe adversity that is caused by sickness or by anything else. He wants you to "worship Him" just as the Israelites did when they "...stood up to praise the Lord, the God of Israel, with a very loud voice" (II Chronicles 20:19).

Are you sick? Does your future look bleak? You should "praise the Lord with a very loud voice." Do not be timid with your praise. Praise the Lord boldly. "When he had consulted with the people, he appointed singers to sing to the Lord and praise Him in their holy [priestly] garments as they went out before the army, saying, Give thanks to the Lord, for His mercy and loving-kindness endure forever!" (II Chronicles 20:21).

You should "sing to the Lord." You should "give thanks to the Lord." *Do you really believe* that God's "mercy and loving-kindness endure forever?" If you do, why wouldn't you sing to Him, praise Him and thank Him regardless of the symptoms of sickness in your body?

If you will continually praise the Lord and sing to Him and worship Him, you will see that God responds to this praise as He did for King Jehosaphat and his followers. "...when they began to sing and to praise, the Lord set ambushments against the men of Ammon, Moab, and Mount Seir who had come against Judah, and they were [self-] slaughtered" (II Chronicles 20:22).

You *must not be overwhelmed* by the sickness in your body. You should praise God and thank Him because you have enormous gratitude in your heart. You should praise Him and thank Him because you have chosen to live for Him and trust Him with every area of your life, including healing.

You should praise Jesus and thank Him for paying the price for your healing. You should thank Him for the horrible bloody stripes on His body that give you conclusive evidence that the price *has* been paid for your healing. You should thank Jesus for taking your sickness so that you will be made well because He bore the sickness in your body for you (see Isaiah 53:10).

If you really trust Jesus and you comprehend the magnitude of what He has done for you, you will praise Him continually. The psalmist David said, "The Lord is my Strength and my [impenetrable] Shield; my heart trusts in, relies on, and confidently leans on Him, and I am helped; therefore my heart greatly rejoices, and with my song will I praise Him" (Psalm 28:7).

You can be certain that "the Lord is *your* Strength and *your* impenetrable Shield." He will give you the strength you need when you are weak from sickness. You can do *all things* through His strength (see Philippians 4:13). The psalmist told you what will happen when your "heart trusts in, relies on, and confidently leans on the Lord." He said, "I am helped." You should have the same certainty that the Lord will *help you*. Your heart should "greatly rejoice" because of your deep faith in the Lord. You should praise Him by singing songs to Him.

You must not give in to sickness. If you continually fill your heart with the Word of God, you will have a song in your heart at all times regardless of how you feel. Songs of praise and worship will pour out from deep down inside of you regardless of your physical symptoms. You will be like the psalmist who said, "My heart is fixed, O God, my heart is steadfast and confident! I will sing and make melody" (Psalm 57:7).

Is your heart "fixed" on God instead of being focused on the sickness in your body? Is your heart "steadfast and confident?" Songs of praise will flow out of your mouth if you really believe what God's Word says about divine healing. "Then [Israel] believed His words [trusting in, relying on them]; they sang His praise" (Psalm 106:12).

You should follow this example that Moses and the Israelites gave you when they faced a seemingly impossible situation at the Red Sea (see Exodus 14:1-31 and Exodus 15:1-19). Even though they were pursued by a large Egyptian army and the Red Sea was before them and high mountains were on either side of them, they showed their absolute faith in God by praising Him in song. God honored their faith in Him by miraculously parting the Red Sea so they could pass through safely.

You should sing songs of praise because you believe in Jesus Christ your Healer more than you believe in the power of sickness in your body. If you truly trust the Lord you will rejoice.

"...let all those who take refuge and put their trust in You rejoice; let them ever sing and shout for joy, because You make a covering over them and defend them..." (Psalm 5:11).

Please highlight or underline the word "all" in this passage of Scripture. This word includes *you*. Your Father wants *you* to "take refuge and put your trust in Him." He wants you to "rejoice and sing and shout for joy" because you trust Him completely. "It is a good and delightful thing to give thanks to the Lord, to sing praises [with musical accompaniment] to Your name, O Most High" (Psalm 92:1).

The amplification of this passage of Scripture tells you to sing your praise to the Lord "with musical accompaniment." I have found that it is much easier for me to sing praise to the Lord when I have anointed Christian music to accompany my songs of praise. I often put some good praise music on my CD player or cassette player when I am tired and weary and I am tempted to be discouraged. I boldly sing along with this inspired music. As I continue to sing praise music in the midst of my weariness I find that a surge of energy rises up from deep inside of me.

Some of the greatest times of praise and worship I have experienced have been in my car when I play anointed praise and worship music. I often lose myself in worshiping the Lord. I drive along in absolute ecstasy. This glorious praise music takes me right into the heavenlies. My heart sings with joy. The problems of the day melt into insignificance. No health problem or any other problem in this world can stand up in the face of continued praise and worship.

You should sing songs of vibrant praise to God instead of being tired of feeling sick and tired. Find the best praise music you can and join your voice with that anointed music. If you do not know where to obtain excellent worship music, you can purchase anointed praise and worship music from the Gaither Collection at www.gaither.com. You can call them toll-free at 1-800-955-8746. I am a big fan of Bill Gaither and his group. You also can obtain anointed praise and worship music from Integrity Music at www.integritymusic.com. You can call them toll-free at 1-800-533-6912.

You cannot boldly sing praise to God and worry at the same time. Continual songs of praise always will drive anxiety out of your mind and heart. "...ever be filled and stimulated with the [Holy] Spirit. Speak out to one another in psalms and hymns and spiritual songs, offering praise with voices [and instruments] and making melody with all your heart to the Lord, at all times and for everything giving thanks in the name of our Lord Jesus Christ to God the Father" (Ephesians 5:18-20).

Do you want to constantly "be filled and stimulated with the Holy Spirit?" You *will* be filled with the Spirit *if* you "offer praise with voices and instruments and make melody to the Lord with all of your heart at all times." You will be stimulated by the Holy Spirit if you continually give thanks to God in the name of Jesus Christ.

There is no better place to be when you are sick and tired than to be in the presence of the Lord. If you praise the Lord continually, you can be certain that you will come into His presence. "...You are holy, O You Who dwell in [the holy place where] the praises of Israel [are offered]." (Psalm 22:3).

This passage of Scripture says that God lived in the praises of the Israelites. He will live in your praise today. You will come into God's presence if you continually praise Him and thank Him. "Let us come before His presence with thanksgiving..." (Psalm 95:2).

When you are sick you must draw as close to the Lord as you possibly can. The Bible repeatedly tells you how to enter into God's presence. You come into His presence by thanking Him and praising Him continually. "Enter into His gates with thanksgiving and a thank offering and into His courts with praise! Be thankful and say so to Him, bless and affectionately praise His name!" (Psalm 100:4).

This passage of Scripture is filled with encouraging promises from God. You should be unreserved in your expression of love to God. You will enter into the "gates" of God's courtyard "with thanksgiving" if you continually offer up a sacrifice of thanksgiving. You will come into His courts if you praise Him continually. If you really are thankful you should "say so to God." You should "bless and affectionately praise His name."

You are in dangerous territory when you are outside the presence of God. You are right where your loving Father wants you to be when you come into His presence and stay there. He will reveal Himself to you as you worship Him more and more.

When you are in the Lord's presence you will understand that you do not have to struggle and strain to do everything yourself. You will see your precious Lord more and more as He truly is. You will be able to comprehend His tremendous healing power. You will learn to live in His presence and His supernatural anointing where miracles take place.

You will always experience the joy of the Lord when you are in His presence. Joy will rise up inside of you as you continually thank Him and praise Him. "Consider it wholly joyful, my brethren, whenever you are enveloped in or encounter trials of any sort" (James 1:2).

Please highlight or underline the words "trials of any sort." These words *include* the sickness in your body. What are you instructed to do when you encounter any kind of adversity, including sickness? You are told to "consider it wholly joyful."

You must not allow the sickness in your body to pull you down. Your faith in God should be so strong that you will rejoice in Him continually regardless of this sickness. "Be happy [in your faith] and rejoice and be glad-hearted continually (always)" (I Thessalonians 5:16).

Please highlight or underline the word "always" in the amplification of this verse of Scripture. The word "always" certainly includes the sickness that is in your body now. How are you instructed to react to this sickness? You are instructed to "be happy in your faith." You are instructed to "rejoice and be glad-hearted continually (always)."

Your heart will sing with joy if you *wholeheartedly believe* that Jesus Christ already has paid the price for your healing. Rejoicing will come naturally to you if you really believe this great spiritual truth and do not doubt. "They who sow in tears shall reap in joy and singing…" (Psalm 126:5).

Sometimes the pain in your body may be so severe that tears will pour down your cheeks. You must not give up hope even if you hurt this much. You should praise the Lord and sing to Him continually. You should "sow in tears." You will "reap" a harvest through "joy and singing." This harvest will come because you sowed seeds of praise when you faced a very difficult challenge with your health.

You should not give in to weariness because of the enervating sickness in your body. You should praise the Lord and thank Him for bringing you through such a difficult time. The Lord will give you the strength you need if you praise Him continually and rejoice in Him. "…the joy of the Lord is your strength…" (Nehemiah 8:10).

Where will you receive the strength you need when you are sick and tired? You will receive this strength from "the joy of the Lord" Who lives in your heart. Our precious Lord never is tired and weary. He never gives up His joy. You will come into His presence and be strengthened by His joy if you praise Him and worship Him continually.

Continual praise and thanksgiving bring you into the presence and power of God. Continual words of doubt and unbelief block the mighty power of God. Some Christians either block or delay God's answers to their prayers because they do not obey His instructions to praise Him and thank Him continually. Praise often provides God with the connection that touches His mighty power. Healing is *not* something you *will* receive. Healing is something *you already have received*. Praise and thanksgiving often will bring you into the healing presence of the Lord.

You have learned that continual praise brings you into the presence of the Lord. If you praise the Lord continually you will be in His presence continually. You should be like the psalmist who said, "My mouth shall be filled with Your praise and with Your honor all the day" (Psalm 71:8).

Worshiping the Lord as part of a congregation in church is good, but worshiping the Lord continually when you are by yourself and your body aches with pain is exactly what your Father wants you to do. You do not have to be in a church to worship God. Your "mouth should be filled with praise" throughout "all the day."

You can praise the Lord when you are taking a shower, driving your automobile, walking or doing odd jobs. You can praise the Lord if you are confined to your bed by the sickness in your body. The opportunities to praise the Lord are endless if you really have a heart to praise Him. "From the rising of the sun to the going down of it and from east to west, the name of the Lord is to be praised!" (Psalm 113:3).

How often does God want you to praise Him? He wants you to praise Him "from the rising of the sun until the going down of it." He wants you to praise Him continually throughout every day and night of your life. He wants you to praise Him "from east to west," no matter where you are.

You should praise the Lord from the moment you wake up in the morning until the moment you drop off to sleep at night. You can and should walk in the presence of the Lord continually. Your loving Father wants you to come into His presence early each morning and remain there throughout the day and night. You then should pray and ask Him to guard you and be with you while you sleep.

Continual praise should be a way of life for you. You should do exactly what your Father instructs you to do whether you feel like it or not. You should praise the Lord continually when you are on the mountaintops of life. You should praise Him continually when you are in the depths of valleys in your life. You should be consistent in your praise.

Chapter 36

God Answers Prayer

You have learned many scriptural facts about the relationship between receiving manifestation of healing and opening *your mouth* to speak, praise, worship and sing as your Father has instructed. In this chapter we will carefully study what the holy Scriptures say about praying to God for manifestation of the healing that already has been provided for you. You will learn exactly what your Father instructs you to do. You also will learn why some Christians pray continually for healing and fail to receive an answer to their prayers.

God is omniscient. He knows every minute detail about every one of the billions of people on earth. Your Father knows exactly what you will pray for before you come to Him in prayer. Jesus said, "...your Father knows what you need before you ask Him" (Matthew 6:8).

Not only does your Father know what every person needs, but He often takes action on the answer to your prayers before you pray. "...it shall be that before they call I will answer; and while they are yet speaking I will hear" (Isaiah 65:24).

If you are sick you should immediately turn to God. The *first* thing Christians should do when they are sick is to pray to God. "Is anyone among you afflicted (ill-treated, suffering evil)? He should pray..." (James 5:13).

I believe that sickness is an affliction although this passage of Scripture does not specifically refer to sickness. Christians who are sick should not pray to God *after* they go to a doctor or purchase medication. Some Christians are so indoctrinated in the world's medical system that they do not pray to God with deep and strong faith before they do anything else.

When you pray to God for healing you should anchor your prayers on specific *facts* from His Word. You should carefully follow your Father's specific instructions pertaining to prayer. Prayers of faith that are solidly anchored on God's specific instructions and definite promises are much more effective than vague and general prayers.

When you are sick sometimes you have to wait several days to obtain an appointment with a doctor. The Great Physician is always willing to listen to you instantly. He *never* says, "I am too busy to listen to your prayer right now. Come back later." Your Father is *delighted* when you come to Him with your needs. "…the prayer of the upright is His delight!" (Proverbs 15:8).

When you are sick you should be absolutely certain that your Father already has provided help for you. Prayer is the line of communication between heaven and earth. Prayer is similar to a telephone line that you can use to call your Father. Prayers of faith can open the windows of heaven and close the gates of hell.

Many people in the United States would be awestruck if they could call the President of the United States on the telephone and talk with him. You must understand that *you* have been given the *privilege* of talking *at any time* to the One Who created the President of the United States and every other person on earth. You must appreciate the tremendous privilege of prayer that has been given to you.

Because of the sacrifice of Jesus Christ every person who has asked Him to be his or her Savior is a member of the royal family of God. You can pray to God for healing with *absolute certainty* that He is your loving Father and that you are His beloved child. You should know that healing is your inheritance as God's child.

Your part is to trust your Father for your healing. God's part was completed by Jesus Christ.

You have definite assurance that your Father already answered your prayer for healing more than two thousand years ago. Jesus paid the price for your healing by the sacrifice He made on the cross at Calvary and by the sacrifice He made at the whipping post.

When you are sick your Father does not want you to come to His throne begging and pleading. He wants you to come to His throne with absolute certainty that you are His beloved child. He wants you to come to His throne with prayers of absolute faith that are based on the specific healing promises He has given you.

You must understand the importance of praying to your Father knowing that He *does* hear your prayers and that He already has answered your prayers. When we were studying Scripture meditation we touched briefly on the following passage of Scripture that we now are ready to look at in more detail. "...the prayer [that is] of faith will save him who is sick, and the Lord will restore him..." (James 5:15).

Your Father clearly says that He "will restore him who is sick" *if* this person prays "the prayer that is of faith." Unfortunately, some Christians who are sick pray to their Father without deep, strong and unwavering faith that He already has answered their prayer. Because of this fact we place great emphasis on increasing faith in God in this book and in our book, *Unshakable Faith in Almighty God* and our Scripture Meditation Cards, *Continually Increasing Faith in God*. Each of these publications contains detailed scriptural instructions that will show you exactly what to do to increase your faith in God.

Some Christians may wonder if God really hears them when they pray. Your loving Father wants you to be absolutely certain that He hears you when you come to Him in prayer. "...this is the confidence (the assurance, the privilege of boldness) which we have in Him: [we are sure] that if we ask anything (make any request) according to His will (in agreement with His own plan), He listens to and hears us" (I John 5:14).

Do not wonder if God hears your prayers. Your Father is looking for simple childlike trust from you. This passage of Scripture says that you should have absolute "confidence" and "assurance" that your Father "listens to" and "hears you" whenever you pray. There is one condition to this promise – that you pray "according to His will." God's Word is His will.

You can be assured that your Father listens to every one of your prayers that is based with unwavering faith on specific facts from His Word. This book is filled with facts from the holy Scriptures proving that *healing is God's provision for you.* You can be certain that your Father hears your prayers that are based on specific Scripture pertaining to divine healing. Because of this great spiritual truth you must understand the importance of finding, learning and believing wholeheartedly in Scripture that provides a solid foundation for your prayers.

As you grow and mature in the Lord every one of your prayers should be anchored on the will of God which is the Word of God. Your Father assures you again that you can be confident whenever you pray that He really is listening to your prayer requests. "…the eyes of the Lord are upon the righteous (those who are upright and in right standing with God), and His ears are attentive to their prayer…" (I Peter 3:12).

You become "righteous" before God when you ask Jesus Christ to be your Savior. You are righteous because Jesus has paid the full price for all of your sins. You can be certain that "God's ears are attentive to your prayer." Jesus said, "We know that God does not listen to sinners; but if anyone is God-fearing and a worshiper of Him and does His will, He listens to him" (John 9:31).

Your Father assures you once again that He *does* listen to your prayers when you meet the conditions that His Word specifies. Sinners cannot be assured that God hears their prayers because "God does not listen" to their prayers. You can be certain that your Father "listens to you" if you are "God-fearing and a worshipper of God and do His will."

Isn't it encouraging to know that Almighty God in heaven *really does* listen to your prayers that are prayed according to His will? *If* you meet specific conditions you also can be certain that God *answers your prayers.* "...if (since) we [positively] know that He listens to us in whatever we ask, we also know [with settled and absolute knowledge] that we have [granted us as our present possessions] the requests made of Him" (I John 5:15).

I believe that I John 5:15 is one of the most encouraging passages of Scripture in the entire Bible. In addition to being certain that God listens to your prayers that are prayed according to His will, you now are told that you also can be certain that God *will answer* your prayers. What more could you possibly ask God to do for you?

There is no question that your Father has done His part. There is no question that Jesus has done His part. *You must do your part.* You must learn and do exactly what your Father instructs you to do to receive His guaranteed answer to every one of your prayers.

You do not have to wonder if God will answer your prayers of faith. The amplification of this passage of Scripture says that you can "know with settled and absolute knowledge" that God will answer your prayers. You are told that God *will* grant "the requests made of Him."

The amplification of this passage of Scripture says that the answer to your prayers is "granted you as your present possession." In the spiritual realm God *instantly* answers prayers of faith that are made according to His will. Your Father often requires a great deal of persevering faith to bring His immediate answer to your prayers in the spiritual realm into manifestation in the natural realm. However, you can be certain that your Father does answer your prayers of faith that are according to His will *when you pray.*

You may not see anything happening immediately after you pray. However, when the Word of God tells you that God *will* answer your prayers of faith as your "present possession," you should proceed the same way you would proceed if you received an immediate response in your body. Your words and your actions should be the same as they would be if you received instant manifestation of healing. You do not need to see God's answer to know that your Father already *has done* exactly what His Word says He will do. Faith sees the deed done before it is seen by the visible eye.

In this chapter we have established a scriptural foundation for prayer for healing. In the next chapter we will carefully study many additional facts from the Word of God about the relationship between deep, strong and unwavering faith in God and receiving answers to your prayers.

Chapter 37

You Must Pray with Unwavering Faith in God

In this chapter we will carefully examine what the Bible says about the relationship between deep, strong and unwavering faith in God and receiving an answer to your prayers. We will begin by looking again at three passages of Scripture we already have covered. We will examine each of the statements from Jesus Christ in the context of what He says about the relationship between your unwavering faith in God and receiving the healing He has provided for you.

- "…whatever you ask for in prayer, believe (trust and be confident) that it is granted to you, and you will [get it]" (Mark 11:24)

- "…whatever you ask for in prayer, having faith and [really] believing, you will receive" (Matthew 21:22).

- "If you live in Me [abide vitally united to Me] and My words remain in you and continue to live in your hearts, ask whatever you will, and it shall be done for you" (John 15:7).

We studied these passages of Scripture previously to prove that God still *does* heal today. Anyone who does not believe that God heals today would have to say that the word "whatever" that is included in each of these passages of Scripture does *not* include healing.

In this chapter we will look at these passages of Scripture, not only to emphasize that God heals today, but to explain in detail the relationship that Jesus spoke of between *your* faith in God and receiving the healing He already has provided for you. Mark 11:24 and Matthew 21:22 probably are the same statement that Jesus made that was recorded slightly differently by Mark and Matthew. Each of these passages of Scripture begins with the same words "whatever you ask for in prayer" and ends with words that are similar when Mark says "you will get it" and Matthew says "you will receive."

For the purpose of this chapter we will focus on the middle portion of these passages. Mark 11:24 says that you must "believe, trust and be confident" that the healing you ask for "is granted." Matthew 21:22 says that you must "have faith and really believe." Mark 11:24 and the other two promises from Jesus are *conditional* promises. God requires you to *believe* these promises.

We now are ready to study John 15:7 from the perspective of receiving healing from God. In this passage of Scripture Jesus says essentially the same thing He said in Mark 11:24 and Matthew 21:22, but He goes one step further. The last portion of this passage of Scripture assures you that you can "ask whatever you will and it shall be done for you." The first portion of this passage of Scripture explains the two conditions that *you* must meet to receive the answer to your prayer that the last portion of this passage of Scripture says you will receive.

The first condition is that Jesus instructs you to "live in Him." The amplification of this portion of Scripture says that you "should abide vitally united to Him." You must *abide* in Jesus at all times if you sincerely desire to receive healing from God. Jesus should be in absolute first place throughout every day of your life.

Please focus on the words "vitally united." If something is vital it is absolutely essential. You must understand the *vital im-*

portance of every aspect of your life revolving around the Lord Jesus Christ Who paid such a tremendous price for the forgiveness of your sins and for your healing of the sickness in your body. Nothing in your life should even remotely approach the importance of your continual focus on Jesus. You should have a deep and consuming desire to draw closer to Him throughout every day of your life.

Jesus said that the second condition to this promise is for His Word to "remain in you and continue to live in your heart." In the chapters on meditation you learned the importance of *continually* filling your heart with God's Word. Jesus emphasizes this priority in this passage of Scripture.

These three passages of Scripture are very clear. The all-inclusive word "whatever" in each passage of Scripture confirms that God *has* provided healing through Jesus Christ. You must stay *close* to Jesus at all times. *Every* aspect of your life should focus on Him. *Nothing* in your life should even begin to approach the degree of importance you place on your personal relationship with Jesus.

You have seen that God's ways are very different from the ways of the world (see Isaiah 55:8-9). In the world many people want to see before they believe. Some people say "I'll believe it when I see it." God's Word says that you *first* must *believe* and *then* you will *see*.

Are you believing God for healing? You can spend your time wisely by meditating continually on these three passages of Scripture. Personalize these promises. Highlight or underline the words that promise you *will* receive manifestation of healing *if* you have deep, strong and unwavering faith that your Father already has given you this healing.

Some Christians go to God in prayer asking Him to heal them without including specific Scripture in their request. Some Christians go to God in prayer for healing without a deep inner certainty that God will do exactly what they are asking Him to do. You must not make either of these mistakes.

The Bible says that it is *impossible* to please God *without faith* (see Hebrews 11:6). Some Christians are praying to God to heal them, but they are not praying with deep, strong and unwavering faith in Him. Their Father is not pleased with these prayers.

The Bible explains that doubt and unbelief actually can *block the Lord from answering your prayers.* I explained in Chapter Sixteen that the sixth chapter of Mark tells you how Jesus went back to His home town of Nazareth after performing many healing miracles elsewhere. Jesus must have had a special desire to perform miracles of healing for the people He had lived with for many years. However, the people in Nazareth did not believe that Jesus was the Messiah. Their doubt and unbelief *blocked Jesus* from performing healing miracles (see Mark 6:1-6).

Some Christians are *blocking God* from giving them the healing He so much wants to give them because they are begging, pleading, wishing and hoping when they pray. These children of God are wasting their breath because they are *not* praying prayers of faith. Their prayers are no more effective than the prayers of unbelievers.

Your faith places you in God's presence and power and enables you to receive God's provision. If you have money on deposit in a bank do you beg and plead for the teller to give you money? No, you do not. When you go to the bank you quietly and confidently ask for what you already know is available to you.

Your Father wants you to come to Him with quiet and calm confidence to receive what you know He already has provided for you. You must understand that prayers of doubt and unbelief actually are a sin against God. "...whatever does not originate and proceed from faith is sin [whatever is done without a conviction of its approval by God is sinful]" (Romans 14:23).

You know that disobedience to any of the Ten Commandments is sin. You must understand that lack of faith in God is just as much a sin as any of the sins that are listed in the Ten Commandments. Your prayer life will only be effective when your prayers are solidly anchored on the Word of God and if your prayers are prayers of faith and not prayers of doubt and unbelief.

This chapter is filled with facts about praying to your Father with deep, strong and unwavering faith that He will answer. If you have strong faith in God, your words and actions in the days, weeks and months after you pray should continually indicate that you are *absolutely certain* that your loving Father answers your prayers of faith.

Now that we have established a scriptural foundation for effective prayer we are ready to look into the holy Scriptures to learn additional facts about prayer. In the next chapter we will discuss why, if you really have deep, strong and unwavering faith in God, you should thank Him *when you pray*.

Chapter 38

Thank God As You Pray Earnestly

When you pray for healing you should emphasize the answer you desire, *not* the problem. Your Father already knows everything about the sickness in your body. Instead of dwelling on the sickness you should simply acknowledge the sickness. The remainder of your prayer should be based on God's *answer* to the problem. I believe that each of your prayers for healing should be solidly anchored on promises in God's Word.

This book is filled with many specific promises from God to give you a solid foundation for your prayers for healing. As you go through this book you might want to highlight, underline or put an asterisk next to the specific passages of Scripture you definitely want to focus on when you pray.

Your Father is pleased when you come to Him with a prayer of faith based on specific promises in His Word. God stands behind every one of His promises. I do not believe you can do anything that is more beneficial than to continually come to your Father with absolute faith that He will answer your prayer because He always honors His promises. You have seen that God's promises often are conditional. If you do what your Father requires you to do you can be certain that He will do what He says He will do.

You will be very familiar with God's healing promises *if* you have faithfully obeyed your Father's instructions to renew your mind in His Word each day and to meditate on His Word through-out the day and night. Your heart should be *filled* with God's heal-ing promises. When you pray, these promises should pour out of your mouth from the abundance of your heart (see Luke 6:45). Your voice should ring with your absolute certainty that God's Word is true and that your loving Father always is faithful to His Word.

You must not worry about the sickness in your body. Instead of worrying you should pray with faith that you will receive heal-ing from God. "Do not fret or have any anxiety about anything, but in every circumstance and in everything, by prayer and peti-tion (definite requests), with thanksgiving, continue to make your wants known to God" (Philippians 4:6).

This passage of Scripture says that you should "not fret or have any anxiety about anything." The word "anything" includes sickness. Your Father instructs you to come to Him in prayer "in every circumstance." The words "every" and "everything" that are used in this verse of Scripture include sickness.

The amplification says that your prayers should consist of "definite requests." Your Father wants you to be specific when you pray. You will be very specific if you pray each of your prayers for healing based on healing Scriptures.

Please highlight or underline the words "with thanksgiving." You have learned about the relationship between praise, giving thanks and divine healing. Your Father wants you to *thank Him when you pray* even though you have not yet received manifesta-tion of healing.

All Christians are children of God. Your Father has told you that *you already have been healed.* Pray thanking Him that He sent Jesus Christ to take your sin and your sickness on Himself. You should not wait until *after* you have received healing in your body to thank God. The Bible clearly instructs you to thank God when you pray.

What would you do if a loving family member or close friend called to tell you that he (or she) had sent you a gift of $100 in the mail? Would you thank this person at that time or would you say something absurd like, "First of all I want to be certain that the post office delivers your check to me. Then I want to be certain that your check clears the bank. Then when I finally have the money in my hand, I will say thank you."?

You *would not think* of treating a loving family member or friend this way. If a loved one says that he or she has sent a gift in the mail, you would thank this person *at that time*. You should do the same when you pray to your loving Father in heaven. Your Father has given you many specific healing promises. He wants you to *believe* that He *will* do exactly what He says He will do. He wants you to show your faith in Him by thanking Him when you pray.

You then are instructed to "continue to make your wants known to God." This portion of Scripture instructs you to continually come to God in prayer. If you have deep and strong faith in God you should show your confidence in Him by thanking Him each time you pray.

You will experience a tremendous breakthrough in the effectiveness of your prayer life when you come to the place of gratitude that flows out of your heart to God. Your Father wants each of your prayers to be "Thank You" prayers. He wants you to habitually thank Him whenever you pray for healing or for any other need.

The next verse tells you that obeying these specific instructions from God will quiet you and calm you. "...God's peace [shall be yours, that tranquil state of a soul assured of its salvation through Christ, and so fearing nothing from God and being content with its earthly lot of whatever sort that is, that peace] which transcends all understanding shall garrison and mount guard over your hearts and minds in Christ Jesus" (Philippians 4:7).

You show your gratitude by thanking your Father when you pray. You will come closer to God if you continually pray out of a heart that is filled with gratitude. You will receive more of His peace because you are in His presence. When you gratefully thank

Him as you pray you *will* experience "that peace which transcends all understanding." God's supernatural peace is *so great* that you cannot even begin to explain it with the limitations of your human understanding.

When you move into this supernatural peace of God your Father promises that His peace will "garrison and mount guard over your heart and mind in Christ Jesus." God's supernatural peace will protect your heart and your mind from any concern about the sickness in your body.

You have seen that God emphasizes through repetition. Your Father tells you in another passage of Scripture the importance of thanking Him when you pray. "Be earnest and unwearied and steadfast in your prayer [life], being [both] alert and intent in [your praying] with thanksgiving" (Colossians 4:2).

Your Father wants you to be very determined when you pray. He does not want you to give in to fatigue. He wants you to "be earnest and unwearied and steadfast in your prayer life." He wants your faith in Him to be deep, strong and unwavering. He wants you to be "alert and intent" when you pray. Once again you are instructed to pray "with thanksgiving."

You have just seen that Colossians 4:2 instructs you to be "earnest" when you pray. Your Father uses this same word in another passage of Scripture when He tells you how you should pray to Him. "...The earnest (heartfelt, continued) prayer of a righteous man makes tremendous power available [dynamic in its working]" (James 5:16).

The amplification after the word "earnest" tells you that this word means "heartfelt and continued." If you continually pray from your heart these prayers "make tremendous power available" to you. The amplification of this passage of Scripture tells you that this power is "dynamic in its working."

You must understand the enormous spiritual power that is released when you pray in this manner. All Christians are "righteous" because Jesus Christ paid the full price for our sin. Your Father wants you to *pour your heart into your prayers.*

You should not just go through the motions of a religious exercise. You must understand that, whenever you pray, you have been given the privilege of talking directly to Almighty God in heaven. Believe that your earnest prayers of faith will open the doors of heaven and cause the mighty hand of God to move on your behalf. There is no comparison between fervent prayer and religious prayer. Fervent prayer pours out of your heart. Religious prayer is rote that comes from the mind and is not connected to Jesus Christ.

The next two verses instruct you to pray like Elijah. "Elijah was a human being with a nature such as we have [with feelings, affections, and a constitution like ours]; and he prayed earnestly for it not to rain, and no rain fell on the earth for three years and six months. And [then] he prayed again and the heavens supplied rain and the land produced its crops [as usual]" (James 5:17-18).

Elijah was a mighty man of God, but he was a human being just like you. Because Elijah prayed "earnestly" his prayers were powerful enough to stop rain from falling "for three years and six months." Then, at a later time when rain was needed, Elijah once again prayed earnestly from his heart and "the heavens supplied rain and the land produced its crops as usual."

We can say for certain that Elijah knew God intimately. Elijah knew God so well that He took him to heaven in a whirlwind in a supernatural phenomenon (see II Kings 2:1-15). Your Father wants you to continually draw closer to Him so that your prayers will be anointed before Him as Elijah's prayers were. A close and intimate relationship with God is the greatest of joys. Healing is part of God's nature.

Chapter 39

Additional Instructions
Pertaining to Prayer

In this chapter we will study additional instructions from the Word of God regarding prayer for healing. The Word of God gives you specific instructions about joining your faith with the faith of other Christians. This kind of prayer is called a prayer of agreement. Jesus said, "…if two of you on earth agree (harmonize together, make a symphony together) about whatever [anything and everything] they may ask, it will come to pass and be done for them by My Father in heaven" (Matthew 18:19).

This passage of Scripture explains the importance of two Christians agreeing together in prayer. Jesus used the word "whatever." The amplification says "anything and everything." There cannot be any question that this statement *includes* agreement in prayer for healing in your body because this healing obviously is included in the all-inclusive words "whatever, anything and everything."

Jesus promises you that the answer to your prayer "will come to pass and be done for *you*" by God in heaven. If you are seriously ill I recommend that you prayerfully compile a list of all other Christians with strong faith whom you believe will agree in prayer with you. You then should contact each of these Christians, explain your need and ask this person to continually agree with you in prayer for manifestation of healing in your body. I have used email many times to ask other Christians with strong faith to pray for a person who needs healing.

If I was severely ill I would make a list of every Christian I know who has strong faith in God. I would telephone each of these people or send each of them an email message explaining my need. I would ask each of these people to join their faith with my faith. I cannot tell you how encouraging it would be to know that many other Christians with deep, strong and unwavering faith in God were joining with me in my prayers.

Do not give up if you fail to receive manifestation of healing soon after you and the other Christians begin to pray. Communicate often with these people. Bring them up to date. Let them know that you are persevering with unwavering faith in God. Ask these Christians to continue in their prayer of agreement with you.

The power of agreeing in faith with other Christians is phenomenal. I believe that these prayers have a synergistic effect. I believe that the faith of two Christians with strong faith continually agreeing together in prayer is not a "one plus one" type of faith. I believe that faith in God multiplies *exponentially* when you agree in prayer with other Christians who have deep, strong, unwavering and unshakable faith in God.

The twelfth chapter of Acts gives you an excellent example of the tremendous power of the prayer of other people. Because we have so much to fit into this chapter I will not include all of these verses. I will summarize what this portion of Scripture teaches you about the power of other people's prayers. If you want to read this Scripture please open your Bible to Acts 12:4-11.

This portion of Scripture tells about an instance where the apostle Peter was imprisoned. Peter was sound asleep the night before he was scheduled to be executed. Peter was chained between two soldiers. Other soldiers stood guard.

An angel suddenly appeared and awakened Peter. The chains that were holding him fell off his wrists. The angel then led Peter out of the cellblock and took him to the main gate of the prison. This gate supernaturally opened and Peter walked to safety.

After Peter left the prison he went to a home where many people were fervently praying for him. Acts 12:16 says that the Christians in this house were "amazed" to see the magnificent answer to their prayers. You must not underestimate the enormous spiritual power of people who are fervently praying for you.

In addition to agreeing in faith with other people as you pray the Bible also gives you specific facts about the importance that God places on *your* continual prayers for *other* people. God often will bless you when you pray continually for *others* even though you are sick or going through adversity yourself. "...the Lord turned the captivity of Job and restored his fortunes, when he prayed for his friends..." (Job 42:10).

Anyone who has studied the Bible knows that Job experienced severe adversity. Job was released from these problems "when he prayed for his friends." God will bless you when you *consistently* put Him first, other people second and yourself last.

One of the best things you can do when you are sick is to get your attention off yourself and to pray for other people. Your Father does not want you to be self-centered. He wants your life to be centered around Him and a sincere desire to reach out to other people. I believe the majority of your prayers should be for other people, not for yourself.

Your Father often will bless you for your unselfishness in prayer just as He blessed Job. God will use your selflessness as a spiritual channel to bless you. You cannot do anything for needy people that is more important than to pray for them continually and fervently with deep, strong and unwavering faith in God. You show your love for God and your love for other people by continually praying for others.

This type of prayer is called intercession. All Christians should pray continually for their unsaved loved ones and friends. You engage in spiritual battle with your prayers of faith for the eternal salvation of these people. The eternal destiny of these people is at stake. You must be relentless and persevering.

For many years I have prayed whenever I hear an ambulance siren. We hear many sirens in Florida because of the high percentage of elderly people who live here. Whenever I hear a siren I know that someone is in trouble. I always intercede for every person who is affected in any way by the reason for the siren.

I include all members of that person's family. I pray for their eternal salvation. I ask God to bless them. I ask God to meet their every need. I believe I average praying this prayer approximately three times a day. That means that I pray more than one thousand times each year for other people because I have heard a siren.

Hardly a day goes by when I do not lay my hands on my daily newspaper to pray for the needs of people I read about. Whenever I see someone who has been in an accident or I am made aware of anyone who has a need, I pray for that person.

I am not saying these things to glorify myself. Our Father clearly instructs us to intercede for other people. If you are sick I believe you need to intensify your prayers for other people who have needs. The world says, "God helps those who help themselves." I believe that God helps His children who keep Him first at all times and continually reach out to others with love and compassion.

I have compiled a prayer list that contains the names of people I pray for consistently. This list changes often, but it always involves prayer requests for more than fifty people. More than half of the people on this prayer list need healing. I pray for healing for these people. I also pray for several Christian ministries, for government leaders, for our country and for a mighty move of revival throughout the world. "...keep alert and watch with strong purpose and perseverance, interceding on behalf of all the saints (God's consecrated people)" (Ephesians 6:18).

You should "keep alert and watch with strong purpose and perseverance" for other people who need your prayers. "...far be it from me that I should sin against the Lord by ceasing to pray for you…" (I Samuel 12:23).

Samuel was a judge in Israel. Part of his responsibility was to pray for Israel. Samuel took this responsibility very seriously. He knew that he would "sin against the Lord" if he "ceased to pray" for Israel. You should feel the same way about your commitment to pray for needy people.

In addition to praying for other people, the Bible instructs you to confess your faults to other people. A *definite relationship* exists between receiving healing from God and openly admitting your faults and shortcomings. "Confess to one another therefore your faults (your slips, your false steps, your offenses, your sins) and pray [also] for one another, that you may be healed…" (James 5:16).

As you examine scriptural instructions about the relationship between praying for other people and receiving manifestation of healing yourself, you must not disregard what this passage of Scripture says. Please read the last part first – "that you may be healed." *What* does your Father instruct you to do to receive this healing? He instructs you to "confess to one another your faults" and "to pray for one another."

Another mistake that many people make when they are sick or when they pray for any other reason is to routinely repeat the same words over and over again when they pray. Jesus said, "…when you pray, do not heap up phrases (multiply words, re-peating the same ones over and over) as the Gentiles do, for they think they will be heard for their much speaking" (Matthew 6:7).

Your Father does not want you to pray in a perfunctory man-ner. He wants you to pray fervently from your heart. You must have full realization that you are speaking directly to Almighty God through Jesus Christ. Your prayers should not be stiff, for-mal and religious. You should talk to your loving Father as natu-rally and spontaneously as you would talk to another human be-ing. Your Father wants you to have a close and intimate relation-ship with Him. He wants you to pray to Him continually.

Some Christians complicate prayer. Your Father does not require you to pray complicated prayers. He wants to hear simple prayers of faith that come from your heart. When young children ask their parents for help they do not complicate their requests. Their requests are very simple. Your Father wants you to do the same when you make requests to Him. He does not want long and formal prayers. Your Father wants you to come to Him with simple childlike trust.

You should set aside specific time each day for prayer. You should have a specific place where you pray. Jesus said, "…when you pray, go into your [most] private room, and, closing the door, pray to your Father, Who is in secret; and your Father, Who sees in secret, will reward you in the open" (Matthew 6:6).

There is no question that Jesus wants you to go to a specific place for your daily prayer time. He instructs you to "close the door" to this room. Your Father listens to these prayers and answers them. He "will reward you" for your fervent prayer.

You should not limit your prayers to the time you pray in this specific place. Your Father wants you to persevere by praying constantly. "…be unceasing in prayer [praying perseveringly]…" (I Thessalonians 5:17). Your Father wants you to pray at all times and in all places. "…in every place men should pray…" (I Timothy 2:8).

Be "unceasing" in your prayers. Pray in "every place" you can pray. Prayer should be a way of life to you. You have many opportunities each day to intercede for other people. You must not allow these opportunities to go by without praying.

Is prayer a chore to you or a comfort? Prayer should not be a chore. You should be *extremely grateful* for the precious privilege you have been given to come to God Himself with your prayers. Jesus died to give you the privilege of praying directly to God. You should talk with your Father several times each day. You should reach out continually with bold faith when you pray to God.

The best way to learn to pray effectively is to pray often. The more you learn what the Word of God says about prayer and follow these specific instructions, the more effective your prayers will be. Christians who pray effectively are Christians who have spent many hours in prayer.

This chapter contains many scriptural instructions on prayer. Although this book is about divine healing, these instructions apply to prayer in every area. In the next chapter we will look into the Word of God to learn that God is *not* a far away, distant God. You will see that your loving Father wants you to constantly be aware that He is very close to you at all times.

Chapter 40

The Great Physician Lives in Your Heart

You have learned that Jesus Christ is your Healer. Jesus is the Great Physician. Have you asked Jesus to be your Savior? If you have, you can be absolutely certain that the Great Physician lives in *your* heart. You can be certain that God is not far from you. "Am I a God at hand, says the Lord, and not a God afar off?" (Jeremiah 23:23).

How can you have faith that God will heal you if you believe He is far away and that He is too busy to be concerned with any one person? The Bible teaches that God sits on His throne in heaven and that Jesus sits next to Him. However, God is *omnipresent*. He is able to be in an *infinite number* of places at the same time. He is "not a God afar off." "...He is not far from each one of us..." (Acts 17:27).

Please highlight or underline the words "each one of us." The words "each one" include *you*. There is no question that God is not far from you. Your absolute certainty of this magnificent truth should pervade your consciousness throughout every day of your life.

When I was a little boy doctors used to make house calls. I can remember the doctor coming to our home when we were sick. Very few doctors make house calls today. The Great Physician makes house calls. The Great Physician is with *you* twenty-four hours a day. He already knows every detail about the sickness in your body. He already has provided healing for this sickness. All that He requires is for you to exhibit persevering faith in Him.

The Bible is filled with facts telling you that God the Father lives in your heart if you have received Jesus Christ as your Savior. "One God and Father of [us] all, Who is above all [Sovereign over all], pervading all and [living] in [us] all" (Ephesians 4:6).

God is the "Father of us all." The word "all" includes *you.* If you are a Christian you can be absolutely certain that God in heaven is *your Father.* You know that God is "above all" in heaven. There is no question that God is "sovereign over all." God is omnipotent. He has all power. The amplification says that God is "pervading all." He is omnipresent. God is diffused throughout the earth.

This passage of Scripture also says that God is "living in us all." The word "all" in this portion of Scripture means that God lives inside of *you.* If you have asked Jesus Christ to be your Savior you can be absolutely certain that your Father lives in your heart.

Some people who are seriously ill are devastated by fear because of the severity of the sickness in their bodies. Your Father is *not* afraid of the sickness in your body. He does not want you to be afraid. "...Be not afraid, neither be dismayed, for the Lord your God is with you wherever you go" (Joshua 1:9).

Why would you be afraid of the sickness in your body if you are *absolutely certain* that "the Lord your God is with you wherever you go?" You are not alone. God is with you throughout every minute of every hour of every day of your life.

You can be certain that your loving Father is right there with you when your body aches with pain. He does not want you to be afraid. He wants you to trust Him completely to help you. "Fear not [there is nothing to fear], for I am with you..." (Isaiah 41:10).

Your Father does not want fear caused by sickness or fear caused by any other circumstance to affect you. He specifically says to you, "Fear not." The amplification says "there is nothing to fear." The word "nothing" *includes* the sickness in your body.

If you are sick and you are going through an excruciatingly difficult time you will be encouraged to know that God promises that He will bring you safely through this ordeal. "When you pass through the waters, I will be with you, and through the rivers, they will not overwhelm you. When you walk through the fire, you will not be burned or scorched, nor will the flame kindle upon you. For I am the Lord your God, the Holy One of Israel…" (Isaiah 43:2-3).

Please highlight or underline the *three times* the word "through" is used in this passage of Scripture. Your Father wants you to know that He will bring you safely *through* the difficult times caused by sickness in your body *if* you trust Him completely and absolutely refuse to waver in your faith in Him. As you are trusting God, He is protecting you.

There is no question that the Bible repeatedly teaches that God the Father lives in *your* heart. The Bible also teaches that His Son Jesus Christ lives in your heart. "May Christ through your faith [actually] dwell (settle down, abide, make His permanent home) in your hearts…" (Ephesians 3:17).

Please highlight or underline the words "through your faith." Do you *really believe* that this passage of Scripture tells the absolute truth when it says that Jesus "makes His permanent home in *your* heart?" "…Do you not yourself realize and know [thoroughly by an ever-increasing experience] that Jesus Christ is in you?…" (II Corinthians 13:5).

If you will carefully obey all of the specific scriptural instructions that are given in this book you will "realize and know thoroughly by an ever-increasing experience that Jesus Christ is in you." As you set aside precious time each day to be alone with Jesus you will progressively become more and more aware of His indwelling presence. The apostle Paul was absolutely certain that Jesus lived in his heart. Paul said, "…it is no longer I who live, but Christ (the Messiah) lives in me…" (Galatians 2:20).

Paul no longer lived for himself. He chose to crucify his life to yield to the indwelling Jesus Christ to control his life. The same Jesus Christ Who died for *your sins* and paid the price for *your healing* lives inside of *you*. Jesus is the Healer. The same Jesus Who healed so many people during His earthly ministry lives in *your* heart today. Trust Him completely for your healing.

You have seen that God the Father lives in your heart. You have seen that Jesus Christ makes His home in your heart. The Bible also teaches that the Holy Spirit lives in your heart. "...if anyone does not possess the [Holy] Spirit of Christ, he is none of His [he does not belong to Christ, is not truly a child of God]" (Romans 8:9).

Every person who has asked Jesus to be his or her Savior becomes "a child of God." Every person who asks Jesus to be his or her Savior "possesses the Holy Spirit." The Holy Spirit lives in *your* heart if Jesus is your Savior. This passage of Scripture says that you are "*not* truly a child of God" if you do not possess the Holy Spirit.

Jesus explained to His disciples at the Last Supper that the Holy Spirit would take up residence in their hearts. He referred to "...the Spirit of Truth, Whom the world cannot receive (welcome, take to its heart), because it does not see Him or know and recognize Him. But you know and recognize Him, for He lives with you [constantly] and will be in you" (John 14:17).

Unbelievers cannot receive the Holy Spirit until they open their hearts to Jesus Christ. However, each person who has asked Jesus to be his or her Savior does receive the Holy Spirit. The same Holy Spirit Who was *so powerful* that He was able to "raise Jesus from the dead" lives in *your* heart. "...the Spirit of Him Who raised up Jesus from the dead dwells in you..." (Romans 8:11).

You can receive manifestation of the healing that already has been provided for you through the impartation of divine power through the Holy Spirit. His anointing can impart healing. This chapter is filled with facts showing you that God the Father, God the Son and God the Holy Spirit live in *your heart*. "…you are in Him, made full and having come to fullness of life [in Christ you too are filled with the Godhead – Father, Son and Holy Spirit – and reach full spiritual stature]…" (Colossians 2:10).

Your Father wants you to "come to fullness of life." The amplification in this passage of Scripture says that "*you* are filled with the Godhead - Father, Son and Holy Spirit." The words "full," "fullness" and "filled" are used four times in this passage of Scripture. You must realize the fullness of spiritual power that lives inside of you.

God the Father is the first person of the Godhead. Jesus Christ is the second person of the Godhead. The Holy Spirit is the third person of the Godhead. Your heart will *sing with joy* if you are *absolutely certain* that God the Father, God the Son and God the Holy Spirit make their residence in your heart.

You should *never* allow sickness to seem to be more severe than the mighty and powerful Godhead in your heart. Your perspective is wrong if you maximize the sickness in your body and minimize the mighty power of God the Father, God the Son and God the Holy Spirit Who live in you.

If you *really believe* that God the Father, God the Son and God the Holy Spirit live in you, you should speak and act accordingly. Many Christians who are very sick would speak much differently if they had this *absolute certainty* deep down in their hearts. The greatest power in the entire universe lives in your heart. Absolutely *refuse* to allow sickness, no matter how severe it may be, to seem to be more powerful than God the Father, God the Son and God the Holy Spirit.

Personalize each passage of Scripture in this chapter. Put your name in every Scripture that says "you." Speak these mighty promises boldly. Meditate continually on this Scripture. Steadily increase your faith that the greatest power in the entire universe really does live in your heart. Enjoy God. Love Him. Thank Him.

Chapter 41

Come Close to God

Now that you have learned many facts about God living in your heart you must understand the importance of continually drawing closer to Him. *What good* does it do you to have God living in your heart if you do not have a close relationship with Him? A close relationship with God is not a nice to have. A close relationship with God is an absolute necessity. "...Seek Me [inquire for and of Me and require Me as you require food]..." (Amos 5:4).

Food obviously is a necessity. You cannot live indefinitely without food. This passage of Scripture says that you are "required" to seek God. Continually drawing closer to God is vitally important if you are sick and sincerely want to receive healing from God.

Your loving Father wants to have a close relationship with each of His children, but He will never force Himself on you. If you have a sincere desire to draw close to God you can be certain that He will come close to you. "...come close to God and He will come close to you..." (James 4:8).

Please highlight or underline the words "will come close to you" in this passage of Scripture. Your part is to continually do everything you can to "come close to God." *If* you do your part you can be absolutely certain that "He *will* come close to *you*."

You should set aside a significant amount of precious time each day to draw closer to God. No matter how busy you might be or what challenges you face, *nothing* should be more important to you. "...seek, inquire for, and require Me daily and delight [externally] to know My ways..." (Isaiah 58:2).

This passage of Scripture instructs you to "seek" God, to "inquire for Him and require" Him. *How often* does your Father want you to set aside time to draw closer to Him? This passage of Scripture tells you that you should seek a closer relationship with Him "daily." You will "delight" in God and you will "know His ways" if you obey these specific instructions. You will learn exactly what your Father instructs you to do to receive the healing He already has provided as you continually draw closer to Him and trust Him more and more.

In the last chapter we studied Scripture that informed you that God is not far away from you. The fall of Adam *separated* every person on earth from God. The shed blood of Jesus Christ enables you to draw *close* to God. "...now in Christ Jesus, you who once were [so] far away, through (by, in) the blood of Christ have been brought near" (Ephesians 2:13).

You "once were so far away," but now you have "been brought near" to God. You *must not forfeit* the precious privilege you have been given of continually drawing closer to God. Unbelievers *cannot* enjoy the privilege of fellowshipping with God. Christians can fellowship with God, but this wonderful privilege will not do you any good *unless* you take full advantage of it. "...[this] fellowship that we have [which is a distinguishing mark of Christians] is with the Father and with His Son Jesus Christ (the Messiah)" (I John 1:3).

The amplification of this passage of Scripture tells you that continual fellowship with God "is a distinguishing mark of Christians." Unfortunately, many Christians go through their entire lives without even beginning to develop a close and intimate relationship with "the Father and with His Son Jesus Christ."

Many Christians go to church each week, but they do *not* spend time *daily* drawing closer to the Lord as Isaiah 58:2 instructs us to do. They may spend a few minutes in prayer each day, but they are not students of the Bible (see II Timothy 2:15). They do not worship the Lord continually (see Psalm 113:3) and they do not know and obey all of the other scriptural instructions that are contained in this book. "…God is great, and we know Him not!..." (Job 36:26).

What good does it do you to have the precious privilege of drawing closer to God that Jesus paid for with His shed blood if you do not partake of this wonderful opportunity? Many of God's children "know Him not." Many Christians are so busy doing things *they* think are important that they fail to obey God's instructions to draw closer to Him on a daily basis.

Some Christians think they know the Lord well. They think they have a close relationship with the Lord. The *only* way you ever will know for certain how well you really know the Lord and how much you really trust Him is by your actions when you face severe sickness or any other adversity. "They profess to know God [to recognize, perceive and be acquainted with Him], but deny and disown and renounce Him by what they do…" (Titus 1:16).

Paul told Titus to rebuke the factions in the church that were defiling and polluting the Truth. This same principle applies today. You can only show how intimately you know God by your daily Bible study and meditation, by your time in prayer, by listening to God and by obeying His instructions.

Christians who are seriously ill show by their words and actions whether they really do have an intimate relationship with the Lord. Unfortunately, some Christians have fallen into many of the ways of the world. Some of us place far *too much* attachment to people, places, things and events when our primary goal should be to continually draw closer to our precious Lord.

Our generation is a restless generation. Some people cannot even begin to think of being still to spend time with the Lord.

They have to be doing something continually. They are always on the go.

These people must be entertained. If they find themselves alone they often pick up the telephone just to talk to someone. When they are alone they turn on a radio, a CD, a television set, a DVD or some other form of noise. Our generation is the noisiest generation in history. Being quiet before the Lord is unnatural for many Christians.

Many families live a very stressful lifestyle. Both parents often are extremely busy. Parents with children have the additional pressure of trying to meet all of the deadlines of their children's activities. Substantial daily quiet time with the Lord often seems to be impossible to these busy people.

Our Father never intended for our lives to be so hectic. Many Christians spend far too much of their time and energy on activities that have absolutely *no* eternal significance. They use their busyness as an excuse for not doing the one thing their Father wants them to do *more* than anything else – to draw closer to Him and to come into His presence continually.

Ask yourself how much time *you* actually have spent being totally quiet before the Lord without any external influence. Many Christians must honestly say that they spend little or no time being quiet before the Lord. *Sickness is a great equalizer.* Many Christians who do not have a close relationship with the Lord suddenly find that sickness or some other form of severe adversity causes them to radically change their priorities. Hopefully they have not waited too long. You should follow the example of the psalmist who said, "…my inner self thirsts for God, for the living God…" (Psalm 42:2).

Do you have a hunger and thirst deep down within yourself for a close personal relationship with "the living God?" This relationship is available to all Christians. *You can be as close to God as you really want to be. You determine how close you will be to God.* God sets no limits on how close He will be to you. You make this decision on a daily basis.

Your Father does not want you to be separated from Him. He wants you to reach out to Him each day. He already has the answer to every problem you will ever face. However, He has given you freedom of choice. If you choose not to draw close to Him on a daily basis, He will honor this choice even though He knows you are headed for severe problems if you fail to come close to Him and stay close to Him.

You cannot draw closer to God without continually turning *away* from the ways of the world (see Romans 12:2). Many Christians do not even begin to understand how much they are influenced by the ways of the world because the choices they make seem so normal and natural to them. Also, many other Christians they know are making similar choices.

Unfortunately, many Christians will not draw close to God *until* they face a severe crisis. Many Christians have not even taken the first step to establish a close relationship with the Lord because everything is going relatively well in their lives. Some of us need to face severe sickness or other adversity to become motivated to do what we *should* have been doing all along – we must draw closer to God on a *daily* basis.

Severe illness can be a very lonely experience. Your loving family members and your friends care about what you are going through, but they can only do so much. Some of your friends will visit you when you are sick. They may offer simplistic solutions to your problem. They may say such things as "Hang in there," "It's all going to work out for the best" and "Time will take care of everything."

This kind of advice may be true, but it lacks spiritual substance. You must have a solid scriptural foundation to persevere with unwavering faith when you are sick and tired and your body aches with pain. If you are very sick you may be in a position where *only the Lord* can give you what you need. Many sick people are overwhelmed by the sickness in their bodies. We each can decide to draw closer to God *every day* and persevere in our faith until we ultimately walk in the victory over sickness that Jesus won for us (see Chapter Two).

Christians who are severely ill need an indomitable spirit that cannot be dominated by sickness or anything else in the world. This kind of spirit can only be developed by constantly drawing closer to the One Who is completely indomitable and absolutely undefeatable.

You must not allow sickness to drive a wedge between you and God. Just the opposite should be true. Nothing is more important for a severely ill person than to come close to God and stay close to Him every day. I have heard many people thank God for the illness or other adversity that caused them to seek Him and draw closer to Him. I have experienced this wonderful blessing because of adversity I have faced in my life.

One advantage that most severely ill people have is that they have *a lot of discretionary time.* The things that used to interest them greatly *pale into insignificance* compared to the severity of the sickness that is ravaging their bodies. Sometimes these people can make up for time in the past when they did not draw close to the Lord by spending prodigious amounts of time alone with the Lord in prayer, in worship and in His Word each and every day.

God's grace often will prevail if you are *humble, teachable and repentant* because you have not drawn closer to Him in the past. "The Lord is close to those who are of a broken heart and saves such as are crushed with sorrow for sin and are humbly and thoroughly penitent" (Psalm 34:18).

This passage of Scripture applies to sinners who come to God and repent of their sins. This statement also can apply to Christians who are seriously ill. Do you have "a broken heart" because of the ravage of sickness in your body? Are you "thoroughly penitent" about your failure to draw closer to the Lord? You may be very surprised at what the Lord will do in your life if you are humble and repentant and if you are absolutely determined to draw closer to Him throughout each and every day.

Do your best one day at a time to obey the specific scriptural instructions that are contained in this book. Faithfully obeying these instructions from God *will* help you to draw closer to Him. You ultimately may come to the conclusion that sickness actually was one of the best things that ever happened to you. You may realize, as many Christians who have faced adversity and drawn closer to the Lord have realized, that you never would have developed this close relationship *unless* you had received a wakeup call caused by sickness or other adversity.

You must understand that sickness and other trials and tribulations actually are *opportunities* to know God much more intimately. Many times the problems that seem so bad will enable you to develop a relationship with the Lord that will sustain you during severe sickness or other adversity (see our Scripture Meditation Cards and our eighty-five minute cassette tape titled *A Closer Relationship with the Lord.*)

Your precious Lord will become much more important to you. You will realize that your life really has no meaning without Him. His love can and will comfort you and strengthen you if you actually seek a closer relationship with Him. As you continually draw closer to the Lord He will calm you and reveal great new truths to you.

In this chapter we have studied some basic facts from the Bible about the absolute necessity of drawing closer to God. In the next two chapters you will learn many vital facts from the holy Scriptures that will tell you *how* to draw closer to God. You will learn that trusting the Lord completely when you are very sick is directly related to the closeness of your relationship with Him.

Chapter 42

The Vital Importance of a Close Relationship with the Lord

Jesus Christ lives in the heart of *each* person who has asked Him to be his or her Savior. Every aspect of your life should revolve around your continual consciousness of His indwelling presence. You must stay close to Jesus if you sincerely desire to receive the healing He has provided for you. Jesus said, "...Whoever lives in Me and I in him bears much (abundant) fruit. However, apart from Me [cut off from vital union with Me] you can do nothing" (John 15:5).

Do *you* "live in Jesus?" Does "Jesus live in you?" Is your life centered around your burning desire to come closer to Him? If so, you will "bear much abundant fruit." Manifestation of healing is abundant fruit.

Some Christians live their lives "apart from Jesus." They do not have a continual consciousness of His indwelling presence. They do not understand that a close relationship with Jesus is a "vital union." When something is *vital*, it is absolutely necessary. Without this close union "you can do nothing." You should not expect to receive manifestation of healing if you are unwilling to consistently set aside time to draw closer to Jesus Who paid such an enormous price for your healing.

If you are seriously ill you cannot do anything that is more important than to draw close to the Lord and stay close to Him. "...let us be zealous to know the Lord [to appreciate, give heed to, and cherish Him]..." (Hosea 6:3).

If you understand the vital importance of staying close to the Lord you will be "zealous" to know Him intimately. People who are zealous are completely devoted to their cause. Do you really "appreciate, give heed to, and cherish" your relationship with the Lord? Is a close relationship with the Lord vitally important to you? "...You will seek Me, inquire for, and require Me [as a vital necessity] and find Me when you search for Me with all your heart" (Jeremiah 29:13).

The amplification of this passage of Scripture refers to "requiring the Lord as a vital necessity." A close relationship with the Lord is not a nice to have. The words "require" and "vital" are strong and emphatic words. They leave no room for doubt. You *will* "find the Lord when you search for Him with all your heart." "...Seek My face [inquire for and require My presence as your vital need]..." (Psalm 27:8).

God instructs you to "seek His face." Once again the amplification uses the words "require" and "vital." Develop a deep and constant desire to continually seek the Lord and to come into His presence.

Now that you have seen the vital importance of drawing closer to the Lord I would like to ask you *if you know the secret* of a wonderful close relationship with the Lord. The Bible tells you exactly what this secret is. "The secret [of the sweet, satisfying companionship] of the Lord have they who fear (revere and worship) Him..." (Psalm 25:14).

The "secret of sweet satisfying companionship" with the Lord is to "fear Him." The world uses the word "fear" in a negative context when they speak of being afraid of someone or something. There is *nothing* negative about fearing the Lord. If you fear the Lord you hold Him in absolute awe and reverence. Every aspect of your life revolves around Him. You should be overwhelmed with the privilege you have been given to draw closer to the Creator of the universe. You should "revere and worship" Him continually.

You can understand from personal experience the relationship that exists between knowing a person intimately and trusting that person completely. Do you trust someone in a matter of utmost importance if you do not know this person well? Most people in the world do not place complete trust in strangers. The same principle applies in the spiritual realm.

Please stop now and think of the one person who is closer to you than anyone else. Place the name of this person firmly in your mind before reading further. Do you have this person's name in the forefront of your consciousness? Please imagine that this person made a specific promise to you. If this person who is closer to you than anyone else in the world promises you something *would you believe* him or her? *Of course you would.*

Trust is based on intimacy. I know Judy very well. I would never doubt the veracity of anything she told me. Judy is impeccably honest. There is no such thing as a fib or a little lie with her. I trust Judy completely. If she tells me something I *know* she is telling the truth.

You should have the *same trust in the healing promises in the Word of God*. If you know the Lord intimately you will *know* that *every one* of His healing promises is absolutely reliable. You will be willing to place all of your trust in Him. No matter how sick you might be or how much your body might ache with pain, your relationship with the Lord should be *so intimate* that your faith in Him will not waver in the slightest.

Christians who are healthy sometimes are caught up in the ways of the world. If you are seriously ill you *must turn away* from the world. You should devote *every possible moment* to drawing closer to the Lord. The more you are in the world, the weaker your faith in the Lord will be. The more you turn away from the world and draw closer to the Lord, the stronger your faith will be. How can you expect to have deep, strong and unwavering faith in the Lord if you only have a shallow surface relationship with Him or no personal relationship at all?

Deep faith comes out of a close and intimate relationship with the Lord. Shallow faith comes from a shallow relationship with the Lord. No faith comes from no personal relationship with the Lord. You cannot expect to have deep, strong and unwavering faith in the Lord if He is not the absolute center of your life. He must be in absolute first place. The Lord must be ahead of *every* person and *everything else* in your life including all of the beloved members of your family.

You *should* have a close, loving and intimate relationship with the members of your family. However, these relationships should not be nearly as close as the intimacy of your personal relationship with the Lord. Your attitude should be similar to the psalmist who said, "…it is good for me to draw near to God; I have put my trust in the Lord God and made Him my refuge…" (Psalm 73:28).

This passage of Scripture shows you the relationship between "drawing near to God" and "putting your trust in Him." The Lord God will be your "refuge" if you are close to Him. If you trust Him completely you will turn away from focusing on the discomfort caused by sickness in your body.

Many people read healing Scripture and try to get these promises from God to work without realizing that the manifestation of God's promises is dependent upon the closeness of our relationship with Him. If you do what your Father has told you to do and continually study and meditate on His Word you will know Him more intimately because God and His Word are the same (see John 1:1).

You cannot have deep, strong and unwavering faith in the Lord unless He is very real to you. He must be so real to you that you will not hesitate for one moment to trust Him completely for healing in your body based on the promises in His Word. "Let us all come forward and draw near with true (honest and sincere) hearts in unqualified assurance and absolute conviction engendered by faith (by that leaning of the entire human personality on

God in absolute trust and confidence in His power, wisdom, and goodness)…" (Hebrews 10:22).

When this passage of Scripture begins with the words "let us all," the word "all" definitely includes *you*. You are instructed to "come forward and draw near" to the Lord. You must have a "true, honest and sincere" desire to draw closer to the Lord. If you are close to the Lord you will have "unqualified assurance and absolute conviction" that He already has provided healing because of the sacrifice Jesus has made for you.

The amplification of this passage of Scripture tells you that faith in God comes from "leaning the entire human personality on God in absolute trust and confidence in His power, wisdom and goodness." *Do you lean this much on God* to give you manifestation of healing from sickness?

I do not know of any other passage of Scripture in the Bible that presents stronger emphasis on the relationship between drawing close to God and trusting Him completely. Please stop and meditate carefully on this passage of Scripture. Speak this passage of Scripture over and over again. Meditate on it. Personalize it. Get these instructions from God *deep down in your heart*.

You will *not* be dismayed by the symptoms of sickness in your body *if* you have consistently set aside significant amounts of time to draw closer to Jesus. "…let us run with patient endurance and steady and active persistence the appointed course of the race that is set before us, looking away [from all that will distract] to Jesus, Who is the Leader and the Source of our faith [giving the first incentive for our belief] and is also its Finisher [bringing it to maturity and perfection]…" (Hebrews 12:1-2).

You are here on earth for a reason. This passage of Scripture speaks of "the appointed course" of your life. It compares what you do with your life to "the course of a race." You are instructed to be patient and persistent in your desire to carry out the assignment the Lord has given you. For more information on this subject you might want to read our book titled *God's Will for Our Lives* and study our Scripture Meditation Cards and listen to our eighty-five minute cassette tape that each are titled *Find God's Will for Your Life.*

You are instructed to "look away from all that will distract" you. Many people who are very sick are distracted by the sickness in their bodies. You must not focus on the sickness in your body. You are instructed to focus continually on "Jesus Who is the Leader and the Source of your faith." This portion of Scripture concludes by saying that Jesus is the "Finisher" of your faith. The amplification tells you that Jesus will bring your faith "to maturity and perfection."

Jesus is the only One Who is able to perfect your faith. He knows what perfect faith is. You saw an example of His perfect faith on the cross at Calvary and at the whipping post. How can you expect Jesus to help you perfect your faith if you only have an arm's length relationship with Him? You should not expect Jesus to help you perfect your faith in Him unless you have faithfully set aside significant amounts of time to develop a close and intimate personal relationship with Him.

You must have an intimate relationship with God. Some Christians stay at the outer gates. Your Father wants you to come into His presence. He created you to know Him more and more deeply. Knowing God intimately should be the first and highest priority in your life.

You should not strain or struggle to develop faith in the Lord Jesus Christ as your Healer. Your faith in Jesus should be natural, normal and spontaneous. As you continually draw closer to Jesus you will *know* how great and magnificent He is. You will be absolutely certain that Jesus is *infinitely more powerful* than the sickness in your body, no matter how powerful the sickness may seem to be.

An intimate relationship with the Lord comes as the result of many precious hours of quiet time alone with Him. Moses said to the Lord, "…show me now Your way, that I may know You [progressively become more deeply and intimately acquainted with

You, perceiving and recognizing and understanding more strongly and clearly]..." (Exodus 33:13).

When you do something progressively you do it incrementally over a period of time. Do you have a deep and sincere desire to know the Lord "progressively and to become more deeply and intimately acquainted" with Him? Do you deeply desire to "perceive and recognize and understand Him more strongly and clearly?"

Your heart will sing with joy regardless of any pain or discomfort in your body if you truly have a close relationship with the Lord. "...let him who glories glory in this: that he understands and knows Me [personally and practically, directly discerning and recognizing My character]..." (Jeremiah 9:24).

Do you "glory" in the Lord? Does your heart rejoice because of your intimate relationship with the Lord regardless of the circumstances you face? Do you "know Him personally and practically?" Do you "directly discern and recognize His character?"

We pray that these two chapters have helped *you* to draw *closer* to the Lord so that *your* heart constantly will sing with joy because of the closeness of your relationship with Him. We urge you to go back over these chapters and spend a great deal of time meditating on the scriptural contents because this Scripture will help you to draw closer to God and live in His healing power in His presence.

This book tells Christians who are sick exactly what they should do to draw closer to the Lord. If you would like more detailed information on a close relationship with the Lord please order our Scripture Meditation Cards and the accompanying eighty-five minute cassette tape that each are titled *A Closer Relationship with the Lord.*

Chapter 43

Precious Quiet Time with the Lord

Christians who are severely ill face an extremely serious predicament. Some of these people are in a situation where the world's medical system has not provided an answer. They need God's wisdom and instruction. If you face a life-threatening sickness *nothing is more important* than to get as much quality time with the Lord as you possibly can.

In Chapter 41 you saw that James 4:8 says that, if you come close to God, He *will* come close to you. Do you *really believe* that the same God Who created heaven and earth and everyone and everything in the entire world wants to spend intimate time each day with *you*? *Why* would any Christian who is severely ill miss out on the precious opportunity to draw closer to God throughout each day of his or her life?

Your loving Father wants you to set aside time each day to receive wonderful revelation from Him. This precious quiet time with the Lord is important in the life of every Christian, but it is especially important for all Christians who suffer from serious illness.

There are two spiritual forces at work in the universe today – God and Satan. You have seen that God *will* come close to you *if* you come close to Him. Satan always wants the opposite of what God wants. If you make the quality decision to draw closer to the

Lord each day you can expect Satan and his demons to oppose this decision and to try to influence you against this resolve.

Satan's mission is to steal, kill and destroy (see John 10:10). He wants you to *suffer* when you are sick. The last thing Satan and his demons want is for you to continually draw closer to God. They know that this close and intimate relationship and the trust that will develop from this relationship will bring hope, life, vitality and healing.

You probably will find that many distractions will occur if you make the decision to spend quiet time with the Lord. Your telephone may ring during this time. Other people may want to see you about seemingly urgent matters. You may find that family members and friends try to intrude because they cannot comprehend the importance of you turning away from everyone and everything else to draw closer to the Lord each day.

Make the decision that you will *not* give in to Satan and his demons. Do not be surprised when you face opposition as you begin spending time with the Lord. Spending precious quiet time alone with the Lord is unnatural for many Christians.

We live in a generation where many people are continually on the go. They feel that they have to be doing something. Their spiritual sensitivity is dulled because of their preoccupation with worldly activities.

Christians who are seriously ill *cannot afford this limited spiritual perception.* You are in a serious situation if you are very sick. Whether it is unnatural for you or not, *you must take the first step* to spending quality quiet time alone with the Lord each day. Refuse to give up if you experience difficulty at first. Be absolutely *determined* to come close to God just as James 4:8 instructs you to do.

As soon as you experience God's presence you will count your focused time with Him as your most precious time each day. This wonderful time is vitally important for you. Truly believe that you will receive healing from the Lord as you continually draw closer to Him.

Many Christians cannot even begin to perceive the depth of what takes place in the presence of the Lord. Jesus is your example in every area of your life. Jesus knew the importance of turning away from everyone and everything to spend quiet time alone with His Father. Jesus often arose very early in the morning to spend precious quiet time with God. "...in the morning, long before daylight, He got up and went out to a deserted place, and there He prayed" (Mark 1:35).

In addition to spending time alone with His Father in the early morning hours, Jesus often spent quality time with His Father in the evening. "...after He had dismissed the multitudes, He went up into the hills by Himself to pray. When it was evening, He was still there alone" (Matthew 14:23).

There is no question that Jesus wanted to heal people. Sometimes He had to *turn away* from crowds of people who wanted healing because He desired to be alone with His Father. "...the news spread abroad concerning Him, and great crowds kept coming together to hear [Him] and to be healed by Him of their infirmities. But He Himself withdrew [in retirement] to the wilderness (desert) and prayed" (Luke 5:15-16).

Even though "great crowds" came to "hear Jesus and to be healed by Him," Jesus showed the importance He placed on quiet time with God. He *turned away* from these needy people to pray to His Father. Do *you* place this same kind of priority on your quiet time with the Lord?

These passages of Scripture tell you that Jesus prayed. This book is filled with many other scriptural instructions telling you what you can do in your quiet time alone with the Lord. In addition to praying you can worship the Lord continually, speak the precious name of Jesus Christ constantly and study and meditate on the holy Scriptures. You can fill your eyes, your ears, your mind, your mouth and your heart with encouraging promises and instructions from God's Word. You also can be absolutely quiet before the Lord, listening for Him to speak to you.

Some Christians who are not experiencing significant challenges in their lives believe that they can omit quiet time with the Lord. Because they do not notice any immediate penalty they often continue to exclude this time with the Lord from their busy daily schedules. Christians who are seriously ill cannot afford to make this mistake. You must steadily increase your faith in the Lord to overcome the effects of the enervating sickness in your body.

I started spending daily quiet time with the Lord thirty-two years ago when I faced severe financial problems and impending bankruptcy. I was paralyzed with fear. When the man who led me to Jesus told me that I needed to saturate myself in the Word of God each day, I was determined to do exactly what he told me to do. I added prayer time and worship to my daily Bible study and meditation.

For many months I did not miss a day. Eventually the peace and wisdom that came into my life from drawing closer to the Lord produced positive results. My seemingly impossible financial situation improved significantly. I then became careless. Sometimes I would miss a day. However, I learned then and I have known ever since that *I soon notice the difference* when I do not spend daily quiet time with the Lord. If you develop this quality habit in your life and you then begin to miss time with the Lord, I can guarantee that you will become aware of the difference.

You must learn how to be still before the Lord. You learn how to be still by being still. Even though this quiet time may not be natural for you when you begin, you should be determined to do what the Bible instructs you to do. The more you are still before the Lord, the more natural it will be for you to continue to be still before Him. Before long you will gladly turn away from people, places, things and events to enjoy your precious daily time with the Lord.

When you are continually still before the Lord He will cause you to be quiet and calm deep down in your heart. You will experience what the psalmist David experienced when, speaking of the Lord, he said, "…He makes me lie down in [fresh, tender] green pastures; He leads me beside the still and restful waters. He refreshes and restores my life (my self)…" (Psalm 23:2-3)

The Lord wants to bring *you* into "fresh, tender green pastures." You can and will be led to "the still and restful waters" in spite of the sickness in your body. God *will* "refresh and restore your life" if you refuse to focus on the symptoms of sickness in your body and, instead, spend a considerable amount of quality time with Him each day.

Once you break through and begin to experience the presence of God you will *yearn* to spend more time in His presence. You will gladly turn away from everyone and everything to draw closer to Him. You will be absolutely determined to draw closer to the Lord each and every day.

You must develop a solid foundation for your faith for healing. Many Christians experience difficulty in trusting God for healing because they have *not* taken time to get to know Him intimately. Casual Christians do not have strong faith in God. Deep, strong and unwavering faith in God requires a solid foundation of significant time alone with Him over a sustained period of time. You need to do more than just know the healing promises in the Word of God. You need to know the Healer intimately.

In this book I am explaining what the Bible teaches pertaining to healing. I do not spend time with God because I want something from Him. I spend time with God because I love Him. I want to know Him more intimately. I want to be in His presence continually. Healing comes as a result of a close relationship with the Great Physician.

We believe you will come to the point where the healer, Father God, becomes more important than the healing. Your Father will refresh you during this time with Him. He will encourage you. The restlessness that you may experience because of the symptoms of sickness will subside as you spend wonderful time alone with the Lord each day. Some Christians never break through the initial barrier of spending time alone with the Lord. If you persevere and the Lord quiets, calms and refreshes you, you will want *more* of this quietness, calmness and refreshing.

No one will have to urge you to spend quiet time alone with the Lord. You will yearn for as much time as you can make each day to be alone with Him. You will plan your day carefully to include as much time as possible with the Lord.

Approach your quiet time with the Lord with an attitude of expectancy. Believe that the Lord will touch you in a wonderful way as you draw closer to Him. The Bible instructs you to "...pursue that consecration and holiness without which no one will [ever] see the Lord" (Hebrews 12:14).

When this passage of Scripture speaks of "pursuing consecration" it refers to setting aside time to seek holiness. You should consistently turn away from the strident clamor and noise of the world to come face to face with God each day. You should turn off the television sets, radios, CDs and DVDs of the world so that you can draw closer to your precious Lord.

You cannot experience holiness in the ways of world. You can only experience holiness as you turn away from people, places, things, events, worries and cares and continue to draw closer to the One Who can and will calm you, quiet you and give you manifestation of the healing you are trusting Him for.

I ask each person reading this book, "How much time are *you* spending with the Lord each day?" Are you absolutely certain that God lives in *your* heart? Are you completely focused on drawing closer to Him each day?

The last three chapters have been filled with scriptural principles that will help you to develop a closer relationship with the Lord. In the next two chapters you will learn how this vital relationship will help you if you receive an unfavorable diagnosis of severe illness or incurable disease from a physician.

Chapter 44

If the Doctor Gives You Bad News

In this chapter we will discuss dread disease and terminal illness. Although many of our comments will be about a diagnosis of incurable illness, the same principles will apply if you have been diagnosed with a severe illness that may not necessarily be diagnosed as terminal.

You must understand that the word "incurable" was created by human beings because of the limitations of medical science. This word is not in the Bible. There is *no* such thing as an incurable illness to God because God knows no limitations whatsoever.

If a doctor says that you are terminally ill, you do not have to accept this verdict. God has healed *many* people who have been diagnosed as being terminally ill. He will heal many more of His children of very severe sickness if they have absolute faith in Him regardless of what a doctor has told them.

Jesus healed leprosy during His earthly ministry even though leprosy was supposedly incurable. You must not allow *any* diagnosis to override your absolute faith that God *already* has healed you. You must not limit God. The mighty power of God is *much greater* than you can possibly comprehend. The Bible speaks of "...Him Who, by (in consequence of) the [action of His] power that is at work within us, is able to [carry out His purpose and] do superabundantly, far over and above all that we [dare] ask or think [infinitely beyond our highest prayers, desires, thoughts, hopes, or dreams]" (Ephesians 3:20).

Please note that this passage of Scripture speaks of "the action of His power that is at work within us." You have read many facts from the Bible about the indwelling presence of God. Instead of focusing on a dire diagnosis from a physician you should focus continually on Almighty God Who lives in *your heart* and His mighty power that *will* work within you.

You must not limit God Who is able to "do superabundantly, far over and above all that you dare ask or think." God can do much more regarding the sickness in your body than you think He can. Know that the power of the living God is at work inside of you.

God does not have degrees of difficulty. If your doctor gives you a dire diagnosis God does not sit on His throne and wring His hands saying, "How can I possibly heal that incurable sickness?" God can heal what the world describes as incurable illness just as easily as He can heal what the world's medicine diagnoses as minor illness.

Refuse to allow the seeming severity of the sickness in your body to control your mind, your heart and your mouth. Be determined to obtain God's perspective on this sickness. Jesus told you exactly how God looks at what human beings say is incurable illness when He said, "...With men this is impossible, but all things are possible with God" (Matthew 19:26).

Please highlight or underline the words "all things" in this passage of Scripture. These two words include the sickness in your body *even if* your doctor says this sickness is incurable. Your doctor is telling you that human beings do not know any way to cure your illness. God's perspective is very different from the perspective of the world. You must not limit God. "...with God nothing is ever impossible and no word from God shall be without power or impossible of fulfillment" (Luke 1:37).

Please highlight or underline the words "nothing is ever impossible." The word "nothing" *includes* the sickness in your body.

The key to receiving healing from God comes from your heart being filled with the Word of God because this passage of Scripture tells you that "no word from God shall be without power or impossible of fulfillment." The supernatural power of the living Word of God that should fill your heart to overflowing is *much greater* than the sickness in your body.

If you have been given a dire diagnosis by your doctor open your mouth and speak Luke 1:37 over and over again. Personalize this passage of Scripture. Meditate on it continually. You may need to speak this passage of Scripture and the other Scripture in this chapter hundreds of times.

You must purge your consciousness of any thoughts of incurable disease. Be *determined* to look at the sickness in your body from God's perspective instead of the limited perspective of human beings. "...Behold, You have made the heavens and the earth by Your great power and by Your outstretched arm! There is nothing too hard or too wonderful for You" (Jeremiah 32:17).

Know that the same God Who "made the heavens and the earth by His great power" lives in *your heart.* Refuse to allow the severity of the sickness in your body to seem to be more powerful than God because "*nothing* is too hard" for Him. If God was able to create heaven, earth and every person on earth He certainly can heal the sickness in your body, regardless of what a physician may have told you.

God replied to Jeremiah shortly after he spoke these words of faith. God affirmed that *nothing* is too difficult for Him. "Then came the word of the Lord to Jeremiah, saying, Behold, I am the Lord, the God of all flesh; is there anything too hard for Me?" (Jeremiah 32:26-27).

Please highlight or underline the word "anything" in this passage of Scripture. This word *includes* the sickness in your body. God is telling *you* here just as He told Jeremiah that He can and will give you manifestation of healing regardless of what your doctor may have told you. Jesus said, "...all things can be (are possible) to him who believes!" (Mark 9:23).

Once again, please highlight or underline the words "all things." You can be certain that these words *include* the sickness in your body. You have learned that Jesus already has provided total healing for your body. An important key as to whether you will receive manifestation of the healing that already has been provided to you is given in the words "to him who believes."

How deep, strong and unwavering is your faith in God? How certain are *you* that God *will* give you manifestation of healing regardless of what your doctor may have told you? Meditate continually on Mark 9:23 and the other passages of Scripture in this chapter. Be *determined* to constantly *increase* your faith in God by obeying the specific scriptural instructions for increasing your faith in God that are contained in this book.

For more than thirty years I have meditated over and over again on the following passage of Scripture *whenever* I face any situation that seems to be overwhelming. "I have strength for all things in Christ Who empowers me [I am ready for anything and equal to anything through Him Who infuses inner strength into me; I am self-sufficient in Christ's sufficiency]" (Philippians 4:13).

Once again, please highlight or underline the words "all things." You can be certain that Jesus has provided you with His strength so that you can overcome incurable illness or any other obstacle to the degree that you trust in His mighty strength and power. The amplification of this passage of Scripture says that you are "ready for anything and equal to anything."

These words are very powerful. *You* can be "ready" for the sickness in your body that definitely is included in the word "anything." *You* can be "equal to" the sickness in your body through the strength of Jesus Christ. There is no sickness that cannot be overcome by the mighty and powerful strength of Jesus Christ Who lives in *your* heart. Believe that Jesus will "infuse inner strength" into you.

Christians who focus continually on Jesus *will* be strengthened. Jesus is your Healer. The more you focus on Him and meditate on what Philippians 4:13 says about His mighty power in you, the more you will be building up your most holy faith in Christ Jesus.

Every aspect of your life should revolve around Jesus. You should constantly be aware of His magnificent indwelling presence. You should never forget the enormous victory He won for you on the cross at Calvary. You always should be conscious of the total victory over sickness He won for you at the whipping post. Some Christians allow the sickness in their bodies to seem like a big, big sickness and forget that Jesus is all-powerful (see Matthew 28:18). *You must not make this mistake.*

You should not look at the diagnosis of a physician or the pain and discomfort in your body the way that unbelievers look at severe sickness. When most people receive a very severe prognosis from a physician and the symptoms of sickness in their body clamor for attention, they focus continually on the sickness. If these people have what the world calls an incurable illness they probably will experience death in the not too distant future.

If there ever was a time when you need to turn away from the diagnosis of a physician and the pain and discomfort in your body, this is that time. You must identify *solely with God and His Word* instead of focusing on what a doctor says or the symptoms of sickness. You must not take the path of least resistance.

God designed your mind so that you cannot think about more than one thing at a time. You will make a tremendous mistake if you allow thoughts of sickness, discomfort and a doctor's diagnosis to overcome the *facts* from the Word of God that are contained in this book. Satan wants you to focus on yourself, the sickness in your body and what your doctor said. Jesus wants you to focus on Him, His mighty power, His indwelling presence and the *facts* in His Word that tell you that He *already* has provided healing for you.

You cannot afford to dwell on the sickness in your body. Once the problem has been identified you need to turn *completely away* from the diagnosis and the symptoms. You should focus your time, effort, thoughts, words and actions on Jesus Christ, your Healer, Who lives in your heart.

Many sick people think sickness. Jesus wants you to think health. Daniel did not focus on the lions when he was in the lion's den. He focused on God. If you are tempted to focus on the severity of the sickness in your body you might want to carefully read the sixth chapter of the Book of Daniel. *See for yourself* how Daniel faced a seemingly impossible situation. See for yourself that Daniel focused on God and that God sent an angel to shut the lions' mouths so they could not hurt Daniel.

The same God Who brought Daniel safely through this seemingly impossible situation lives in your heart. He will bring *you* through a seemingly impossible situation *if* you focus continually on Him and trust completely in Him. A direct relationship exists between the seeming severity of sickness in your body and the amount of time you should invest focusing on God.

You should be consumed with Jesus your Healer. You should focus on Him throughout every day and night of your life. You should meditate continually on the many encouraging *facts* from the Word of God that are contained in this book. This focus should permeate your consciousness throughout every hour of every day of your life. You should be like the psalmist who said, "Unto You do I lift up my eyes, O You Who are enthroned in heaven" (Psalm 123:1).

You must work diligently on a daily basis to continually increase your faith in God. This chapter is filled with facts from the holy Scriptures telling you exactly what your Father wants you to do when you face a dire diagnosis from a physician and severe pain and discomfort in your body. In the next chapter we will carefully study the Word of God to learn more specific facts about how to stay focused on God.

Chapter 45

Receive God's Perfect Peace

You have learned that many people who are sick are consumed by the sickness in their bodies. They think about this sickness continually. The continual pain and discomfort in their bodies keep this sickness at the forefront of their consciousness.

Your Father wants you to do *exactly the opposite*. He wants you to focus continually on *Him* because you *trust Him completely*. "You will guard him and keep him in perfect and constant peace whose mind [both its inclination and its character] is stayed on You, because he commits himself to You, leans on You, and hopes confidently in You. So trust in the Lord (commit yourself to Him, lean on Him, hope confidently in Him) forever; for the Lord God is an everlasting Rock [the Rock of Ages]" (Isaiah 26:3-4).

If you refuse to focus on the symptoms of sickness and instead keep your "mind stayed on God," your Father promises to "guard" you. He promises to "keep you in perfect and constant peace." Do you deeply desire to receive these wonderful blessings from God? God *always* does what He says He will do.

You must understand that this promise is a *conditional* promise. You must keep your mind "stayed on God" if you want your Father to guard you and keep you in perfect peace regardless of the sickness in your body. You will not think about sickness because you have "committed yourself to Him," because you "lean on" Him and because you "hope confidently in Him." You *can* "trust in the Lord" Who is "the everlasting Rock of Ages."

When you are sick your Father does not want you to forsake the supernatural peace He has provided for you. Satan's demons will try to get into your mind when you are sick and weary. They will attempt to influence you to focus on the pain and discomfort of sickness. They will try to get you to think about how much worse this sickness might become in the future. If the sickness is severe enough they will constantly attempt to put thoughts of death into your mind.

Unfortunately, some Christians do exactly the opposite of what Isaiah 26:3 instructs them to do. They keep their minds focused on the sickness in their bodies, their worries, their anxieties and their fears instead of keeping their minds stayed on God. Perfect peace comes from *keeping* your mind stayed on God and trusting completely in Him. *A complete lack of peace* comes from keeping your mind stayed on sickness and failing to place your trust in God.

Anyone who has not grown in faith before sickness arrives may have a very difficult time developing faith because of the energy drain of the sickness. You must be strong in your faith in God to be ready for whatever may come into your life. In these last days before Jesus returns we all must increase our faith in God (see our book, *Unshakable Faith in Almighty God,* and our Scripture Meditation Cards and cassette tape that each are titled *Continually Increasing Faith in God.*)

You have learned the biblical account of what Moses did when he brought more than two million Israelites to the edge of the Red Sea. Moses and his followers faced a seemingly impossible situation. The Red Sea was in front of them. They were surrounded by high mountains on both sides. Pharaoh and his mighty army were behind them.

What did Moses do? Did he focus on the seemingly impossible dilemma he faced? "…he never flinched but held staunchly to his purpose and endured steadfastly as one who gazed on Him Who is invisible" (Hebrews 11:27).

How was Moses able to persevere with unwavering faith in God when he faced such a seemingly impossible situation? Moses "never flinched." When you flinch you draw back from something that is perceived to be difficult or dangerous.

Moses persevered in his faith in God. He "held staunchly to his purpose and endured steadfastly." How was Moses able to persevere in faith? *He was able to persevere "because he gazed on Him Who is invisible."*

You must do the same thing with the sickness in your body. You must not flinch. You must persevere in your faith in God. Instead of focusing on the sickness you should focus continually on "Him Who is invisible."

You do not have to be able to see God with your natural eyesight to trust Him. If you have faithfully obeyed your Father's instructions to continually fill your mind and your heart with His Word and to draw closer to Him every day, you will trust Him even though He is invisible to your natural eyesight. *God will be more real to you* than the sickness in your body or anything else on earth. You will see Him as your Healer.

God brought Moses safely through this seemingly impossible problem. He parted the water in the Red Sea so that more than two million Israelites could walk through it. He then closed the Red Sea so that Pharaoh and his army were destroyed.

You must trust God as Moses did with every aspect of your life. Christians who are sick should focus more and more on Jesus. "He must increase, but I must decrease. [He must grow more prominent; I must grow less so]" (John 3:30).

These words that John the Baptist spoke concerning Jesus Christ at the beginning of His earthly ministry apply to you today. Jesus is your Healer. Your focus on Him "must increase." Your focus on the sickness in your body "must decrease."

How do you accomplish this goal? You have previously seen that Jesus Christ and the Word of God are the same. "In the beginning [before all time] was the Word (Christ), and the Word was with God, and the Word was God Himself" (John 1:1).

If you focus continually on the Word of God you focus continually on Jesus Christ Who is your Healer. You must understand that the Word of God is much more than just words written on paper. The supernatural power of God's living Word will rise up in your heart if you have faithfully obeyed your Father's instructions to meditate continually on His Word. You will not allow the bad news that was given to you by a physician to override all of the good news that is contained in the Word of God. You will not allow the pain and discomfort in your body to stop you from continually immersing yourself in the Word of God.

Many people who are severely ill live in a great black spiritual cloud that is caused by Satan's influence. They are surrounded by the spiritual darkness because of their constant focus on sickness. Instead of allowing Satan to envelop you with darkness you must focus on the supernatural light of the living Word of God. "Your word is a lamp to my feet and a light to my path" (Psalm 119:105).

This passage of Scripture is the theme verse of Lamplight Ministries. God has given you His Word to serve as "a lamp to your feet and a light to your path." You will walk continually in the light of God if you focus on God's Word instead of focusing on the sickness in your body. Satan's demons will not be able to pull you into the spiritual darkness that people who constantly focus on sickness live in.

Many people are held prisoner by sickness. They think continually of the diagnosis they have been given and they think constantly of the pain and discomfort in their bodies. Everything else is pushed into second place in their lives. The last thing they feel like doing is to meditate on the Word of God.

There is no place in the Word of God where you are instructed to do what you feel like doing. The Word of God is filled with specific instructions telling you exactly what to do when you face severe illness or any other problem. Unfortunately, some Christians "...reject and turn their backs on the Truth" (Titus 1:14).

Paul spoke of disorderly and unruly men who were deceived and deceived others. This same principle applies to Satan's deception in your life today. Christians who are sick must not be deceived by ignorance of the supernatural living Word of God and its mighty power. Instead of "turning your back on the Truth" you should turn your eyes and ears toward the Truth. This book is filled with magnificent Truth from the supernatural living Word of God. You must not allow sickness to cause you to reject the Truth of God's Word.

The worse you feel, the *more* you need to focus on what the Word of God says about divine healing. You must not allow pain and discomfort to rule your life. When your body aches with pain you should be like the psalmist who said, "Trouble and anguish have found and taken hold of me, yet Your commandments are my delight" (Psalm 119:143).

I do understand that the pain caused by sickness may become so unbearable that you cry out for the relief of death and the peace of heaven. At this point other Christians with strong faith in God must undergird you throughout every day with prayer for your healing. Trust God for healing until your last breath. At that time you will know that your healing has come because death is the ultimate healing for every Christian.

Until and unless you reach this point you must focus on the fact that Jesus already has healed you. The psalmist refused to focus on the "trouble and anguish" in his life. Instead, he focused on God's Word which was "his delight." If you can even begin to comprehend the immense power of the supernatural living Word of God that is explained throughout this book, your heart will sing with joy regardless of the symptoms of sickness. Like the psalmist you will be *delighted* with the Word of God. You will keep it in first place where it belongs, far ahead of what the doctor has told you and far ahead of the pain and discomfort you are experiencing.

Christians who persevere in meditating on healing Scripture and speaking healing Scripture will find that the supernatural power of God's living Word will keep them strong in spirit. They should see changes in their health. This process does not happen overnight. You must get in there and fight the good fight of faith (see I Timothy 6:12). Hold fast to your goal of improved health with your focus on Jesus Christ your Healer.

Faith in God increases by continually meditating on God's Word. Fear increases by continually meditating on sickness. You should do what Jesus told you to do when He said to a man named Jairus whose daughter had died, "...Do not be seized with alarm and struck with fear; only keep on believing" (Mark 5:36).

If your daughter had already died as Jairus' daughter had died, would you be strong enough to persevere in your faith in God instead of being filled with fear? Jesus honored the faith of Jairus and raised his daughter from death (see Mark 5:37-43). The same Jesus Christ lives in your heart today if you are a Christian. You must not allow the sickness in your body to cause you to "be seized with alarm and struck with fear."

Please highlight or underline the words "only keep on believing." The word "only" means that Jesus wants you to do *just one thing* – He wants you to *keep on believing*. He does not want you to give up. "...we take comfort and are encouraged and confidently and boldly say, The Lord is my Helper; I will not be seized with alarm [I will not fear or dread or be terrified]..." (Hebrews 13:6).

Jesus "is your Helper." He went to the cross to *help you*. He went to the whipping post to *help you*. Jesus won a total, complete and absolute victory over sin, death and sickness. He wants you to "take comfort and be encouraged" by these scriptural facts. Jesus wants you to "confidently and boldly say" that "He is your Helper."

Jesus does *not* want you to be "seized with alarm." He does *not* want you to "fear or dread or be terrified." "...He shall not be afraid of evil tidings; his heart is firmly fixed, trusting (leaning on and being confident) in the Lord. His heart is established and steady, he will not be afraid…" (Psalm 112:7-8).

The words "evil tidings" could include the bad news of a dire prognosis from a physician. These words definitely refer to Satan's demons and the evil thoughts they will try to put into your mind. You "will not be afraid" if "your heart is firmly fixed." Your heart will be "established and steady" if you "trust, lean on and have confidence in the Lord."

Instead of dwelling on sickness you should *give this sickness to the Lord* because you trust Him completely. "Commit your way to the Lord [roll and repose each care of your load on Him]; trust (lean on, rely on, and be confident) also in Him and He will bring it to pass" (Psalm 37:5).

Your Father wants you to "commit" every aspect of your life to Him. He wants you to "roll" the sickness in your body on Him. He has instructed you to "repose your cares on Him." He does not want you to attempt to carry the heavy "load" of severe illness. He *will* carry this heavy load *if* you will *give* it to Him and *leave* it with Him. Your Father wants you to "trust, lean on and be confident in Him." If you obey these instructions "He will bring it to pass." He will take your burden. You can trust Him with it.

You must live your life one day at a time as Jesus has instructed you to do (see Matthew 6:34). You must not be concerned about anything that happened in the past. You must not worry about what the future might hold. You need to trust Jesus completely to *bring you through today.*

If trusting Jesus one day at a time is too difficult, trust Him one hour at a time. Focus continually on Him for the next hour trusting Him to bring you through that hour. Then repeat this process.

Your loving Father will be pleased if you persevere in your faith in Him when your body aches with pain. He will be pleased if you obey His instructions to constantly fill your mind and your heart with His supernatural living Word instead of dwelling on the sickness in your body and a physician's diagnosis pertaining to this sickness.

Have you been given a dire diagnosis by your doctor? Does your body ache with pain? This book is filled with health instructions and *spiritual medicine* from the Word of God. Fill your eyes, your ears, your mind, your heart and your mouth continually with this magnificent supernatural medicine that your loving Father has provided for you.

Chapter 46

Why Do You Want God to Heal You?

An important fact for you to consider in regard to receiving healing from God is to ask yourself *why* you are asking to be healed. Is your prayer for healing simply because you want to be free from pain so that you can enjoy life?

Sometimes God will heal you because of His love, grace and mercy even if you are not in the center of His will for your life. On the other hand, some people may fail to receive an answer to their prayers for healing because they ask God for the wrong reasons.

I believe that your primary motivation in asking God for healing from sickness should be a deep and consuming desire to carry out God's will for your life. I believe that our Father wants each of His children to have a deep, constant and sincere desire to seek, find and carry out His assignment for their lives.

I believe that only a small percentage of Christians are in the center of God's will for their lives. Some Christians spend their entire lives pursuing personal goals with little or no thought to God's will for their lives. Your Father has a definite, specific and precise plan for the lives of each of His children. He very much wants to reveal His plan to you.

Many people fail to receive an answer to their prayers because they have the wrong motivation when they pray. "…You do not have, because you do not ask. [Or] you do ask [God for them] and yet fail to receive, because you ask with wrong purpose and evil, selfish motives. Your intention is [when you get what you desire] to spend it in sensual pleasures" (James 4:2-3).

You saw in a previous chapter that some people do not pray to God for healing from sickness. God cannot answer because "they do not ask." How can God give anyone an answer to prayer if this person does not pray?

I believe that most Christians who are very sick do ask God to heal them. Sometimes these people give up before they receive their healing. This passage of Scripture also says that some of us do not receive an answer to our prayers because we "ask with the wrong purpose and evil, selfish motives."

Some people do not receive an answer from God because they want God to heal them so they can engage "in sensual pleasures." If you are praying to God for healing in your body are you asking Him to heal you primarily so that you can pursue personal desires? Are you asking Him to heal you so that you can successfully carry out His assignment for your life?

God created the earth for us to enjoy, but I do not believe the pursuit of pleasure should be your primary goal when you pray for healing. Your motive when you pray is very important. Your Father knows your innermost thoughts. You could not deceive Him for one second. I believe you are much more likely to receive an answer to your prayers for healing when you pray with a deep and sincere motivation to serve God and to serve others by doing what your Father has called you to do with your life.

If you have grown and matured over the years as a Christian you will turn more and more away from selfish desires to seek God's plan for your life. "Shun youthful lusts and flee from them, and aim at and pursue righteousness (all that is virtuous and good, right living, conformity to the will of God in thought, word, and deed)…" (II Timothy 2:22).

This passage of Scripture instructs you to turn away from "youthful lusts." You should not allow the things you desired when you were young and immature to continue to predominate as you grow older. You should "flee from" these immature desires. Instead, you should "aim at and pursue righteousness."

The amplification of this passage of Scripture says that righteousness is "all that is virtuous and good, right living, conformity to the will of God in thought, word and deed." Do the words in this amplification accurately describe the reason why *you* are asking God to heal you? Instead of asking God for healing so that you can pursue personal goals you should be determined to "…offer and yield yourself to God…" (Romans 6:13).

Do you "offer" yourself to God? Do you willingly "yield" control of your life to the Holy Spirit Who lives in your heart? You must understand that you actually "rebel" against God if you seek to pursue selfish goals instead of seeking His will for your life. "Woe to the rebellious children, says the Lord, who take counsel and carry out a plan, but not Mine…" (Isaiah 30:1).

When Jesus explained what today we call the Lord's Prayer He emphasized that every person on earth should seek to do God's will just as everyone in heaven does God's will. Jesus said, "…Your will be done [held holy and revered] on earth as it is in heaven" (Luke 11:2).

The amplification of this passage of Scripture tells you that God's will for your life should be "holy and revered." God has a holy plan for the lives of each of His children. You should be in absolute awe that your Father has a definite plan for your life. You should seek God's plan for your life with deep reverence. You should yearn to be in the center of His will.

God gave you specific gifts and talents when He created you. You received these gifts and talents because of God's grace. You did not earn and do not deserve the talents God has given you. Your Father has given you these special talents to carry out His plan for your life. "Having gifts (faculties, talents, qualities) that differ according to the grace given us, let us use them…" (Romans 12:6).

You will make a big mistake if you do not *use* the "gifts, faculties and talents" that God has given you because of His grace. Did you fervently seek God's will for your life before you were sick? If you did you have a strong motivation to ask for healing. If you have not yet made this commitment now is the perfect time for you to fervently seek God's will for *your* life. Now is the time to fervently dedicate yourself to receiving healing so that you will be able to carry out the assignment God has given you.

If you are committed to seeking, finding and carrying out God's will for your life you should know that God promises to give you the strength and energy you need to do what He has called you to do. "[Not in your own strength] for it is God Who is all the while effectually at work in you [energizing and creating in you the power and desire], both to will and to work for His good pleasure and satisfaction and delight" (Philippians 2:13).

You must understand that God does *not* require you to do everything He has called you to do "in your own strength." You have seen that God lives inside of you. If you fervently seek God's will for your life God will "all the while effectually be at work in you." The amplification of this portion of Scripture says that He will "energize and create in you the power and desire" to devote your life to work "for His good pleasure and satisfaction and delight."

Please note that God does not promise to give you strength to work for *your* pleasure. If you sincerely seek God's will for your life God promises to give you *the power* you require to do what He has called you to do. This power *includes* healing so that you can successfully carry out God's assignment for your life. Your Father wants you to be like the apostle Paul who said, "…I do not run uncertainly (without definite aim)…" (I Corinthians 9:26).

Your Father does not want you to "uncertainly" pursue vague personal goals. He wants you to live your life with "definite aim" as you pursue the assignment that you are certain He has given you. You must understand that God had a specific plan for your life before He created you in your mother's womb. "Your eyes saw my unformed substance, and in Your book all the days [of my life] were written before ever they took shape, when as yet there was none of them" (Psalm 139:16).

Think about the enormity of this statement. Know that Almighty God had a specific plan for "all the days of *your* life" before you were born. "...we are God's [own] handiwork (His workmanship), recreated in Christ Jesus, [born anew] that we may do those good works which God predestined (planned beforehand) for us [taking paths which He prepared ahead of time], that we should walk in them [living the good life which He prearranged and made ready for us to live]...." (Ephesians 2:10).

Your spirit came alive when you were "recreated" because you asked Jesus to be your Savior. You were "born anew." Everything in your life was new, fresh and different (see II Corinthians 5:17). At that time you were given full access to the "good works which God predestined and planned beforehand for you." Your Father wants you to "take paths which He prepared ahead of time."

God created each of us to be special, unique and different. There is no one else in the entire world like you. You are *one of a kind*. You can see the accuracy of this statement by the knowledge that every person on earth has different fingerprints. In recent years DNA evidence has become very important in our legal system. No two people have the same DNA.

Know that you are special and unique. Know that your Father has a specific plan for *your* life that is different from the plan He has for the life of *anyone else*. Be *determined* to draw closer and closer to God as you go through the challenges you face with the sickness in your body. As you seek manifestation of healing from God also seek revelation that you may not have sought before as to exactly what God wants you to do with the remainder of your life.

Many Christians miss out on finding God's plan for their lives because they are not consistently quiet before Him to hear Him clearly. You may find that the very sickness that has caused your normal life to change frees you to draw much closer to the Lord. You will be able to hear His voice telling you exactly what He wants you to do with your life when you are able to function again.

You will hear the Lord's voice clearly when you spend precious time alone with Him day after day, week after week and month after month. As you continue to draw closer to Him He will continue to fill in the details to show you more about what He wants you to do with your life, how He wants you to do it and what He will do in you and through you. "Acquaint now yourself with Him [agree with God and show yourself to be conformed to His will] and be at peace; by that [you shall prosper and great] good shall come to you" (Job 22:21).

If you are very sick you may have much more discretionary time to "acquaint yourself" with God. If you are extremely ill you may have a perfect opportunity to think about what God has planned for the remainder of your life. As you come closer to God you will be "conformed to His will and be at peace."

You will "be at peace" if you faithfully obey these instructions. If you consistently seek God's will you will "prosper and great good shall come to you." Prosperity from God's perspective is not limited to financial prosperity. God's prosperity includes manifestation of healing from sickness. You *will* experience "great good" if you devote your life to serving God and other people.

You must understand that your life does *not* belong to you. Your life belongs to Jesus Christ. "...you are not your own. You were bought with a price [purchased with a preciousness and paid for, made His own]. So then, honor God and bring glory to Him in your body" (I Corinthians 6:19-20).

Your life is "not your own." Your life was "bought with a price" – the enormous price that Jesus paid on the cross at Calvary. Your primary goal should be to "honor God and bring glory to Him." Your reason for desiring healing should be to bring glory to God.

Chapter 47

Live Your Life to Serve Jesus Christ

Jesus Christ is your example in every area of your life. Whenever you want to know what your Father in heaven wants you to do you often can look at the earthly ministry of Jesus to follow His example. Jesus knew why He was sent to earth. He said, "…I have come down from heaven not to do My own will and purpose but to do the will and purpose of Him Who sent Me" (John 6:38).

Jesus "came down from heaven not to do His own will and purpose but to do the will and purpose of God Who sent Him." You are here for the same reason. "…[if] One died for all, then all died; and He died for all, so that all those who live might live no longer to and for themselves, but to and for Him Who died and was raised again for their sake" (II Corinthians 5:14-15).

Please note that the word "all" is used *four times* in the first portion of this passage of Scripture. God is emphasizing that He is speaking to every person on earth. The word "all" includes *you*. Jesus died for you so that you will "live no longer to and for yourself." Jesus wants you to live for Him because He "died and was raised again for your sake."

God's will for your life often is obvious. Parents who are raising children are called upon by God to do their very best to raise their children based on biblical principles. "Train up a child in the way he should go [and in keeping with his individual gift or bent], and when he is old he will not depart from it" (Proverbs 22:6).

All parents of young children who are threatened by severe illness have *definite reason* to ask God for healing to successfully complete the assignment of raising their children. Many people have other family responsibilities that are part of God's will for their lives. These responsibilities should cause them to persevere in faith and refuse to give up as they hold fast to God for healing.

There is no question that your loving Father wants you to do your very best to raise your children according to the instructions in His Word. This goal is part of God's general will for the lives of *all* of His children who are parents.

One of the primary times that Christians should fervently seek God's will for their lives is when they have an empty nest – after their children have grown and gone out on their own. I do not know of any place in the Bible that speaks of retirement. God does not instruct us to pursue pleasure as our primary goal.

Retirement is a worldly concept, not a Christian concept. When you retire from your secular vocation you should retire from secular employment to working for God. When you retire you will have additional time to carry out God's will for your life by devoting to God a good portion of the time you used to devote to your vocation.

The onset of sickness is especially prevalent in people of retirement age. I believe that many Christians who have sought and found God's will for their lives and are completely devoted to doing what God has called them to do will live much longer and fuller lives than older people whose lives are devoted to selfish goals.

Some older people find that their lives are increasingly empty. They do not have a vibrant purpose. They are just existing, waiting to die. Their lives have been devoted to a pursuit of pleasure. Their lives are forlorn when illness overtakes them and they no longer are able to pursue pleasure.

You cannot persevere against severe illness during the final years of your life unless you have a strong desire for healing that transcends earthly desires such as the pursuit of pleasure and the accumulation of wealth. If severe sickness comes upon you during your final years, the emptiness of worldly goals will *not* give you the motivation you must have to persevere in faith to receive the healing Jesus has provided for you.

Christians who are in the center of God's will and become seriously ill during their final years of life *must not give in* to the symptoms of sickness. If you know what God has called you to do and if you definitely have not completed this assignment, you can and should trust your loving Father to give you the strength you need one day at a time to continue to do what He has called you to do.

God's ways are very different from the ways of the world (see Isaiah 55:8-9). Some worldly leaders are very proud. Jesus said that leaders who are in the center of God's will are here to *serve others*. He said, "…whoever wishes to be most important and first in rank among you must be slave of all. For even the Son of Man came not to have service rendered to Him, but to serve, and to give His life as a ransom for (instead of) many" (Mark 10:44-45).

Jesus came to earth "to serve" others. He gave His life as a "ransom for" *you.* If you truly want to be in the center of God's will you will be highly motivated to do whatever He has called you to do to serve Him and serve others. You are called to be "…servants (slaves) of Christ, doing the will of God heartily and with your whole soul; rendering service readily with good will…" (Ephesians 6:6-7).

Please note that the word "slave" is used in both Mark 10:44 and Ephesians 6:6. A slave is a person who belongs to someone else. You should turn completely away from the opinion that your life is yours to do with as you will. This philosophy ultimately will lead to heartache. True fulfillment can only come from doing the will of God.

Your Father wants you to have a fervent desire to serve Him. If you truly seek His will you will yield control of your life to the Holy Spirit so that He can and will guide you continually into the center of God's will for your life. "...be aglow and burning with the Spirit, serving the Lord" (Romans 12:11).

Are *you* "aglow and burning with the Spirit" because of your intense desire to "serve the Lord?" Is this goal the primary reason you are believing God for healing? Refuse to give up. Persevere with unwavering faith that you will be able to complete the unfinished tasks that have been assigned to you by God.

I have had challenges with my eyesight in recent years. I am trusting God completely for excellent eyesight during the remainder of my life so that Judy and I can continue writing these Scripture-filled books that have helped so many people around the world. This book is the seventeenth Christian book I have written either by myself or co-authored with Judy. Judy and I also have co-authored ten sets of Scripture Meditation Cards.

On my seventy-fourth birthday I had lived a total of almost 27,000 days on this earth. I have much more time on earth behind me than I have ahead of me. I am *very determined* that the days I have left will be *completely dedicated* to serving Jesus. I will persevere in faith during each day of the remainder of my life to continue to write these books. I am completely consumed with doing what God has called me to do.

I suggest that you take a hard look at your own life. Multiply the number of years you have lived by 365. Then estimate the minimum number of years you can reasonably expect to live to complete God's assignment for you. Multiply this number by 365.

Take a hard look at how many days you have lived and how many days you reasonably might expect to live. What is the primary purpose of the remaining days in *your* life? Will you pursue pleasure as many people do when they grow older; or will you be completely dedicated to use *every one* of the days you have remaining to draw closer to Jesus so that you can seek, find and carry out His will for your life?

This book is filled with scriptural *facts* about the magnificent healing that Jesus has provided for you. Be *determined* to be healed so that you will live long enough to completely carry out the assignment God has given you. Refuse to give in because you have reached a certain age or because you are sick and tired. Seek God with your whole heart. Focus on seeking God rather than seeking healing. He will give you the strength you need to do what He has called you to do.

Satan and his demons do everything they can to stop older Christians from doing what God has called them to do. Satan knows that older Christians are not far from living eternally in the glory of heaven. Satan and his demons know that they will suffer eternally in the lake of fire. They are very envious of all Christians who will live eternally in heaven. They are determined to do everything they can to stop each of us from seeking, finding and successfully completing God's assignment for our lives.

If you were Satan and you wanted to choose Christians to attack wouldn't you focus primarily on Christians who are in the center of God's will for their lives? These Christians are the greatest threat to Satan. If you are pursuing God's will for your life you can be certain that Satan and his demons will do everything they can to stop you.

Doctors know that the will to live is extremely important for people who are very sick. Many sick people, whether they are Christians or not, have a strong desire to live because they are determined to finish something that is very important to them. The will to live is especially important to Christians who are completely devoted to carrying out God's will for their lives. If you are extremely sick you may be tempted to give in to this sickness *unless* you have an overwhelming desire to live so that you can carry out God's assignment for your life.

The psalmist spoke of his complete dedication to live and not die. He said, "...I shall not die but live, and shall declare the works and recount the illustrious acts of the Lord. The Lord has chastened me sorely, but He has not given me over to death" (Psalm 118:17-18).

The psalmist knew that the time for his death had not yet arrived. He was determined to live to do what the Lord had called him to do with the remainder of his life. You should have the same attitude the apostle Paul had. Paul said, "...none of these things move me; neither do I esteem my life dear to myself, if only I may finish my course with joy and the ministry which I have obtained from [which was entrusted to me by] the Lord Jesus..." (Acts 20:24).

Paul knew that imprisonment and suffering awaited him. He knew that his death was imminent. Nevertheless, he was determined not to give in to adversity. Paul was determined to "finish his course with joy" to successfully complete "the ministry which was entrusted to him by the Lord Jesus."

Follow Paul's example. Refuse to give in to sickness. Be determined to successfully complete the assignment God has given to you.

Chapter 48

Trust Completely in God's Timing

In the next three chapters we will discuss the patience and perseverance that we often must exhibit before we receive manifestation of the healing that already has been provided for us. The Bible is filled with many stories of instant healing when Jesus prayed for people who were sick. There is no question that God *does* perform instant healing miracles. However, my experience has shown me that, for every person who receives instant healing, a large number of people will need to persevere in faith before they receive healing from God.

The Word of God is filled with promises telling you what God *will* do for you, but these promises *never* tell you *when* God will do what He promises to do. If you have studied and meditated on the scriptural contents of this book you know what God already has done regarding healing. Some of the things you can do to stop the manifestation of healing that Jesus Christ has provided for you are failure to obey factual information pertaining to divine health, ignorance of God's promises, failure to obey your Father's specific instructions regarding healing, failure to believe with deep, strong and unwavering faith that He will do what He says He will do and/or lack of patience and perseverance.

Your faith must not waver during the time that elapses between praying for healing and receiving manifestation of healing. God's timing is very specific. Daily weather reports tell you exactly when the sun will rise and set each day and exactly when the moon will change four times each month. "[The Lord] appointed the moon for the seasons; the sun knows [the exact time of] its setting" (Psalm 104:19).

God also causes ocean tides to come in and go out on a definite, precise schedule. You must appreciate the magnificent precision of God's timing. "[Even the migratory birds are punctual to their seasons.] Yes, the stork [excelling in the great height of her flight] in the heavens knows her appointed times [of migration], and the turtledove, the swallow, and the crane observe the time of their return. But My people do not know the law of the Lord [which the lower animals instinctively recognize in so far as it applies to them]" (Jeremiah 8:7).

This passage of Scripture says that birds know exactly when to migrate. They know when to fly from the north to the south and when to fly north again. Many human beings "do not know" God's timing that these "lower animals instinctively recognize" because many of us impatiently try to figure everything out with the limitations of our intellectual understanding.

We do *not* know how long the manifestation of healing will take. Once again I want to emphasize that the Word of God tells you what God will do, but it never tells you *when* He will do it. Meditate continually on what the Word of God says about healing. *Leave the timing of this healing up to God.*

God has created a miraculous self-healing body for each of us. You have learned through experience that God has specific times to heal various ailments. If you cut your hand you know that this cut usually will not heal instantly. If you break a bone in your leg you know that it will take time to knit. You must not try to figure out God's timing. "...It is not for you to become acquainted with and know what time brings [the things and events of time and their definite periods] or fixed years and seasons (their critical niche in time), which the Father has appointed (fixed and reserved) by His own choice and authority and personal power" (Acts 1:7).

Paul was speaking of not knowing when the kingdom would be restored to Israel. This same principle of not knowing God's exact timing also can apply to your healing today. Please highlight or underline the words "it is not for you" in this passage of Scripture. *Refuse to question God's timing* for manifestation of the healing that already has been provided for you.

The Bible is filled with instructions that tell you to wait on the Lord. We will look at a few of these instructions as they pertain to healing. When the Bible instructs you to wait on the Lord or to wait for the Lord this instruction means that you should exchange your human weakness for God's strength. No matter how weary you might be you can trust the Lord to give you the strength you have to have. "Have you not known? Have you not heard? The everlasting God, the Lord, the Creator of the ends of the earth, does not faint or grow weary; there is no searching of His understanding. He gives power to the faint and weary, and to him who has no might He increases strength [causing it to multiply and making it to abound]" (Isaiah 40:28-29).

God "does not grow weary." He wants you to look to Him when you are "faint and weary." When you "have no might" He will "cause your strength to multiply and make it abound" according to your faith in Him. God goes on to give you additional promises. "Even youths shall faint and be weary, and [selected] young men shall feebly stumble and fall exhausted; but those who wait for the Lord [who expect, look for, and hope in Him] shall change and renew their strength and power; they shall lift their wings and mount up [close to God] as eagles [mount up to the sun]; they shall run and not be weary, they shall walk and not faint or become tired" (Isaiah 40:30-31).

Please carefully study and meditate on the facts in this magnificent passage of Scripture. If you "wait for the Lord" you will "expect, look for and hope in Him." You will not give up. If you wait on the Lord faithfully and patiently you "shall not faint and be weary." You will be given supernatural spiritual energy to persevere when even "selected young men shall feebly stumble and fall exhausted."

Absolutely refuse to give up. Keep your faith in God strong by continually saturating yourself in the Bible, including the Scripture contained in this book. Believe that the Lord will "renew your strength and power." Believe that He will give you the strength you must have to carry out the assignment He has given you.

You *will* be able to fly above the problems caused by sickness in your body just as eagles are able to "lift their wings" to fly above a storm. When eagles see a storm coming they set their wings so that the winds of the storm will lift them and carry them above the storm. If your faith in the Lord is strong and if you wait on Him you will be like these eagles. You will be able to "mount up close to God." You will be able to fly above the storm of sickness in your body if you wait on the Lord and persevere in faith.

God will give you the strength to persevere. You will be able to "run and not be weary." You will "walk and not faint or become tired." These promises are given to God's children who *wait for Him*. "Wait and hope for and expect the Lord; be brave and of good courage and let your heart be stout and enduring. Yes, wait for and hope for and expect the Lord" (Psalm 27:14).

All of your hope should be based on the Lord. When you see repetition in the Bible this repetition is used to emphasize what the Lord is trying to tell you. This short passage of Scripture tells you *twice*, at the beginning and at the end, that you should "wait for and hope for and expect the Lord." You should "be brave and of good courage" while you are waiting. Your heart should be "stout and enduring." You should pour encouragement into your heart by continually meditating on Scripture. You must not give up.

In this chapter we have studied some basic scriptural facts about God's timing and persevering in your faith in Him. If you would like more information in this area you might want to read our book *Never, Never Give Up*. The first five chapters of this book are devoted to scriptural instructions pertaining to patience. The remainder of this book contains thirteen chapters that are filled with facts explaining what the Bible instructs you to do in the area of perseverance.

Chapter 49

Ask and Keep on Asking

Your Father does not want you to stop trusting Him if you are going through a prolonged period of suffering from sickness. You must not give up. Your Father loves you. He already has provided healing for you. Continue to pray with faith for healing. "Be unceasing in prayer [praying perseveringly]..." (I Thessalonians 5:17).

Some people think that continually praying to God with the same request shows a lack of faith. I disagree. The Bible consistently tells you to *keep on praying.* Your Father wants you to be "unceasing in prayer." You should "pray perseveringly" when you are sick. "Rejoice and exult in hope; be steadfast and patient in suffering and tribulation; be constant in prayer" (Romans 12:12).

If you are sick and you see no indication of manifestation of healing you should "rejoice and exult in hope." You must not give up hope. Live with a zeal and a joy in the Lord. Your Father instructs you to be "steadfast and patient" if you are "in suffering and tribulation." He instructs you to "be constant in prayer." Jesus emphasized the importance of continued prayer when He said, "...they ought always to pray and not turn coward (faint, lose heart, and give up)" (Luke 18:1).

Jesus does not want you to "lose heart and give up." He does not want you to be discouraged. Jesus said, "Keep on asking and it will be given you; keep on seeking and you will find; keep on knocking [reverently] and [the door] will be opened to you. For everyone who keeps on asking receives; and he who keeps on seeking finds; and to him who keeps on knocking, [the door] will be opened" (Matthew 7:7-8).

Please highlight or underline the word "everyone" in this passage of Scripture. This word includes *you* and the sickness in your body. These words that Jesus spoke to a crowd of people on the side of a mountain many years ago are fully applicable to your prayers for healing today.

Please highlight or underline the words "keep on" or "keeps on" in Matthew 7:8. These words are used *six times* in this one passage of Scripture. I have explained many times that God uses repetition in the Bible for the purpose of emphasis. Receive by faith the healing God has provided for you no matter how long you are required to persevere.

Jesus went on to give you additional instruction to "keep on" praying. He said, "…what man is there of you, if his son asks him for a loaf of bread, will hand him a stone? Or if he asks for a fish, will hand him a serpent? If you then, evil as you are, know how to give good and advantageous gifts to your children, how much more will your Father Who is in heaven [perfect as He is] give good and advantageous things to those who keep on asking Him!" (Matthew 7:9-11).

Many parents who are unbelievers "give good gifts and advantageous things" to their children. If unbelievers give these gifts to their children "how much more will your Father Who is in heaven give good things to *you*?" The words "good and advantageous things" *include healing*. Do what Jesus told you to do. Keep on asking Him. "…think of Him who endured from sinners such grievous opposition and bitter hostility against Himself [reckon up and consider it all in comparison with your trials], so that you may not grow weary or exhausted, losing heart and relaxing and fainting in your minds" (Hebrews 12:3).

Compare your suffering with the price that Jesus paid at the whipping post to provide healing for *you*. He took your sickness upon Himself. Think of the price that Jesus paid on the cross for your sins to provide you with eternal salvation in heaven. Try to understand the incomprehensible suffering that Jesus went through when He took the sins of the entire human race upon Himself. The amplification of this passage of Scripture instructs you to "consider it all in comparison with your trials."

You *must not* "grow weary or exhausted, losing heart and relaxing and fainting in your mind." You must not allow the debilitating effects of sickness to pull you down and cause you to be discouraged; instead, you should focus continually on Jesus and the price He paid for you. You must be determined that the tremendous price Jesus paid for your healing will *not* be in vain.

The Bible gives many examples of persevering faith. The following passage of Scripture shows the tremendous perseverance of the apostle Paul. His perseverance should be an example to you. Paul said, "We are hedged in (pressed) on every side [troubled and oppressed in every way], but not cramped or crushed; we suffer embarrassments and are perplexed and unable to find a way out, but not driven to despair; we are pursued (persecuted and hard driven), but not deserted [to stand alone]; we are struck down to the ground, but never struck out and destroyed" (II Corinthians 4:8-9).

Please highlight or underline the words "but not" and the words "but never" that are used *four times* in this passage of Scripture. Once again I want to emphasize that repetition is used for the purpose of emphasis. Paul absolutely refused to give up when he faced extreme hardships and he was "perplexed and unable to find a way out." Paul was "not driven to despair."

If you would like to study and meditate on additional passages of Scripture that will help you to persevere, I recommend Luke 11:5-10, Luke 18:1-8, Mark 2:3-12 and James 5:11. Anyone who studies and meditates on these passages of Scripture plus the other Scripture references in these chapters on patience and perseverance will clearly see that your loving Father does *not* want you to give up no matter how much pain and discomfort you have.

Throughout this book we have emphasized the importance of meditating continually on all of God's promises that are contained in this book. The worse the symptoms in your body are, the more you should fill your eyes, your ears, your mind, your heart and your mouth with the power of God's supernatural living Word. You *cannot* dwell on sickness and how long it is taking to be healed if you keep your attention focused on God.

Many people will be excited when they first read all of the encouraging Scripture in this book. They will be excited about receiving healing from God. However, some of these people will not persevere because they will not obey God's instructions to renew their minds *each day* in His Word (see II Corinthians 4:16 and Ephesians 4:23). They will not persevere because they will not obey God's instructions to meditate on His Word throughout *every* day and night (see Joshua 1:8 and Psalm 1:2-3).

When your body aches with pain you cannot persevere in faith based on the Bible study and meditation you did last week and last month. You need a *fresh supply* of the supernatural spiritual food of the living Word of God throughout every day and every night. Christians who are very sick should do their very best to *immerse themselves* in the holy Scriptures continually

You must understand that the Word of God is *much more powerful* than thermonuclear power or any other power on earth. You will make a big mistake if you stop focusing on the Word of God because you allow the symptoms you are experiencing in your body to seem to be more powerful than God's supernatural Word.

You need to continually fight against pain and discomfort with encouraging facts from the Word of God that will help you to persevere in faith. The Word of God is filled with the supernatural power of Almighty God. The Word of God *is* able to lift you up and strengthen you when your body aches with pain.

I have explained the absolute necessity of establishing a daily routine that you follow when you are sick. You must have a definite and specific program of Bible study and meditation that you *stick to* day in and day out, week in and week out and month in and month out until God gives you manifestation of healing. "...continue to hold to the things that you have learned and of which you are convinced..." (II Timothy 3:14).

Paul was speaking to Timothy about knowing the Word of God pertaining to salvation through Jesus Christ. This same principle applies to your faith in God for healing. If you faithfully obey your Father's instructions to continually renew your mind in His Word and to meditate on His Word throughout the day and night, you will be absolutely "convinced" that you have been healed. You will "continue to hold to the things you have learned." You will not give up.

The Word of God is your lifeline. The Word of God can and should be a constant source of encouragement. You must study and meditate on God's Word continually so that you *will* develop patience, endurance, steadfastness and perseverance. Your heart should be so filled with God's supernatural living Word that you *will* wait for as long as is necessary.

This chapter is filled with more facts from the holy Scriptures telling you exactly how to *persevere in faith* as you continue to trust God for your healing. In the next chapter you will learn additional facts from the Word of God that will enable you to persevere and endure patiently with unwavering faith in God.

INTENTIONALLY BLANK

Chapter 50

Absolutely Refuse to Give Up

There is no question that God *already* has provided the answer to His promises in the Bible through the sacrifice of Jesus Christ. "…as many as are the promises of God, they all find their Yes [answer] in Him [Christ]…" (II Corinthians 1:20).

This passage of Scripture tells you that *all* of God's promises "find their Yes answer in Christ." The word "all" includes healing in your body. You are fighting a very serious battle if you are severely ill. You must persevere in faith. "…thanks be to God, Who in Christ always leads you in triumph [as trophies of Christ's victory]…" (II Corinthians 2:14).

Please highlight or underline the word "always" in this passage of Scripture. You learned in Chapter Two that Jesus won a total, complete and absolute victory over sickness. There are no "ifs" and "buts." This victory has been given to *you*. God will "always lead you in triumph as trophies of Christ's victory" *if* you persevere and absolutely refuse to give up. The apostle Paul said, "…he who believes in Him [who adheres to, trusts in, and relies on Him] shall not be put to shame nor be disappointed in his expectations" (Romans 9:33).

Do you *really believe* what the Word of God says about healing? Do you "adhere to, trust in and rely on God?" If you do you "shall not be put to shame nor be disappointed in your expectations." Shortly after that Paul made a similar statement. He said,

"...No man who believes in Him [who adheres to, relies on, and trusts in Him] will [ever] be put to shame or be disappointed" (Romans 10:11).

Once again you have learned that repetition in Scripture is used for the purpose of emphasis. Paul said almost exactly the same thing in Romans 10:11 as he did in Romans 9:33. If you would like to look up Psalm 34:22, Isaiah 28:16, Isaiah 49:23 and Jeremiah 17:7 you will receive similar encouragement from these passages of Scripture. There is no question that your Father in heaven is emphasizing that you *never* will be disappointed *if you* do not give up. Your Father wants you to "...hold fast and firm to the end your joyful and exultant confidence and sense of triumph in your hope [in Christ]" (Hebrews 3:6).

Are you determined to "hold fast and firm to the end?" Jesus *has* paid the full price for healing in your body. He wants you to have "joyful and exultant confidence and sense of triumph" in the victory He has won for you over the sickness in *your* body.

You read many *facts* in Chapter Two about the tremendous price Jesus paid to provide healing for *you*. You often are required to pay a price yourself. The price you have to pay is to obey God's specific instructions for health and healing. The price you have to pay often includes adding great perseverance to your faith for as long as God requires you to persevere. Your Father wants you "...[to exercise] every kind of endurance and patience (perseverance and forbearance) with joy" (Colossians 1:11).

What kind of perseverance does God require from you? Please highlight or underline the word "every." Your Father wants you to "exercise every kind of endurance and patience, perseverance and forbearance with joy." Your Father does *not* want you to give up your joy.

Your Father wants you to exhibit bulldog tenacity while you patiently, faithfully and joyfully focus on Jesus and not on the sickness in your body. When you are sick you should do everything you possibly can do to get better. You should follow all of the scriptural instructions in this book. Walk through every door of hope.

Study and meditate on God's Word constantly. Immerse yourself in the holy Scriptures. Pray continually. Praise the Lord throughout every day and night of your life. Set aside precious time each day to be still before the Lord to draw closer to Him.

There is nothing wrong in seeking medical help from a physician. You should do your best to eat wholesome food. You should drink a lot of water. You should exercise if you can. You should get plenty of rest. Be certain that you do not harbor bitterness, resentment or unforgiveness. When you have done everything you know how to do and you cannot do any more, God tells you what to do. "…having done all [the crisis demands] to stand [firmly in your place]" (Ephesians 6:13).

This passage of Scripture applies to standing against Satan and his demons. The "having done all" portion applies to putting on all of the armor of God. This spiritual principle also is applicable to what you should do if you are sick.

The word "stand" in this passage of Scripture refers to the military word "stand." When an army moves forward and takes a certain amount of ground the goal is to "stand" – to hold onto the ground they have acquired. Your Father wants you to "stand firmly in place" after you have done everything you know how to do. You must not give up.

There is only one place to go when you have done everything you know how to do in the natural realm. You must go into the spiritual realm. You should be very still when you "stand" in the spiritual realm. You should be calm. You should be quiet. You should be confident.

One of the best ways to find God is to come to the end of yourself. In the spiritual realm there is *no better place to be* than at the end of self. When you cannot do one more thing in the natural realm you have come to the point where you must *let go completely* and *give* the sickness *to God* and *leave* it with Him. *Stand* in faith for as long as He requires you to stand. "…stand firm in your faith (your conviction respecting man's relationship to God and divine things, keeping the trust and holy fervor born of faith and a part of it). Act like men and be courageous…" (I Corinthians 16:13).

This passage of Scripture tells you to "stand firm in your faith." You are instructed to "keep the trust and holy fervor born of faith." You will have absolute faith in God and His Word if you continue to increase your faith in God every day while you wait to receive manifestation of the healing that Jesus already has provided for you. Your faith in God will not waver whether or not you see results. You will persevere in faith.

Giving up is not an option. If you are going through a difficult time with sickness you must hold on tightly one hour at a time and one day at a time. You need to close the door to yesterday and close the door to tomorrow and focus only on today (see Matthew 6:34). You need to trust God completely to bring you through *this day* without allowing your thinking to go past that point. As you move forward one hour at a time and one day at a time you must focus continually on the Word of God, speaking God's healing promises over and over and over again. Visualize your body being healed and made whole through Christ Jesus.

You must not get caught up with thoughts about what the sickness in your body could develop into tomorrow or next week or next month. This heavy load is *far too much* for you to deal with. This is why Jesus instructed you to live your life one day at a time.

Be determined to persevere through tonight. Persevere diligently one hour at a time. Set your eyes on the end of today. Stand firmly on your faith in God to bring you safely through this day. Refuse to concern yourself with what might happen tomorrow.

You are what the Word of God says you are. If the Word of God says you are healed *then you are healed*. There is *no question* about what the Word of God says. You need to fill your heart continually with the Scripture contained in this book. You need to speak the Word of God continually. Keep on speaking healing

Scripture week after week, month after month and, if necessary, year after year. You must not give up.

The Holy Spirit *will help you* while you persevere in faith. He will help you to hold on and not give up. "...through the [Holy] Spirit's [help], by faith anticipate and wait for the blessing..." (Galatians 5:5).

If you have asked Jesus Christ to be your Savior the Holy Spirit lives in your heart. He will "help" you "by faith to anticipate and wait for the blessing." The word "blessing" in this passage of Scripture describes the total gospel of Jesus Christ which *includes* healing for your body. When you anticipate that something will happen you expect it to happen. You will persevere if your faith is strong.

The previous three chapters have been filled with facts from the holy Scriptures that tell you how to endure with patient and persevering faith if you are required to wait for the manifestation of healing that Jesus already has provided for you. Go back over the Scripture in these chapters again and again. These facts come from God Himself. They will give *you* the encouragement *you* need to persevere in faith one day at a time, absolutely refusing to give up.

Chapter 51

Keep Your Healing after You Receive It

This book is filled with specific instructions from the Bible instructing you what to do to receive manifestation of the healing Jesus has provided for you. You are not guaranteed to keep your healing after you receive it. You must learn *how* to keep this healing. In this chapter you will learn facts from the holy Scriptures that will show you how to keep your healing instead of losing it and becoming sick again.

Most sickness is caused either by disobedience to God's principles pertaining to good health or by the influence of Satan. "...the Lord said to Satan, Have you considered My servant Job, that there is none like him on the earth, a blameless and upright man, one who [reverently] fears God and abstains from and shuns all evil [because it is wrong]? And still he holds fast his integrity, although you moved Me against him to destroy him without cause" (Job 2:3).

God was willing to allow Satan to attempt to defeat Job because God knew that Job would persevere. God blessed Job abundantly after the ordeals he went through (see Job 42:10-17). One of these ordeals was the sickness that Satan was able to put on him. "...Satan went forth from the presence of the Lord and smote Job with loathsome and painful sores from the sole of his foot to the crown of his head" (Job 2:7).

The Old Testament definitely tells us that Satan could put sickness on people. If you have asked Jesus Christ to be your Savior you are able to partake of the New Testament victory that Jesus won over Satan. You must learn the facts about your authority over Satan and not allow him to have power over you in any area, including sickness.

You should expect that Satan and his demons will do everything they can to try to put sickness and depression back on you after you have received healing. You must know how to resist Satan. "Be well balanced (temperate, sober of mind), be vigilant and cautious at all times; for that enemy of yours, the devil, roams around like a lion roaring [in fierce hunger], seeking someone to seize upon and devour. Withstand him; be firm in faith [against his onset—rooted, established, strong, immovable, and determined]…" (I Peter 5:8-9).

This passage of Scripture urges you to be "well balanced" and to be "vigilant and cautious at all times." You must understand that Satan and his demons always are looking for "someone to seize upon and devour." You are instructed to be "firm in faith against his onset – rooted, established, strong, immovable and determined."

How are you able to resist Satan's demons if they try to put sickness back on you? We are ready to look again at a passage of Scripture we have studied before. "…the Word of God is [always] abiding in you (in your hearts), and you have been victorious over the wicked one" (I John 2:14).

The best defense against Satan's attacks in any area is to continually fill your mind and your heart with the supernatural living Word of God. God did not tell you to renew your mind each day (see II Corinthians 4:16 and Ephesians 4:23) only until you receive manifestation of healing. Your Father wants you to *continue* to renew your mind in His Word throughout each day during the remainder of your life. God did not tell you to meditate throughout the day and night on His Word (see Joshua 1:8 and Psalm 1:2-3) only until you receive manifestation of healing. Your

Father wants you to *continue* to meditate on His Word throughout each day and night for the remainder of your life.

Your mind and your heart should be filled continually with the Word of God. Satan's demons have no defense against minds and hearts that are consistently being filled with the power of the supernatural living Word of God.

Now that you have seen what the Bible says about resisting Satan and his demons when they try to put sickness back on you, you are ready to learn some facts about the other primary cause of sickness which is sin. Sin is anything that is in disobedience to the instructions of God. If you truly desire to keep your healing you should continually study the Word of God to learn everything you can about how your Father wants you to live. You should do your very best to obey these instructions from God so that you will not sin and give sickness an opportunity to come back on you.

The best way to resist sin is to continually yield control of your life to the Holy Spirit. The Holy Spirit takes up residence in the heart of each person who has asked Jesus Christ to be his or her Savior. "...because you [really] are [His] sons, God has sent the [Holy] Spirit of His Son into our hearts, crying, Abba (Father)! Father!" (Galatians 4:6).

You saw in Chapter Eight that Galatians 5:16 tells you to continually allow the Holy Spirit to control your life. The fruit of the Holy Spirit will be produced in your life if you do your very best each day to yield control of your life to the Holy Spirit. "...the fruit of the [Holy] Spirit [the work which His presence within accomplishes] is love, joy (gladness), peace, patience (an even temper, forbearance), kindness, goodness (benevolence), faithfulness, gentleness (meekness, humility), self-control (self-restraint, continence)..." (Galatians 5:22-23).

Unforgiveness, resentment, bitterness, anxiety, worry, fear and all other negative attitudes can give Satan and his demons a foothold to try to bring sickness back on you. Satan will not be able to put sickness back on you if all of this fruit is constantly being produced in your life by the Holy Spirit.

There is no question that many people bring sickness upon themselves because of the choices they make. The Bible explains that some people become sick as a result of sin. "Some are fools [made ill] because of the way of their transgressions and are afflicted because of their iniquities" (Psalm 107:17).

Many people are made sick in the first place because of sin. Sin also can cause you to be sick again after you have been healed. If you have received healing from God you should do your very best to eat healthy food, exercise regularly and drink a lot of pure water. You should carefully follow the instructions on divine health that are included in Chapter Three through Chapter Eight.

You also should do your very best to fill your mind and your heart each day with the Word of God and to yield control of your life to the Holy Spirit so that you will not sin. After Jesus healed a man who had been sick for thirty-eight years "...He said to him, See, you are well! Stop sinning or something worse may happen to you" (John 5:14).

These words that Jesus spoke to a man who had just been healed apply to every person who receives healing from God. You must "stop sinning or something worse may happen to you."

I have seen God heal many people by giving them an instant healing miracle. Unfortunately, some people who are healed instantly lose their healing soon afterward. People who receive a miracle of healing or receive healing primarily from someone else's faith must do what God's Word tells them to do. They must consistently increase their own faith in God so that they can keep the healing they have received.

This book is filled with specific scriptural instructions that explain how to receive manifestation of healing from God. You should obey these same instructions *after you* have received manifestation of healing. Christians who have been healed should pray continually, worship God continually, set aside precious time to be alone with the Lord each day, draw closer to the Lord each day and study and meditate on God's Word continually.

When Jesus healed ten lepers only one of them returned to thank Him (see Luke 17:11-19). You must not be like the nine lepers who did not thank Jesus. You should tell other people how you were healed. You should give all of the glory to the Lord. Jesus said, "…Go home to your own [family and relatives and friends] and bring back word to them of how much the Lord has done for you, and [how He has] had sympathy for you and mercy on you" (Mark 5:19).

Tell "your family and relatives and friends how much the Lord has done for you" because of His "sympathy for you and mercy on you." Give Jesus the glory He deserves. Sickness is much more likely to come back on you if you are ungrateful. Gratitude provides healing energy.

You should have a constant attitude of gratitude because of the eternal salvation you have received as a result of the enormous price Jesus paid for you on the cross at Calvary. If you have received healing from Jesus you should praise Him and thank Him continually. The deep inner gratitude that fills your heart should pour out of your mouth constantly (see Matthew 12:34).

You should give Jesus the honor, glory and recognition He deserves for the tremendous price He paid at the whipping post and on the cross so that you could be healed. You should constantly be aware of the healing miracle that has taken place in your life. You should not forget for one moment what Jesus has done for you.

You have learned that the Word of God is God's medicine. People in the world often stop taking medication if their health improves. You should *continue* to take God's medicine for the rest of your life. Taking God's medicine is an important key to receiving healing. Taking God's medicine is vitally important to staying healed.

The older you get, the more easily sickness can overtake you. I believe that, the older you get, the more important studying and meditating continually on the Word of God becomes. There is no question that Christians who have been healed and get into God's Word and stay there are able to maintain their healing and walk in divine health much better than Christians who do not faithfully study and meditate on the Word of God.

The Word of God is preventive medicine. You must keep strengthening yourself spiritually to maintain the healing you have received. Faith in God never remains constant. Your faith in God is either increasing or decreasing. You must obey all of the Bible's instructions, including the ones in this book, so that your faith in God will *remain strong* after you have received manifestation of healing.

Your heart should be filled with God's Word. The Word of God that abundantly fills your heart should pour out of your mouth continually. If symptoms return after you have received healing you should boldly speak the Word of God and the name of Jesus Christ.

If sickness tries to come back at you, you should speak boldly to that sickness in the name of Jesus Christ. You should tell the sickness in your body to leave. You must understand the importance of the supernatural power of the mighty name of Jesus Christ when you speak to sickness, absolutely refusing to allow it to come back on you.

You have seen the emphasis that the Bible places on the importance of praying for other people when you were believing God for healing. You should continue to pray for others after you have received healing. Every aspect of your life should be devoted to drawing closer to God and living in accordance with His will for your life.

Conclusion

We have spent thousands of hours doing research for this book and writing it. The book is filled with many Scripture references pertaining to divine health, divine healing and increasing your faith in God. We believe that any person who is sick will be blessed by the scriptural contents of this book.

You have seen that God has done His part to provide you with everything you need to receive healing from the sickness in your body. You have seen that Jesus Christ has paid the full price for you to receive healing in your body. You have in your possession a comprehensive step-by-step outline of exactly what the holy Scriptures instruct you to do to receive healing from the sickness in your body. Do you want to receive healing badly enough to do *exactly* what your Father instructs you to do?

Some people fail to receive healing from God, not because God is saying "No," but because they are saying "No." Some Christians who are sick will look at the detailed scriptural instructions contained in this book and think, "That is a lot of work." Daily quiet time with the Lord, renewing your mind in the Word of God each day, meditating on the holy Scriptures throughout the day and night and the other specific scriptural instructions in this book *are what you should have been doing all along.* These instructions are not just for divine healing. They are instructions our Father has given to every one of His children whether they are sick or not.

The only reason these instructions will seem like a lot of work to some Christians is because they have not already been doing what their Father has instructed them to do each day. Many Christians today are relatively complacent. When things are going well in their lives they do not spend quiet time with the Lord each day, renew their minds in the Word of God daily, meditate continually on the holy Scriptures and obey the other scriptural instructions that have been given in this book. They do not see any need to pay this price each day.

Sickness is a great equalizer. When you are sick you should have a deep desire to learn *exactly* what your Father tells you to do to receive the healing He already has provided for you. You then should do exactly what He instructs you to do in His Word. Because you want so badly to get rid of the pain and discomfort in your body, you probably are willing to pay much more of a price to obey these scriptural instructions each day than you would have paid before you were sick. We pray that you will make the quality decision now to learn and obey each of the specific instructions your Father has given you pertaining to divine healing.

This book is not a book just to be read. This book is a book to be *studied*. This is not a book to read just one time. This is a book to read over and over again as you carefully study and then meditate on all of the scriptural instructions your Father has given you.

We recommend that you highlight or underline everything in this book that you believe you need to study and meditate on. If you want to write notes there is some room at the top and bottom of each page and at the beginning and end of most chapters. Once you have highlighted or underlined meaningful scriptural instructions and written notes, you then are ready to go back over the facts from God's Word and meditate on these facts from the Word of God over and over again. You are ready to test your knowledge with the comprehensive Study Guide at the end of this book.

The scriptural contents of this book are not only for people who are sick. Christians who are healthy can use many of these instructions and promises during each day of their lives. If you like what you have read in this book we suggest that you go to the back of the book to carefully read about our other books, Scripture Meditation Cards and cassette tapes.

We have devoted more than thirty years to provide you with detailed scriptural instructions on a wide variety of subjects. If you will carefully study the explanation of our other publications and cassette tapes you may find additional scriptural instruction that will help you to receive the healing that Jesus *already* has provided for you.

Please pray about sharing this book with other people. You have a sphere of influence of people you know well. Some of these people are sick and need healing. Giving this book to these people could be the most important thing you could do to help them. Some of them could live eternally in heaven as they read, understand and do what the salvation message in this book instructs them to do.

The order forms in the back of this book will tell you about the liberal quantity discounts we give if you purchase five to ten copies of our books. Additional discounts are given if you purchase more than ten copies.

We pray that this book has been a tremendous blessing to you. We pray that *many people will receive healing and wholeness from God* because they have studied, learned, meditated on and obeyed the scriptural instructions in this book.

We love you and care about you. We would be excited to hear from you if this book has helped you. Please take a few moments to write to us, call our 800 number, email us or leave a message on our website. Your comments give us the encouragement at the ages of seventy-four and sixty-six to keep on writing more and more books. Thank you and God bless you.

Appendix

This book contains comprehensive biblical instructions that explain how to receive healing from God. These instructions are given to God's children - those human beings who have entered into His kingdom. We ask each person reading this book, "Have you entered into the kingdom of God?"

You do not enter into the kingdom of God by church attendance, baptism, confirmation, teaching Sunday school or living a good life. You *only* can enter into the kingdom of God if you have been "born again." Jesus said, "...I assure you, most solemnly I tell you, that unless a person is born again (anew, from above), he cannot ever see (know, be acquainted with, and experience) the kingdom of God" (John 3:3).

Some people are so caught up with their personal beliefs and their religious denomination that they completely miss God's instructions on how to enter His kingdom. This process begins by admitting that you are a sinner. You then must repent of these sins. Jesus said, "...unless you repent (change your mind for the better and heartily amend your ways, with abhorrence of your past sins), you will all likewise perish and be lost eternally" (Luke 13:5).

Many people miss out on the glory of eternal life in heaven because they are trusting in the goodness of their lives to get them to heaven. With the exception of Jesus every person who has ever lived is a sinner. "...None is righteous, just and truthful and upright and conscientious, no, not one" (Romans 3:10). We all are sinners. "…all have sinned and are falling short of the honor and glory which God bestows and receives" (Romans 3:23).

God does not have degrees of sin. If you have committed one sin you are just as guilty before God as someone who has committed many sins. "For whosoever keeps the Law [as a] whole but stumbles and offends in one [single instance] has become guilty of [breaking] all of it" (James 2:10).

In addition to acknowledging your sins and repenting of them you must take one additional step. "…if you acknowledge and confess with your lips that Jesus is Lord and in your heart believe (adhere to, trust in, and rely on the truth) that God raised Him from the dead, you will be saved. For with the heart a person believes (adheres to, trusts in, and relies on Christ) and so is justified (declared righteous, acceptable to God), and with the mouth he confesses (declares openly and speaks out freely his faith) and confirms [his] salvation" (Romans 10:9-10).

You must do more than just pay mental assent to the crucifixion of Jesus to receive eternal salvation. You must admit that you are a sinner. You must repent of your sins. You must turn away from your sins and go the other way. Repent means to change.

You must believe deep down in your heart that Jesus has paid the full price for all of your sins by taking *your* place on the cross at Calvary. You must believe that Jesus died for you and that He has risen from the dead. You must believe totally, completely and absolutely that you will live eternally in heaven only because of the price Jesus paid for you.

If you really believe these spiritual truths in your heart you will speak them with your mouth. You may feel timid about doing this at first, but speaking continually of Jesus increases your faith and draws others to Him. You should tell other people that you have been born again, that you are a Christian and that you trust completely in Jesus for your eternal salvation.

You were born physically on the day your mother gave birth to you. You must have a second birth to be born spiritually. "You have been regenerated (born again), not from a mortal origin (seed, sperm), but from one that is immortal by the ever living and lasting Word of God" (I Peter 1:23).

Why do you have to be born of the Spirit? You were born into the world with a body and a soul. The spirit of man was separated from God when Adam and Eve sinned. You live your life only in the body and your soul until the Spirit of God plants Himself in your heart. At that moment you are born of the Spirit. You are born again.

Jesus became a man and lived a sinless life to become the required sacrifice for your sins. Jesus is your bridge back to God. God sees you as righteous not because you are good, but because you are in Christ Jesus. The blood of Jesus, the sinless sacrifice, was required to enable you to come into God's holy presence.

God does not reveal Himself to you through your intellect. He reveals Himself to your heart. You may be an adult in the natural realm, but you need to start all over again as a child in the spiritual realm. You must have childlike faith. Jesus said, "…unless you repent (change, turn about) and become like little children [trusting, lowly, loving, forgiving], you can never enter the kingdom of heaven [at all]" (Matthew 18:3).

The following prayer will result in your spiritual birth if you truly believe these words in your heart and if you boldly confess them to others with your mouth. "Dear Father God I come to You in the name of Jesus Christ. I admit that I am a sinner. I am genuinely sorry for my sins. I want to change my ways. Please help me. Please forgive me. I believe in my heart that Jesus is Your Son and that He died on the cross to pay for my sins. I believe that You raised Him from the dead and that He is alive today sitting at Your right hand. I trust completely in Jesus as my only way of receiving eternal salvation. Thank You, Lord Jesus. Thank You, Father. Amen."

You have been born again if you prayed this prayer from your heart and if you confessed these heartfelt beliefs with your mouth. You have been given a fresh new start "…if any person is [ingrafted] in Christ (the Messiah) he is a new creation (a new creature altogether); the old [previous moral and spiritual condition] has passed away. Behold, the fresh and new has come!" (II Corinthians 5:17).

You now have entered into the most precious relationship of all. Your previous spiritual condition changed when you were born into Christ Jesus. You are not the same person you were before. You are a child of Father God.

Begin to talk with your Father each day. Pray to Him continually. Study the Bible daily. Meditate on the Word of God continually. Praise God and thank Him each day.

Pray asking the Lord to guide you to the church He wants you to join (see Hebrews 10:25). Find other Christians who love God. Fellowship with them. Speak to others of your relationship with God. This new relationship that began when you asked Jesus to be your Savior will grow and grow and your new life will be a very wonderful life where you constantly will draw closer to God.

Please contact us and let us know that you have become a child of God. We would like to pray for you and welcome you as our new brother or sister in Christ Jesus. We love you and bless you in the name of our Lord Jesus Christ. We would be so pleased to hear from you.

Study Guide

What Did You Learn From This Book?

The questions in this Study Guide are carefully arranged to show you how much you have learned about divine health and divine healing. This Study Guide is not an academic test. The sole purpose of the following questions is to help you increase your *practical knowledge* pertaining to divine health, divine healing and increasing your faith in God.

Page reference

1. Why does the Bible say that you should learn everything you possibly can about divine health and divine healing? (Hosea 4:6) 18

2. If you are sick how does your Father want you to approach His Word in regard to learning facts about divine health and divine healing? (Isaiah 66:2) 18

3. What does the Bible say about the relationship between the sin of Adam, death and the victory of Jesus Christ? (I Corinthians 15:22 and I Corinthians 15:45) 24

4. Has *any* person except Jesus Christ ever lived such a good life that he or she is not regarded by God as a sinner? (Romans 3:23, James 2:10 and Romans 3:12) 24-25

God do? How does this story apply to you regarding the sickness you have in your body? (Acts 16:22-26)

185. What does the Bible teach about the enormous power of praising the Lord in the biblical account of King Jehosaphat and his followers as they faced mighty foes? How does this magnificent story apply to you in regard to the sickness in your body? (II Chronicles 20:15-22)

186. The psalmist David trusted completely in the Lord to give him the strength and protection he needed. David was absolutely certain that the Lord would help him. How did he show his gratitude to the Lord? (Psalm 28:7)

187. How will you react to sickness and any other adversity if your heart is solidly "fixed" on God and you trust Him and His Word completely? (Psalm 57:7 and Psalm 106:12)

188. How did Moses and the Israelites react when they faced a seemingly impossible situation with the Red Sea ahead of them, extremely high mountains on either side of them and the mighty Egyptian army behind them? Why should you react in the same way in regard to the sickness in your body? (Exodus 14:1-31 and Exodus 15:1-19)

189. What relationship exists between trusting the Lord completely and actually "singing" your praise to Him? (Psalm 5:11 and Psalm 92:1)

190. Being "filled and stimulated with the Holy Spirit" is important to all Christians. The fullness of the Spirit is especially important to Christians who are sick. What does the Bible instruct you to do to be filled with the Spirit? (Ephesians 5:18-20)

A Few Words About Lamplight Ministries

Lamplight Ministries, Inc. originally began in 1983 as Lamplight Publications. After ten years as a publishing firm with a goal of selling Christian books Lamplight Ministries was founded in 1993. Jack and Judy Hartman founded Lamplight Ministries with a mission of continuing to sell their publications and also to *give* large numbers of these publications free of charge to needy people all over the world.

Lamplight Ministries was created to allow people who have been blessed by our publications to share in financing the translation, printing and distribution of our books into other languages and also to distribute our publications free of charge to jails and prisons. Over the years many partners of Lamplight Ministries have shared Jack and Judy's vision. As the years have gone by Lamplight Ministries' giving has increased with each passing year. Thousands of people in jails and prisons and in Third World countries have received our publications free of charge.

Our books and Scripture Meditation Cards have been translated into eleven foreign languages – Armenian, Danish, Greek, Hebrew, German, Korean, Norwegian, Portuguese, Russian, Spanish and the Tamil dialect in India. The translations in these languages are not available from Lamplight Ministries in the United States. These translations can only be obtained in the countries where they have been printed.

The pastors of many churches in Third World countries have written to say that they consistently preach sermons in their churches based on the scriptural contents of our publications. We believe that people in several churches in many different countries consistently hear sermons that are based on the scriptural contents of our publications. Praise the Lord!

Jack Hartman was the sole author of twelve Christian books. After co-authoring one book with Judy, Jack and Judy co-authored ten sets of Scripture Meditation Cards. Judy's contributions to *God's Wisdom Is Available To You, Exchange Your Worries for God's Perfect Peace, Unshakable Faith in Almighty God* and *Receive Healing from the Lord* were so significant that she is the co-author of these books. Jack and Judy currently are working on several other books that they believe the Lord is leading them to write as co-authors.

We invite you to request our newsletters to stay in touch with us, to learn of our latest publications and to read comments from people all over the world. Please write, fax, call or email us. You are very special to us. We love you and thank God for you. Our heart is to take the gospel to the world and for our books to be available in every known language. Hallelujah!

Lamplight Ministries, Inc.,
PO Box 1307 - Dunedin, Florida, 34697. USA
Phone: 1-800-540-1597 • Fax: 1-727-784-2980
• website: lamplight.net • email: lamplightmin@yahoo.com

We offer you a substantial quantity discount

From the beginning of our ministry we have been led of the Lord to offer the same quantity discount to individuals that we offer to Christian bookstores. Each individual has a sphere of influence with a specific group of people. We believe that you know many people who need to learn the scriptural contents of our publications.

The Word of God encourages us to give freely to others. We encourage you to give selected copies of these publications to people you know who need help in the specific areas that are covered by our publications. See our order form for specific information on the quantity discounts that we make available to you so that you can share our books and cassette tapes with others.

A request to our readers

If this book has helped you we would like to receive your comments so that we can share them with others. Your comments can *encourage other people* to study our publications to learn from the scriptural contents of these publications.

When we receive a letter containing comments on any of our books, cassette tapes or Scripture Meditation Cards we prayerfully take out excerpts from these letters. These selected excerpts are included in our newsletters and occasionally in our advertising and promotional materials.

If any of our publications have been a blessing to you please share your comments with us so that we can share them with others. Tell us in your own words what a specific publication has meant to you and why you would recommend it to others. Please give as much specific information as possible. We will never print your name or street address. We simply use the state or country you live in (example: Illinois).

Thank you for taking a few minutes of your time to encourage other people to learn from the scripture references in our publications.

Books by Jack and Judy Hartman

Receive Healing from the Lord — is solidly anchored on 464 Scripture references. The first two chapters will *prove to you* from the holy Scriptures that Jesus Christ *already* has provided healing for you. The next six chapters are devoted to a study of divine health. The remaining chapters give you detailed instructions from God's Word that tell you exactly what your Father wants you to do to receive the healing He has provided for you.

Exchange Your Worries for God's Perfect Peace — Our Father does not want His children to worry. He wants each of us to be absolutely certain that He has provided for all of our needs, that He lives in our hearts, that He is with us at all times and that He will help us if we have faith in Him. This book contains over 441 Scripture references that explain exactly what we should do to be set free from worry and fear and exactly what we should do to receive God's perfect peace that has been provided for us.

Unshakable Faith in Almighty God is solidly anchored on 411 Scripture references to explain to you exactly what the Bible says about increasing your faith in God. Jack and Judy Hartman believe that difficult times are coming upon the world. They believe that Christians absolutely must learn what the holy Scriptures say about increasing their faith in God.

God's Wisdom Is Available To You explains from 501 Scripture references how to receive the wisdom our Father has promised to give to us. God looks at the wisdom of the world as "foolishness" (see I Corinthians 3:19). You will learn how to receive the revelation knowledge, guidance and wisdom from God that bypasses sense knowledge.

Trust God for Your Finances is currently in its nineteenth printing with more than 150,000 copies in print. This book which has been translated into nine foreign languages contains over 200 Scripture references that explain in a simple, straightforward and easy-to-understand style what the Word of God says about our Father's instructions and promises pertaining to our finances.

Never, Never Give Up devotes the first five chapters to a scriptural explanation of patience and the remaining thirteen chapters to scriptural instruction pertaining to the subject of perseverance. This book is based on almost 300 Scripture references that will help you to learn exactly what our loving Father instructs us to do to increase our patience and perseverance.

Quiet Confidence in the Lord is solidly anchored on more than 400 Scripture references that explain how to remain calm and quiet in a crisis situation. You will learn from the Word of God how to control your emotions when you are faced with severe problems and how to increase your confidence in the Lord by spending precious quiet time alone with Him each day.

What Will Heaven Be Like? explains from more than 200 Scripture references what the Bible tells us about what heaven will be like. Many people have written to tell us how much this book comforted them after they lost a loved one. We have received many other letters from terminally ill Christians who were comforted by scriptural facts about where they would be going in the near future.

Soaring Above the Problems of Life has helped many people who were going through severe trials. This practical "hands on" book is filled with facts from the Word of God. Our Father has given each of us specific and exact instructions telling us how He wants us to deal with adversity. This book is written in a clear and easy-to-understand style that will help you to learn to deal with the adversity that we all must face in our lives.

How to Study the Bible. Many Christians attempt to study the Bible and give up because they are unable to find a fruitful method of Bible study. This book explains in detail the method that Jack Hartman uses to study the Bible. This practical, step-by-step technique will give you a definite, specific and precise system for studying the Word of God. Any person who sincerely wants to study the Bible effectively can be helped by this book and our two cassette tapes on this subject.

Increased Energy and Vitality. Jack and Judy Hartman are senior citizens who are determined to be in the best possible physical condition to serve the Lord during the remainder of their lives. They have spent many hours of study and practical trial and error to learn how to increase their energy and vitality. This book is based on more than 200 Scripture references that will help you to increase your energy and vitality so that you can serve the Lord more effectively.

Nuggets of Faith – Jack Hartman has written over 100,000 spiritual meditations. This book contains some of his early meditations on the subject of increasing our faith in God. It contains 78 "nuggets" (average length of three paragraphs) to help you to increase your faith in God.

100 Years from Today tells exactly where each of us will be one hundred years from now if Jesus is our Savior and where we will be if Jesus is not our Savior. This simple and easy-to-understand book has helped many unbelievers to receive Jesus as their Savior. This book leads the reader through the decision to eternal salvation. The book closes by asking the reader to make a decision for Jesus and to make this decision now.

Conquering Fear – Many people in the world today are afraid because they see that various forms of worldly security are disappearing. Our Father does not want us to be afraid. He has told us 366 times in His Word that we should not be afraid. This book is filled with scriptural references that explain the source of fear and how to overcome fear.

God's Will For Our Lives teaches from the holy Scriptures why we are here on earth, what our Father wants us to do with our lives and how to experience the meaning and fulfillment we can only experience when we are carrying out God's will. God had a specific plan for each of our lives before we were born. He has given each of us abilities and talents to carry out the assignment He has given to us.

Scripture Meditation Cards and Cassette Tapes by Jack and Judy Hartman

Each set of Scripture Meditation Cards consists of 52 2-1/2 inch by 3-1/2 inch cards that can easily be carried in a pocket or a purse. Each set of Scripture cards includes approximately 75 Scripture references and is accompanied by an 85-minute cassette tape that explains every passage of Scripture in detail.

Freedom From Worry and Fear

The holy Scriptures tell us repeatedly that our Father does not want us to be worried or afraid. There is no question that God doesn't want us to be worried or afraid, but what exactly should we do if we have a sincere desire to overcome worry and fear? You will learn to overcome worry and fear from specific factual instructions from the Word of God. You will learn how to have a peaceful mind that is free from fear. You'll learn to live one day at a time forgetting the past and not worrying about the future. You'll learn how to trust God completely instead of allowing worry and fear to get into your mind and into your heart.

Enjoy God's Wonderful Peace

Peace with God is available to us because of the sacrifice that Jesus made for us at Calvary. In addition to peace with God, Jesus also has given us the opportunity to enjoy the peace of God. You will learn how to enter into God's rest to receive

God's perfect peace that will enable you to remain calm and quiet deep down inside of yourself regardless of the circumstances you face. You will learn exactly what to do to experience God's peace that is so great that it surpasses human understanding. The Holy Spirit is always calm and peaceful. We can experience His wonderful peace if we learn how to yield control of our lives to Him.

Find God's Will for Your Life

The Bible tells us that God had a specific plan for every day of our lives before we were born. Our Father will not reveal His will for our lives to us if we seek His will passively. He wants us to hunger and thirst with a deep desire to live our lives according to His will. God's plan for our lives is far over and above anything we can comprehend with our limited human comprehension. We cannot experience deep meaning, fulfillment and satisfaction in our lives without seeking, finding and carrying out God's will for our lives.

Receive God's Blessings in Adversity

The Lord is with us when we are in trouble. He wants to help us and He will help us according to our faith in Him. He wants us to focus continually on Him instead of dwelling on the problems we face. We must not give up hope. Our Father will never let us down. He has made provision to give us His strength in exchange for our weakness. Our Father wants us to learn, grow and mature by facing the problems in our lives according to the instructions He has given us in His Word. We must persevere in faith to walk in the magnificent victory that Jesus won for us.

Financial Instructions from God

Our loving Father wants His children to be financially successful just as loving parents here on earth want their children to be successful. God's ways are much higher and very different from the ways of the world. Our Father doesn't want us to follow the world's system for financial prosperity. He wants us to learn and obey His instructions pertaining to our finances. You will learn how to renew your mind in the Word of God so that you will be able to see your finances in a completely different light than you see them from a worldly perspective. You will be given step-by-step instructions to follow to receive financial prosperity from God.

Receive Healing from the Lord

Many people are confused by the different teachings about whether God heals today. Are you sick? Would you like to see for yourself exactly what the Bible says about divine healing? Study the Word of God on this important subject. Draw your own conclusion based on facts from the holy Scriptures. You will learn that Jesus has provided for your healing just as surely as He has provided for your eternal salvation. You will learn exactly what the Word of God instructs you to do to increase your faith that God will heal you.

A Closer Relationship with the Lord

Because of the price that Jesus paid at Calvary all Christians have been given the awe-inspiring opportunity to come into the presence of Almighty God. These Scripture cards clearly explain the secret of enjoying a sweet and satisfying relationship with the Lord. Many Christians know about the Lord, but He wants us to know Him personally. We should have a deep desire to enjoy a close personal relationship with our precious Lord. He has promised to come close to us if we sincerely desire a close relationship with Him.

Our Father's Wonderful Love

God showed His love for us by sending His beloved Son to earth to die for our sins. Jesus showed His love for us by taking the sins of the entire world upon Himself on the cross at Calvary. The same love and compassion that was demonstrated during the earthly ministry of Jesus is available to us today. Because of the sacrifice of Jesus all Christians are the beloved sons and daughters of Almighty God. God is our loving Father. Our Father doesn't want us to seek security from external sources. He wants us to be completely secure in His love for us. You will learn from the Word of God exactly how faith works by love and how to overcome fear through love.

God is not far away. He lives in our hearts. We must not neglect the gift that is in us. We are filled with the Godhead — Father, Son and Holy Spirit. Why would we ever be afraid of anything or anyone if we are absolutely certain that God is always with us? God's power and might are much greater than we can comprehend. He watches over us at all times. He wants to help us. He wants us to walk in close fellowship with Him. His wisdom and knowledge are available to us. He wants to guide us throughout every day of our lives.

Continually Increasing Faith in God

We all are given the same amount of faith to enable us to become children of God. Our Father wants the faith that He gave us to grow continually. We live in the last days before Jesus returns. We must learn how to develop deeply rooted faith in God. You will learn how to walk in the authority and power you have been given over Satan and his demons. You can walk in victory over the circumstances in your life. You will learn exactly what the holy Scriptures tell us to do to receive manifestation of God's mighty strength and power. You will learn the vital importance of the words you speak. You will learn that there is only one way to control the words you speak when you are under severe pressure in a crisis situation.

Why you cannot combine orders for quantity discounts for Scripture Meditation Cards with other products

We desire to make the purchase of our products as *simple* as possible. However, we are unable to combine orders for our Scripture Meditation Cards with orders for our other products.

The reason for this decision is that the cost of printing and packaging Scripture Meditation Cards is much higher in proportion to the purchase price than the price of printing books. If we wanted to offer the same percentage quantity discount that we offer with our books, the cost for one set of Scripture Meditation Cards would have to be $7. This price was unacceptable to us.

We decided to offer each individual set of Scripture Meditation Cards for a reasonable price of $5 including postage. In order to keep this price for individual sets of Scripture Meditation Cards this low we had to develop an entirely different price structure for quantity discounts. Please see the enclosed order form for information on these discounts.

Cassette Tapes by Jack Hartman

01H   **How to Study the Bible** (Part 1) – 21 scriptural reasons why it is important to study the Bible

02H   **How to Study the Bible** (Part 2) – A detailed explanation of a proven, effective system for studying the Bible

03H   **Enter Into God's Rest** – Don't struggle with loads that are too heavy for you. Learn what God's Word teaches about relaxing under pressure.

04H   **Freedom From Worry** – A comprehensive scriptural explanation of how to become free from worry

05H   **God's Strength, Our Weakness** – God's strength is available if we can admit our human weakness and trust instead in His unlimited strength.

06H   **How to Transform Our Lives** – A scriptural study of how we can change our lives through a spiritual renewal of our minds.

07H   **The Greatest Power in the Universe** (Part 1) – The greatest power in the universe is love. This tape explains our Father's love for us.

08H   **The Greatest Power in the Universe** (Part 2) – A scriptural explanation of our love for God and for each other, and how to overcome fear through love.

09H   **How Well Do You Know Jesus Christ?** – An Easter Sunday message that will show you Jesus as you never knew Him before.

10H   **God's Perfect Peace** – In a world of unrest, many people search for inner peace. Learn from God's Word how to obtain His perfect peace.

11H   **Freedom Through Surrender** – Many people try to find freedom by "doing their own thing." God's Word says that freedom comes from surrendering our lives to Jesus.

12H   **Overcoming Anger** – When is anger is permissible and when is it a sin? Learn from the Bible how to overcome the sinful effects of anger.

13H   **Taking Possession of Our Souls** – God's Word teaches that patience is the key to the possession of our souls. Learn from the Word of God how to increase your patience and endurance.

14H   **Staying Young in the Lord** – Some people try to cover up the aging process with makeup, hair coloring and hairpieces. Learn from the Bible how you can offset the aging process.

15H   **Two Different Worlds** – Specific instructions from the Word of God to help you enter into and stay in the presence of God.

16H   **Trust God For Your Finances** – This tape is a summary of the highlights of Jack's best-selling book, *Trust God For Your Finances.*

17H   **The Joy of the Lord** – Learn how to experience the joy of the Lord regardless of the external circumstances in your life.

18H   **Let Go and Let God** – Our Father wants us to give our problems to Him and leave them with Him because we have complete faith in Him..

19H   **Guidance, Power, Comfort and Wisdom** – Learn the specific work of the Holy Spirit Who will guide us, empower us, comfort us and give us wisdom.

20H   **Go With God** – This tape is based on 35 Scripture references that explain why and how to witness to the unsaved.

21H   **One Day at a Time** – Our Father doesn't want us to dwell on the past nor worry about the future. Learn how to follow biblical instructions to live your life one day at a time.

22H   **Never, Never Give Up** – Endurance and perseverance are often added to our faith as we wait on the Lord, releasing our will to His.

23H   The Christ-Centered Life – Some Christians are still on the throne of their lives pursuing personal goals. Learn how to center every aspect of your life around the Lord Jesus Christ.

24H   Fear Must Disappear – The spirit of fear cannot stand up against perfect love. Learn what perfect love is and how to attain it.

25H   Internal Security – Some Christians look for security from external sources. In this tape, Jack shares his belief that difficult times are ahead of us and the only security in these times will be from the Spirit of God and the Word of God living in our hearts.

26H   Continually Increasing Faith – Romans 12:3 tells us that all Christians start out with a specific amount of faith. In these last days before Jesus returns, we will all need a stronger faith than just the minimum. This tape offers many specific suggestions on what to do to continually strengthen our faith.

27H   Why Does God Allow Adversity? – Several Scripture references are used in this tape to explain the development of strong faith through adversity.

28H   Faith Works by Love – Galatians 5:6 tells us that faith works by love. Christians wondering why their faith doesn't seem to be working may find an answer in this message. A life centered around the love of the Lord for us and our love for others is absolutely necessary to strong faith.

29H   There Are No Hopeless Situations – Satan wants us to feel hopeless. He wants us to give up hope and quit. This tape explains the difference between hope and faith. It tells how we set our goals through hope and bring them into manifestation through strong, unwavering faith.

30H   Walk By Faith, Not By Sight – When we're faced with seemingly unsolvable problems, it's easy to focus our attention on the problems instead of on the Word of God and the Spirit of God. In this tape, Jack gives many personal examples of difficult situations in his life and how the Lord honored his faith and the faith of others who prayed for him.

31H   Stay Close to the Lord – Our faith is only as strong as its source. A close relationship with the Lord is essential to strong faith. In this tape, Jack explores God's Word to give a thorough explanation of how to develop a closer relationship with the Lord.

32H   Quiet Faith – When we're faced with very difficult problems, the hardest thing to do is to be still. The Holy Spirit, however, wants us to remain quiet and calm because of our faith in Him. This message carefully examines the Word of God for an explanation of how we can do this.

33H   When Human Logic is Insufficient – Human logic and reason often miss God. This message explains why some Christians block the Lord because they're unable to bypass their intellects and place their trust completely in Him.

34H   The Good Fight of Faith – In this message, Jack compares the "good fight of faith" with the "bad" fight of faith. He explains who we fight against, where the battle is fought, and how it is won.

ORDER FORM FOR BOOKS AND CASSETTE TAPES

Book Title	Quantity	Total
Receive Healing from the Lord ($14.00)	_____	_____
Unshakable Faith in Almighty God ($14.00)	_____	_____
Exchange Your Worries for God's Perfect Peace ($14.00)	_____	_____
God's Wisdom is Available to You ($14.00)	_____	_____
Increased Energy and Vitality ($10.00)	_____	_____
Quiet Confidence in the Lord ($10.00)	_____	_____
Never, Never Give Up ($10.00)	_____	_____
Trust God For Your Finances ($10.00)	_____	_____
What Will Heaven Be Like? ($10.00)	_____	_____
Conquering Fear ($10.00)	_____	_____
God's Will For Our Lives ($10.00)	_____	_____
How to Study the Bible ($7.00)	_____	_____
Nuggets of Faith ($7.00)	_____	_____
100 Years From Today ($7.00)	_____	_____

Cassette Tapes (please indicate quantity being ordered) • *$5 each*

_____01H _____02H _____03H _____04H _____05H _____06H _____07H
_____08H _____09H _____10H _____11H _____12H _____13H _____14H
_____15H _____16H _____17H _____18H _____19H _____20H _____21H
_____22H _____23H _____24H _____25H _____26H _____27H _____28H
_____29H _____30H _____31H _____32H _____33H _____34H

Price of books and tapes _____
Minus 40% discount for 5-9 items _____
Minus 50% discount for 10 or more items _____
Net price of order _____
Add 15% ***before discount*** for shipping and handling _____
   (Maximum of $50 for any size order)
Florida residents only, add 7% sales tax _____
Tax deductible contribution to Lamplight Ministries, Inc. _____
Enclosed check or money order (do not send cash) _____

(Please make check payable to Lamplight Ministries, Inc. and mail to:
PO Box 1307, Dunedin, FL 34697)

MC____ Visa____ AmEx____ Disc.____ Card # _____

Exp Date _____ Signature _____

Name _____

Address _____

City _____

State or Province _____ Zip or Postal Code _____
(Foreign orders must be submitted in U.S. dollars.)

ORDER FORM FOR BOOKS AND CASSETTE TAPES

Book Title	Quantity	Total
Receive Healing from the Lord ($14.00)	_____	_____
Unshakable Faith in Almighty God ($14.00)	_____	_____
Exchange Your Worries for God's Perfect Peace ($14.00)	_____	_____
God's Wisdom is Available to You ($14.00)	_____	_____
Increased Energy and Vitality ($10.00)	_____	_____
Quiet Confidence in the Lord ($10.00)	_____	_____
Never, Never Give Up ($10.00)	_____	_____
Trust God For Your Finances ($10.00)	_____	_____
What Will Heaven Be Like? ($10.00)	_____	_____
Conquering Fear ($10.00)	_____	_____
God's Will For Our Lives ($10.00)	_____	_____
How to Study the Bible ($7.00)	_____	_____
Nuggets of Faith ($7.00)	_____	_____
100 Years From Today ($7.00)	_____	_____

Cassette Tapes (please indicate quantity being ordered) • *$5 each*

_____01H _____02H _____03H _____04H _____05H _____06H _____07H
_____08H _____09H _____10H _____11H _____12H _____13H _____14H
_____15H _____16H _____17H _____18H _____19H _____20H _____21H
_____22H _____23H _____24H _____25H _____26H _____27H _____28H
_____29H _____30H _____31H _____32H _____33H _____34H

Price of books and tapes   _____
Minus 40% discount for 5-9 items   _____
Minus 50% discount for 10 or more items   _____
Net price of order   _____
Add 15% **before discount** for shipping and handling   _____
   (Maximum of $50 for any size order)
Florida residents only, add 7% sales tax   _____
Tax deductible contribution to Lamplight Ministries, Inc.   _____
Enclosed check or money order (do not send cash)   _____

(Please make check payable to Lamplight Ministries, Inc. and mail to:
PO Box 1307, Dunedin, FL 34697)

MC_____ Visa_____ AmEx_____ Disc._____ Card # _____

Exp Date _____ Signature _____

Name _____

Address _____

City _____

State or Province _____ Zip or Postal Code _____
(Foreign orders must be submitted in U.S. dollars.)

Order Form for Scripture Meditation Cards and Cassette Tapes

Due to completely different price structure for the production of Scripture Meditation Cards and 85-minute cassette tapes, we offer a different quantity discount which cannot be combined with our other quantity discounts. The following prices *include shipping and handling.* $5 per card deck or cassette tape; $4 for 5-9 card decks or cassette tapes; $3 for 10 or more card decks or cassette tapes.

SCRIPTURE MEDITATION CARDS	QUANTITY	PRICE
Find God's Will for Your Life	_____	_____
Financial Instructions from God	_____	_____
Freedom from Worry and Fear	_____	_____
A Closer Relationship with the Lord	_____	_____
Our Father's Wonderful Love	_____	_____
Receive Healing from the Lord	_____	_____
Receive God's Blessing in Adversity	_____	_____
Enjoy God's Wonderful Peace	_____	_____
God is Always with You	_____	_____
Continually Increasing Faith in God	_____	_____

CASSETTE TAPES		
Find God's Will for Your Life	_____	_____
Financial Instructions from God	_____	_____
Freedom from Worry and Fear	_____	_____
A Closer Relationship with the Lord	_____	_____
Our Father's Wonderful Love	_____	_____
Receive Healing from the Lord	_____	_____
Receive God's Blessing in Adversity	_____	_____
Enjoy God's Wonderful Peace	_____	_____
God is Always with You	_____	_____
Continually Increasing Faith in God	_____	_____

TOTAL PRICE _____

Florida residents only, add 7% sales tax _____

Tax deductible contribution to Lamplight Ministries, Inc. _____

Enclosed check or money order (do not send cash) _____

Please make check payable to Lamplight Ministries, Inc. and mail to:
PO Box 1307, Dunedin, FL 34697

MC____ Visa____ AmEx____ Disc.____ Card # _____

Exp Date _____ Signature _____

Name _____

Address _____

City _____

State or Province _____ Zip or Postal Code _____

(Foreign orders must be submitted in U.S. dollars.)

Order Form for Scripture Meditation Cards and Cassette Tapes

Due to completely different price structure for the production of Scripture Meditation Cards and 85-minute cassette tapes, we offer a different quantity discount which cannot be combined with our other quantity discounts. The following prices *include shipping and handling.* $5 per card deck or cassette tape; $4 for 5-9 card decks or cassette tapes; $3 for 10 or more card decks or cassette tapes.

SCRIPTURE MEDITATION CARDS	QUANTITY	PRICE
Find God's Will for Your Life	_____	_____
Financial Instructions from God	_____	_____
Freedom from Worry and Fear	_____	_____
A Closer Relationship with the Lord	_____	_____
Our Father's Wonderful Love	_____	_____
Receive Healing from the Lord	_____	_____
Receive God's Blessing in Adversity	_____	_____
Enjoy God's Wonderful Peace	_____	_____
God is Always with You	_____	_____
Continually Increasing Faith in God	_____	_____

CASSETTE TAPES

Find God's Will for Your Life	_____	_____
Financial Instructions from God	_____	_____
Freedom from Worry and Fear	_____	_____
A Closer Relationship with the Lord	_____	_____
Our Father's Wonderful Love	_____	_____
Receive Healing from the Lord	_____	_____
Receive God's Blessing in Adversity	_____	_____
Enjoy God's Wonderful Peace	_____	_____
God is Always with You	_____	_____
Continually Increasing Faith in God	_____	_____

TOTAL PRICE _____

Florida residents only, add 7% sales tax _____

Tax deductible contribution to Lamplight Ministries, Inc. _____

Enclosed check or money order (do not send cash) _____

Please make check payable to Lamplight Ministries, Inc. and mail to:
PO Box 1307, Dunedin, FL 34697

MC____ Visa____ AmEx____ Disc.____ Card # _____

Exp Date _____ Signature _____

Name _____

Address _____

City _____

State or Province _____ Zip or Postal Code _____

(Foreign orders must be submitted in U.S. dollars.)

The Vision of Lamplight Ministries

Lamplight Ministries, Inc. is founded upon Psalm 119:105 which says, "Your word is a lamp to my feet and a light to my path." We are so grateful to our loving Father for His precious Word that clearly shows us the path He wants us to follow throughout every day of our lives.

From the beginning of our ministry God has used us to reach people in many different countries. Our vision is to share the instructions and promises in the Word of God with multitudes of people in many different countries throughout the world.

We are believing God for the finances to provide the translation of our publications into many different foreign languages. We desire to give our publications free of charge to needy people all over the world who cannot afford to purchase them.

We are believing God for many partners in our ministry who will share our vision of distributing our publications which are solidly anchored upon the Word of God. It is our desire to provide these publications in every foreign language that we possibly can.

We yearn to share the Word of God with large numbers of people in Third World countries. We yearn to share the Word of God with large numbers of people in prisons and jails. These people desperately need to learn and obey God's instructions and to learn and believe in God's promises.

Please pray and ask the Lord if He would have you help us to help needy people all over the world. Thank you and God bless you.